Standards and Dialects
in
English

TIMOTHY SHOPEN
Australian National University

JOSEPH M. WILLIAMS
University of Chicago

under the auspices of the
Center for Applied Linguistics

Standards and Dialects

in

English

Winthrop Publishers, Inc.
Cambridge, Massachusetts

Library of Congress Cataloging in Publication Data

Main entry under title:

Standards and dialects in English.

    Includes bibliographies.
    1. English language—Standardization—Addresses,
essays, lectures. 2. English language—Variation—
Addresses, essays, lectures. 3. English language—
Dialects—United States—Addresses, essays, lectures.
4. Sociolinguistics—Addresses, essays, lectures.
I. Shopen, Timothy. II. Williams, Joseph M.
III. Center for Applied Linguistics.
PE1072.S75   420   80-14647
ISBN 0-87626-817-3

Design by Amato Prudente

Photo Credits

    Page 1: Jacob Riis/Museum of the City of New York
    Page 85: Hella Hammid/Photo Researchers, Inc.
    Page 137: Frank Siteman/The Picture Cube
    Page 175: Constantine Manos/Magnum Photos, Inc.

© 1980 by Winthrop Publishers, Inc.
17 Dunster Street, Cambridge, Massachusetts 02138

Printed in the United States of America.

10   9   8   7   6   5   4   3   2   1

Contents

Illustrations on the Cassette

Side I   (28:53)

Chapter 6: Selections from Bengt Loman's "Conversations in a Negro American Dialect"

Part I: Five Conversations   (11:02)
Conversation 1: Gregory J. (10) and Michael J. (10), cousins   (1:31)
Conversation 2: Jacqueline D. (11) and Michael J.   (0:46)
Conversation 3: Anita P. (10) and Jacqueline D.   (2:31)
Conversation 4: Jacqueline D., Anita P., and Sandy B. (one of the interviewers)   (1:07)
Conversation 5: Anita P., Margy G. (one of the interviewers), Michael J., and Jacqueline D.   (4:30)

Part II: Five Additional Conversations   (11:09)
Conversation 6: Gregory J. and his aunt Patricia J.   (3:13)
Conversation 7: Gregory J. and Patricia J.   (1:39)
Conversation 8: Gregory J. and Margy G.   (2:14)
Conversation 9: Jacqueline D. and Margy G.   (1:56)
Conversation 10: Anita P. and Margy G.   (1:42)

Chapter 7: The Speech of the New York City Upper Class

Part I: Local Features in the Dialect   (6:42)
Section 1.1
How to Say "Coffee" and "Dog" (Passage A)   *(1:14)*
Bryan L. (middle class Californian, student, 24)
Judy E. (lower middle class, secretary, 27)
Robert H. (working class, route manager, 23)
Barbara D. (upper class, book editor, 32)
Robert N. (upper class, college teacher, 31)

Introduction

The Aim of this Book and Its Companion Volume

STANDARDS AND DIALECTS IN ENGLISH has a companion volume, STYLE AND VARIABLES IN ENGLISH. Together they provide an introduction to the English language, especially American English, as part of the culture of those who speak it. Both books are about linguistic variation—this one about the kind that distinguishes communities and social groups from each other, its companion volume about the kind that occurs in the same community and even in the words of a single person. We have provided copious illustrative material, including the cassette that comes with this book, the expression of a variety of English speakers. We hope readers will find themselves involved in the exploration and analysis of this data, and then discover how they might continue with research of their own.

Diversity and Unity

Languages are forever changing, largely because new generations renew them in creative ways. By their structure, languages tend toward certain kinds of change, but at the same time, new generations contribute innovations of their own. In this way, at least until the advent of mass media and rapid transportation, the speech varieties of separate communities have usually become more distinct from each other. That is how the dialects of the single language we call Proto–Indo-European changed over five millennia to become a far-flung family of languages now spoken by half the population of the earth, a family that includes English, Icelandic, Gaelic, Spanish, Russian, Lithuanian, Greek, Albanian, Armenian, Persian, Kurdish, Hindi, Bengali and the language of the gypsies, Romany.

At the same time, people who want to communicate with each other always find means of doing so, and this is a counter-force for linguistic unity. Human beings learn to understand each other's languages or dialects; they borrow from each other and modify their standards in the direction of greater homogeneity; they become actively bilingual or bidialectal; they settle on a common lingua franca. Diversity and unity: each tendency checks the other—and complements the other. Indeed, human societies not only accommodate them both, but need them both.

Standards are conventions for how things are to be done, a defining characteristic of any culture. Shared language standards make communication possible, and they provide a framework for creativity, creativity that can have meaning for more than just the author. There are, however, different kinds of language standards—some flexible on points of grammar with emphasis instead on clarity and liveliness, appropriateness to social context and relevance to topic; others are inflexibly set on just matters of form. Problems arise when the standards reinforce social hierarchies and rivalries and exclude parts of the population from equal opportunity in an already competitive society.

Through accidents of our history, English has become the first language of most—but by no means all—of the population of the United States, and through other accidents of our history some varieties of English have come to carry more prestige than others. A child who learns one of these improves his or her chances for success in education, social mobility and employment; a child who does not can be disadvantaged. But there can be no *general* solution to social inequality in terms of language, in spite of a familiar chain of reasoning that goes: "The language of most poor people is different from that of most affluent people; therefore, it can be seen that the poor are being held back by their language, and if their language could be made like that of affluent people, they would have a better chance." This argument turns the matter on its head. Poverty is a function of the economy, not of language. However much they might want a higher standard of living, most people find identity in the way they speak and do not want to try to sound like someone else, like someone above them on the social ladder. And even if one could change the language of a substantial part of the population, members of opposing social groups would still identify each other through speech. This follows from the nature of language and society: it always has been and always will be the case that distinct social groups develop distinct ways of speaking, and that when they have reason to they notice the differences.

Everyone has a unique way of speaking, as we know from our ability to identify individuals by hearing them talk, but with close acquaintances we tend to overlook the differences. Speakers from the same place or the same social group usually display the distinct variety of a language we call a dialect, but not all dialects attract notice or comment. Which ones people notice depends on attitudes. Tolerance for linguistic variation is a sign of social cohesion, intolerance a sign of competitiveness or even hostility. Some closely knit communities have wide variation in a language, or even more than one language, while other populations divide into antagonistic factions that use relatively small linguistic differences to tell friend from foe.

Language, more than any other kind of behavior, distinguishes humans from other animals; perhaps this is why one of the most common ways in which we belittle each other is in terms of language. The word *barbarian* from ancient Greek *barbaros* was a pejorative name for "foreigner," someone rude and uncivilized. The original reference, though, was to that person's language. It was a mocking imitation of someone who did not speak Greek, whose speech was heard as unintelligible gibberish, as a stammering *bar-bar-bar-bar*. . . . The old Slavs called the Germans *nēmci,* from the adjective *nēm,* "mute." The word meant "mute ones, ones without language." Some of us have the same motive when we accuse others of being sloppy when they say *dem* instead of *them,* or lazy when they say *workin* instead of *working,* or stupid when they say *I didn't see nobody* instead of *I didn't see anybody.* Both Spanish *Yo no vi a nadie* and Russian *Ya ne videl nikogo* translate literally as "I did not see nobody."

Any form of English which is grammatically consistent, clear, and appropriate to a speaker's topic and audience is "Good English," something we need as much of as we can get. Indeed, in our schools, we should include instruction not just in what we call good "institutional" English—the kind that serves government, business, scholarship and the professions. We should also recognize the fact that good English includes a great diversity of forms and styles, and learn to appreciate good speakers and writers wherever they come from and whatever their grammar. We have to learn the value for each of us of being able to express ourselves in a wide range of forms and styles: some appropriate for institutional settings, to be sure, but others as well.

It is true that every society with a rich written tradition eventually develops something it calls a "standard written dialect," which in fact can influence speech as well as writing. We have such a standard—it is our "institutional English"—and we cannot responsibly ignore it when we teach young people to read and write. We should give everyone who wants to the linguistic means to move up the economic and social ladder, and for that one *must* learn "institutional English."

But if our culture then decides that this "institutional English" is the *only* good English, not only does it punish those of us who speak different kinds of good English, it also deprives us of a valuable resource and the capacity to enjoy our cultural diversity. Every dialect reflects the vitality of its speakers: every dialect is a treasury of sounds and words and grammatical forms that allow its speakers to identify themselves and their values. But every dialect is also a treasury of sounds and forms from which other dialects borrow to strengthen their own linguistic resources. We more often borrow words than forms, but to disparage any distinctive feature of a dialect—social or geographical—is to disparage and thereby reject the values and accomplishments of the speakers who use those forms. And by rejecting those values along with the speech that expresses them, we may be rejecting that which can enrich us.

We need have no fear of dialect variation wearing away at our ability to communicate with each other. Relatively homogeneous grammatical standards evolve among those who share a social life, especially one that requires public and thus formal styles of expression. With such widespread communication today in the English-speaking world, this kind of homogenization will very likely increase. But it will happen naturally, and at the same time, smaller groups of people will continue to identify with the special qualities that make their speech distinctive.

Some societies value homogeneity. In many ways we in the United States have rejected it for diversity. There may be some who find social homogeneity appealing and would like to have us the same from coast to coast. But the vast majority of us delight in and take strength from the cultural differences between New Orleans and Chicago, between Appalachia and the Cascades, between New England and New Mexico. Without giving up our institutional standards, we can take the same kind of pleasure in our linguistic diversity. In unity there is strength, but only the kind that allows diversity. Behind our social diversity is a common set of values that we like to believe gives the individual the right to be what he or she wants to be. Behind our acceptance of a relatively unified institutional standard, we can preserve a dedication to linguistic diversity.

The Chapters

The first three chapters of the book study ways in which people have molded standards for English.

Shirley Brice Heath explores in Chapter 1 the changing attitudes toward the language that have come out of American experience, showing that in the early years of the republic there was a widespread belief that a living language was a tool bound to change with the needs of its speakers. Therefore one should expect variation from one part of the country to another and learn English by observing the usage of good speakers and writers in realistic settings. Then she shows how in the mid-nineteenth century educators began to say that good English was fixed in a form that could not be acquired through natural usage, but only through persistent study of a canonized set of do's and don'ts. She shows that the latter view came to hold sway for a century but that now both views have currency and can be seen in competition with each other.

Margaret Shaklee in Chapter 2 examines the evolution of a standard for English in medieval England. She begins at the time of England's emergence from French domination when there was increased social mobility and competition for status by people who spoke different varieties of English. She shows that between the fourteenth and sixteenth centuries the standard in London came to include a number of forms that earlier were restricted to a northern dialect and investigates the economic and social background for this development. She then explores social class dialects in the late fifteenth century and attempts by grammarians soon after that time to codify a standard of correctness.

In Chapter 3, Wayne O'Neil tells how the English spelling system came to be what it is today. He surveys the necessary qualities of a good spelling system and shows how in the time of Old English the spelling was not well conceived for use by native speakers, probably because of the influence of non-native speakers, Irish- and Latin-speaking missionaries. He then traces how some time later, as literacy spread, native speakers took over the spelling system and fashioned it into a more useful implement, one better suited to the nature of the language. He shows the virtues of English spelling in respect to variation, first variation within the sound system, as for the verb *create* in the series *create, creation, creature,* and second variation across dialects where the specific sounds will vary but where the systematic relationships in a series such as *create, creation, creature* will remain the same.

The next two chapters, 4 and 5, are about the innovative way children acquire language skills. They show that children approximate the standards of the adult community only by a many-staged process of recreation, deviating from adult standards not by random "mistakes," but by systematic generalizations of their own.

Timothy Shopen describes in Chapter 4 the English of his son Pablo, especially during the first two years of his life. He recounts innovations by the child in word meanings and discusses the similarity with innovations that have taken place in the history of the language, showing that it is above all the widening of generalizations that characterizes the child's inventions. Then he explores pronunciation and shows again that it is primarily widening that distinguishes the child's generalizations from the adults'. In an afterword, the author gives an example of historical change in English pronunciation for comparison with the child data.

Charles Read in Chapter 5 presents evidence that children's acquisition of English spelling has its own systematic development. He shows particular nonstandard spellings which could not have been learned from adults and which a number of kindergarten and first grade children produce independently of each other. He demonstrates that the children have done some untutored phonological analysis, grouping a wide range of sounds into a system that can be represented by the letters of the alphabet. He explores the principles the children have invented both for the sound system and for its representation in spelling and points to facts that imply that they perceive the sound structure of English differently from adults.

The last three chapters, 6, 7, and 8, are accompanied by a cassette. Each of them explores in some detail a dialect of American English. It is important to hear speakers of the dialects being discussed, because far beyond any other aspect of speech it is the phonetic detail, the accent of a speaker, that can gain notice and identify the person as an insider or an outsider—"one of us," or "one of them."

Timothy Shopen presents in Chapter 6 excerpts from a tape-recorded study by Bengt Loman focusing on four young Black speakers aged 10 and 11 in Washington, D.C. Attention is devoted to the range of speaking styles exemplified on the tape, and we hear how the children speak differently when talking with adults than with each other. Readers are led to explore their own speech, and if they are "standard" speakers they are likely to discover that when they speak informally they share a number of the "nonstandard" features of pronunciation exemplified by these children. What then makes the speech varieties distinctive are differences in degree rather than in kind, and one is prompted to ask whether the dialects might not be less different than they sometimes appear. In other instances the speech of the children is seen to encode grammatical principles that are categorically "nonstandard," but with their own logic and coherence.

Geoffrey Nunberg in Chapter 7 presents a study of the speech of the New York City upper class. After a discussion of the social setting of this class, he involves the reader-listener in an exploration of socially distinctive features of their speech. He shows ways in which upper class speakers resemble working class speakers in New York City, leaving the middle class speaker as the odd one out. On the other hand, he shows subtle speech characteristics that upper class speakers use to make exclusive identification of their fellows. He leads us to investigate changes that have taken place in the upper class standard by comparing speakers of different ages and shows us similarities to upper class speech in other communities along the Eastern seaboard.

The final chapter, 8, comes under the section heading "Dialect Encounters Standard." Here Walt Wolfram and Donna Christian investigate the special problems facing a nonstandard speaker taking a standardized test on abilities involving language skills. They take the point of view of a speaker of Appalachian English and acquaint us with the standard for that dialect. We learn a method for evaluating tests in respect to the population being tested, taking the features of their dialect into account to judge the fairness of individual test items. In an afterword, Joseph M. Williams comments on the historical accidents that have put Appalachian English in the position of a nonstandard dialect.

The Sounds of English

In this book we use symbols for the sounds of English which include the following. For consonant phonemes see Table 1.

Pairs of sounds appearing together in this table contrast just for voicing. For example, the place and manner of [f] and [v] are identical, but the vocal cords vibrate for [v] and not for [f]. Readers can feel and hear the difference by saying a prolonged [fffffffff], then [vvvvvvvvv], while touching their Adam's apple.

Not present in this table is the phoneme [h], a chameleon-like sound that takes the shape of whatever sound follows it and gives its voiceless counterpart, thus a voiceless [ī] in *heat* [hīyt], a voiceless [æ] in *hat* [hæt], and a voiceless [w] in *which* when it is pronounced [hwič]. We use some additional symbols at several points, but explain as we present them.

It might be well to single out some of the consonant symbols for exemplification. See Table 2.

These are symbols for *sounds,* and the correspondence to spelling is not one-to-one. Thus, although the letter *y* is not used, the sound [y] occurs in the word *cute,* and it is this sound that distinguishes *cute* from *coot,* [kyūwt] vs. [kūwt]. The sound [š] is represented by *sh* in *shoe,* but *ti* in *nation, ssi* in *mission, si* in *compulsion, se* in *nausea, sci* in *conscience, shi* in *fashion, ci* in *special, ce* in *ocean, ch* in *machine* and *Chicago, sch* in *Schlitz* and *Schweizer,* and when it combines in the sequence [kš] there is *x* in *luxury* and *si* in *anxious*!

Table 1. *The consonant phonemes of English, except* [*h*]

Manner of Articulation	Bilabial	Labio-dental	Inter-dental	Alveolar	Palato-alveolar	Palatal	Velar
Stops	p b			t d			k g
Affricates					č ǰ		
Fricatives		f v	θ ð	s z	š ž		
Nasals	m			n			ŋ
Central Approximants	(w)			r		y	w
Lateral Approximant				l			

Place of Articulation spans the consonant columns.

And these sounds are phonemes, distinctive sound units that produce contrasts in meaning. Their phonetic realization varies from one speaker to another and from one utterance to another. Some of this variation can be predicted from linguistic context. Just substituting [l] for [r] produces a different meaning both in *fear* and *feel* and in *reef* and *leaf.* The same phoneme [l] contrasts with [r] in each pair but its physical realization is different. An [l] at the beginning of a syllable in English is always 'clear,' and at the end always 'dark.' An [l] at the beginning of a syllable is formed with just the tip of the tongue raised to make contact at the top of the mouth; an [l] at the end of a syllable has the back of the tongue involved as well, humped up to 'color' the

Table 2. *Some of the consonant phonemes exemplified*

Symbols	Examples	Symbols	Examples
θ	*th*ink	č	*ch*ur*ch*
ð	*th*en	ǰ	*j*u*dge*
š	*sh*oe	y	*y*ou
ž	gara*ge*	ŋ	si*ng*

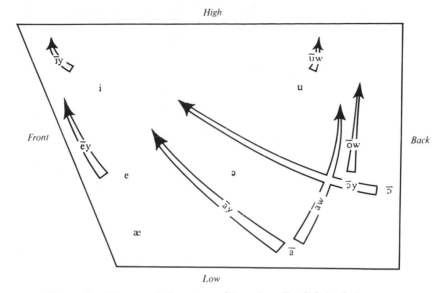

Figure 1. *The vowel phonemes of American English in their approximate articulatory and acoustic positions.*

*Tense vowels have a bar over them, lax vowels do not.
Vowel sounds including one of the semi-vowels [y] and [w] are
glided as shown by the arrows. For many speakers of American
English the glides for the high vowels [īy] and [ūw] are minimal;
for others they are more noticeable. The orientation of the vowel
symbols and arrows refers to acoustic correlates for the gesture
made by the tongue in the mouth, especially the position of the
highest point of the tongue. Thus for [īy] the highest point on
the tongue is as high and as far forward as it ever gets for a
vowel sound, for [ā] as low as it ever gets. Some speakers have
additional vowel contrasts. Many speakers lack one or more of
the contrasts here. For example, before [r] speakers may merge
tense and lax vowels into a single lax pronunciation:* they [ðēy]
combines with are *to give* they're [ðer] *with a lax vowel, sounding exactly as* there [ðer]. *Many speakers have neutralized the
contrast between* [ɔ̄] *and* [ā] *in all positions, saying* cot *and*
caught, hock *and* hawk *all with* [ā].

sound. If you record *feel* on tape and then play the tape backwards
you will hear a peculiar-sounding *leaf* with a dark [l] at the wrong end
of the syllable. You can hear these sounds distinctly in *holy* and *wholly*.
Ho-ly has a clear [l] at the beginning of its second syllable, *whol-ly* has a
dark [l] at the end of its first syllable. The two [l] sounds are *allophones*

Table 3. *The tense and lax vowels of English, in closed and open syllables*

	Vowel Sound	In Closed Syllables	In Open Syllables
Tense	īy	beet	bee
	ēy	bait	bay
	ā	pot	spa
	āy	bite	buy
	āw	bout	now
	ūw	boot	new
	ōw	boat	no
	ɔ̄	bought	saw
	ɔ̄y	void	boy
Lax	i	bit	
	e	bet	
	æ	bat	
	ə	but	
	u	put	

of the same phoneme in that although there is a difference in what the tongue does to articulate them, they are similar sounds and they do not contrast. One cannot substitute one for another in the same position and produce a change in meaning. Some languages have several [l] phonemes, English has just one.

For vowel phonemes we use the system of transcription shown in Figure 1, one suited particularly for American English. The phonetic norms specified there are reference points in terms of which we can describe variation. Speakers always have most of the 'contrasts' of this system, whatever their phonetic norms.

The vowel sounds written with two symbols are all glided: the major syllabic thrust comes at the beginning of the sound and then tapers off as the tongue glides up to a higher position. We have represented a common pronunciation where all glided vowels are tensed, with tenseness indicated by a bar over a vowel symbol, but there is considerable variation here as with other aspects of pronunciation. There is a pronunciation widespread in Canada, where the sound [āy] is tense in words like *why, wide,* and *wives,* but not tense and therefore shorter in duration in words like *white* and *wife,* where the syllable ends with a voiceless consonant.

All vowels with a bar are tense. Vowels that are not tense are called lax. A consistent difference between tense and lax vowels is that the tense vowels are longer in duration. Thus tense [ā] is notably longer in *rod* than the lax [e] in *red.* Only tense vowels can occur in stressed final open syllables (open syllables have no consonant after the vowel). Examples are shown in Table 3.

Acknowledgments

We want to acknowledge the generous support of the National Endowment for the Humanities, the Center for Applied Linguistics, and the Australian National University. At Winthrop Publishers, Paul O'Connell has provided important direction and Clive Martin, Herb Nolan and Pat Torelli have done valuable production work. The person most helpful to us in editing this volume has been one of its authors, Margaret Shaklee.

At the Center for Applied Linguistics, thanks to Begay Atkinson, John Hammer, Roger Shuy, and especially Peggy Good. Peg Griffin, and Diana Riehl. Thanks to the Department of Linguistics at U.C.L.A.—to everyone personally, and especially to Willie Martin. Thanks also to people too numerous to name at the Australian National University. Valuable contributions to the work at various stages have come from Avery Andrews, Charles Bird, Wayles Browne, Bob Dixon, Bill Foley, Talmy Givón, Cliff Goddard, John Haviland, Agnes Huhn, Harold Koch, Val Lyon (who did the map in Chapter 2), Wayne O'Neil, Phil Rose, Pablo Shopen, Carmen Silva, Benji Wald, and Anna Wierzbicka. Grateful thanks to all.

> TIMOTHY SHOPEN
> *Canberra, Australia*
>
> JOSEPH M. WILLIAMS
> *Chicago, U.S.A.*

Standards

Chapter 1

Standard English: Biography of a Symbol

Shirley Brice Heath

Shirley Brice Heath teaches anthropology and linguistics courses at the Graduate School of Education, University of Pennsylvania. She has taught Spanish and English as a second language at the elementary and secondary levels. Her special interests are the social history of language in the United States and the role of ethnography in education.

1. Standards

What does it mean to be a speaker of "good English," "proper English," or "standard English" (SE) in the United States? Both those who speak SE and those who don't, recognize it when they hear it, can readily give examples of what it is *not,* and are able to identify places where it is spoken as well as places where it is not likely to be used. When they try to define SE, however, we are reminded of the blind men trying to describe an elephant by identifying its individual parts. Some tell us SE is the absence of accent; some say it is "correct grammar"; and others say it is characterized by Latinate words and sophisticated sentence structures. Some say SE is reinforced by schoolteachers and dictionaries. Some tell us that most printed English is standard, but only some spoken English is.

We often hear the opinion that "children won't learn to talk right unless they are taught grammar." Closely related to this idea is the assumption that schools and teachers are the only institutions and agents dispensing grammar, and therefore a knowledge of SE depends on successful passage through the educational system. Moreover, to many who judge their own speech acceptable in most contexts, teachers seem to hold special powers of speaking and judging SE. But upon being introduced to an English teacher, those same people will apologize for their language by comments such as, "Oh, I must watch my English around you. If I'm wrong you'll know it." Political candidates worry about not measuring up to models of SE and often admit to "cleaning up" their accents and grammar for public performances.

3

Some or all of these views on SE are held by most of the population in the United States. But we still don't know what SE is or what it means to speak it. We only know that SE is something that is "clean," "good," and recognizable; it involves pronunciation, vocabulary, and syntax; and it is tied to specific contexts in writing and speaking, especially in school. It is an ideal by which some of us monitor our own speaking and writing and by which we are judged by others.

→ Why is SE an ideal in the United States? Why is it so difficult to say what it is? This chapter will present some historical evidence on these questions by examining what those who have attempted to define SE have said about its role in American society and what they have thereby demonstrated about its development as a symbol. Throughout its history, the linguistic and social character of American SE has not been consistently defined. We often get away with carelessly or inconsistently referring to symbols; in some ways "good English" is a symbol not unlike "Uncle Sam," the Star-Spangled Banner, or the screaming eagle. Yet unlike other nationalistic symbols, SE is also believed to be a tool, whose correct use demands that we acquire a set of skills. But tools have to be defined and identified in both their production and use and standardized in their shape, size, and the quality of raw materials from which they are made. As a tool, SE has been variously (and often inconsistently) defined and identified. How "good English" is defined often depends on how United States citizens view its role in their attempts to improve their socioeconomic status. Most symbols require little or nothing of those who acquire them; they are simply accepted or adopted for worship, adornment, or display. Moreover, if a philosophy or set of beliefs is connected with the symbol, our adherence to it can often be superficially demonstrated. Wearing the United States flag in your lapel does not necessarily mean you can recognize portions of the Constitution. SE, on the other hand, is a symbol that requires not just occasional display, but near-constant demonstration. Many believers in SE claim that one should not only be able to use SE, but should also be able to recite its rules. Even those born of parents who speak SE must have their knowledge reinforced by rules and practice provided by nonfamily members and societal institutions.

Two central issues have consistently influenced those who have written about SE—language acquisition and language change. How SE is acquired and how and why it changes have been matters of disagreement for grandparents and grandchildren, literary figures and grammarians, and students and teachers.

As we examine historical attitudes on SE by writers of grammars, books about language, and articles on language in the popular press, we frequently find these two issues uppermost. The authors wished not only to define SE, but to determine how it was learned and

4

what its role could and should be in either promoting or retarding language change.

2. The Beginnings: Principles

During most of the first half-century of United States national history, those who attended schools and colleges studied Latin, not English. Students memorized rules of Latin grammar, recited passages from the Classics, and created oratory styled on the ancients of Greece and Rome. However, what the historian Daniel Boorstin has noted as the pragmatic bent of Americans prompted their citizens to criticize education that emphasized Greek and Latin, rote recitation, and artificial lessons.[1] They wanted to stress English, an understanding of its flexibility, and practical knowledge such as letter writing, account reporting, and conversational debating. It is not surprising, therefore, that the earliest American books on English argued that the rules of the English language should be learned by observing the models of "good" speakers and writers, not by attention to rules learned in school. In 1767, the author of the following passage commented on some current views of achieving "correct English" in both the American colonies and Great Britain.

> I cannot help thinking a living language stands in small need either of a grammar or dictionary. . . . The Syntax and choice of words are best to be learned from good authors and polite company. . . . Let your style be plain and simple, suited to your subject, and to the capacity of those for whose perusal it is intended. (Campbell, *Lexiphanes: A Dialogue*)[2]

This excerpt presents three common themes that ran through books on language for the next fifty years:

• Language, spoken and written, is best learned in realistic settings.

---

1. Daniel J. Boorstin, *The Americans: The Democratic Experience* (New York: Vintage Books, 1973).
2. References for early grammars and periodicals are given in abbreviated form. A majority of these grammars may be found in the Early American Imprint Series; periodicals are most readily located through the American Periodical Series I and II. These are microprint and microfilm copies of the original sources, many of which are now extremely rare. Students of the eighteenth and nineteenth centuries usually discarded their grammar books, or they were passed down from class to class until they were too worn for further use. These books are excellent sources from which to examine language change and shifts in attitudes toward standards.

5

- A living language changes because language must be a tool, changing and changed by the needs of its speakers.
- The essential advantage of English over Latin is its practical merits; it can be made plain and simple and fitted to a wide variety of speakers and uses.

On the basis of examples like this, we may hypothesize that these writers wanted language education that would provide positive, practical benefits for both nation and individual. The United States should promote English as the universal language because of the obvious vocational advantages that accrued to those who mastered its flexibilities. Practical language skills for daily living, commerce, artisanship, and agricultural productivity depended upon education in English. It was openly admitted (even in college commencement speeches!—see the third quote below) that "learned men" who neglected English to spend their time studying Latin and Greek would not have the practical skills needed for the new nation. Local schoolmasters who wrote grammars for regional schools emphasized the important role the "unlearned" (i.e., those not trained in the dead languages) would play in building the new nation:

> It will easily be discovered what language I would wish to introduce, for carrying on this great scheme of business [treaties and diplomatic negotiations]; . . . I shall therefore frankly own, without being actuated by a *national partiality*,. that I think the *English* is the most preferable language, in all respects, to any other amongst the *living* or the *dead*. (*The Monthly Miscellany,* Nov., 1758)

> The Importance of an English Education is now pretty well understood; and it is generally acknowledged, that, not only for Ladies, but for young Gentlemen designed merely for Trade, an intimate acquaintance with the Proprieties, and Beauties of the English Tongue, would be a very desirable and necessary Attainment, far preferable to a Smattering of the learned Languages. (Ash, *Grammatical Institutes,* 1785)

A Charge which ought to be delivered to the Graduates in the Arts, in all the Colleges in the United States:

YOUNG GENTLEMEN,
You have this day received the honours of what is called a learned education. But to be plain with you, these honours are an empty shadow, and your learning is the reverse of a useful education. We have employed four years out of the five, in which you have been under our care in teaching you to read the languages of two nations, with whom you will never converse, and from whose writings you can derive not half the instruction and pleasure, that are contained in the

6

language of your own country. . . . The first and best thing you can do, is to forget all that you have been taught within these walls; afterwards let me advise you to apply yourselves to the study of the English language. It is well known we have neither taught you grammar, orthography, nor composition. (*Universal Asylum and Columbian Magazine,* July–December, 1790)

Often co-occurring with laments that both the nation and individuals were suffering from the inadequate attention given to English was the caution that the language itself was decaying. Like all natural things, language grew, reached its maturity, and then began to deteriorate. Without proper attention, American English would not even reach healthy maturity before it began to decay. The only way to prevent this was to subject the English language to rules and structures devised through the reason and discipline of man. A crucial problem, however, was whether or not these rules derived from the thing itself, or whether there were universal rules that man must discover and impose on language in order to preserve it. This dilemma had led some British to try to establish a national academy that would set the rules for English and sponsor both a dictionary and a critical guide to pronunciation. All attempts to establish government sponsorship of standardization failed. Nevertheless, many individual British speakers turned to popular pronunciation guides and Samuel Johnson's dictionary for their rules. One "critical pronouncing dictionary" recommended both universal rules (derived from analysis of the similarities of current words to ancient words) and specific guidelines drawn from usage. These specific rules were to be based on the combination of any two of the three models: the court, schoolmen and other professionals, and the "multitudes" (Walker, *A Critical Pronouncing Dictionary,* 1798).

3. The Beginnings: Pronunciation and Spelling

In the United States, citizens debated standardized pronunciation and the differences between British and American English among the various regions of the new nation and among individuals of varying social classes. In this early national period, variations in vocabulary and syntax concerned them far less than pronunciation differences. In America, early guides to pronunciation explained the relations between sounds and letters and stated the rules that governed them; speakers were to follow these guides in order to maintain a uniform pronunciation in both oral reading and speaking. Note in the following passage how the author reasons that pronunciation that differed from the norm could be interpreted as a sign of illiteracy and lack of "genius."

> The pronunciation of the southern states of English America is almost as different from that of the New-England states, even among the learned, as any two dialects of the language of any illiterate nation can be supposed to be: and yet both those parts of America abound with men of bright genius, large mental capacities and profound learning. In Great-Britain the pronunciation is much more various than in America; there being scarcely two Shires in which the English is pronounced according to the same dialect. But this is not all: the same person, both in England and America, pronounces differently when he reads, from what he does, when he converses; even when the words, which he reads, and those by which he converses, are numerically and literally the same. . . . The only method, I think, by which the English language can be reduced to an uniformity of pronunciation in reading and speaking, (and in these there should be a perfect uniformity in all languages) is—1. To ascertain, by rules as general as possible, the different sounds of the English vowels, and also the different sounds of the same vowel, accordingly as it is followed by certain consonants. 2. To ascertain, by general rules, all the different sounds of the diphthongs and triphthongs. 3. The sounds of the consonants. 4. To point out, by general rules, the silent letters in the English language. 5. To point out, by general rules, the accented or most forcibly sounded letter in monosyllables;—and the accented letter,—or rather, the most forcibly sounded syllable of words exceeding one syllable. (Carroll, *The American Criterion,* 1795)

Three views represented here are important to note, for they have been consistently asserted since the earliest days of the nation. The first is the most obvious: southern speech is different from northern speech. The second is more subtle: "learning" (experience in formal education and, specifically, exposure to literacy) changes a person's way of talking. The author asserts that people who read can learn to speak properly by listening to "elegant speakers" and comparing their oral pronunciation of individual words with the letters as the word is written.

However, determining in any absolute sense this kind of correspondence depended upon either establishing spelling reforms (making orthography "fit" the sounds of words) or standardizing spelling in accordance with models of pronunciation (i.e. written guides prescribing arbitrary letter-sound correspondences).

Reform of orthography was closely linked with the question of whether the United States should strive for a uniform national pronunciation. Some reformers, such as Benjamin Franklin, wanted an alphabet that would represent a "perfect expression" of English sounds.

In this way, words would represent sounds unambiguously, children and foreigners could more easily learn to read, and regional pronunciations could be recorded. Noah Webster's reforms were not so wide-sweeping as Franklin's; Webster wanted not a "perfect system," but rather simplification and uniformity. He proposed elimination of silent letters, spelling of the *ch* as *k* in words such as *chorus,* and substituting *sh* for *ch* in words of French origin, such as *machine.*

Webster believed pronouncing dictionaries should illustrate "standard" spellings and pronunciations determined not by imitating the British court or theater, but according to American usage. The model of usage was, however, difficult. The following letters suggest the variety of views about who should set standards and free American citizens from "European whim" in matters of orthography and pronunciation. (Remember that "brother Jonathan" was a pseudonym used then for the United States.) In addition, determine the specific pronunciation features about which these citizens were concerned. Which of these features exist in our speech today?

A LETTER TO THE EDITOR:

I am a man of business, and have not much time to examine into criticisms, and the analogy and construction of words; but as I have a serious desire that we should have some kind of standard for the words we are to make use of, I have thought of proposing a convention of the Literati, from the several states, to settle on some general principles of construction, orthography, and pronunciation. . . .

A set of writers have lately sprung up in England, who tell us, there is no need of any rules for spelling, because the best rule is to spell a word out as you pronounce it; very well, then if I am in New England, I will spell "*Keow, Geyown,* etc." If in Philadelphia, "the best *vine* is made from *wines* that grow," etc. And if in the southern states, "have you *hurd whar* the general is."—No, no, say they, these are provincial accents, you must not follow them, you must learn to pronounce as they do at the court of Great Britain; this is the standard of the English language.—Be it so, but how am I to know, at this distance, how they spell and speak there.

A pert blockhead who has become tutor to my son, is teaching him the way in which he says it's done there; but the poor boy makes such a barbarous work of it. . . . I called him the other day to read a letter to me; my friend wished to know if any member of the legislature had passed by my house; the boy began, "Dear sir, has *anne* member of the *legislatcher past* by, etc." "You blockhead," said I, quite angry, "you are reading all false; my friend knows very well there is no *Anne* who is a member of the legislature; they are all *men. Legislatcher,* Ha! what sort of word is that pray? Did you ever hear such a word in your life? Again, my friend does not want to know whether they are beyond my house or not; but whether they *passed* this way or the other." "Pappa," says the child, with all the innocence imaginable, "I'm sure that's the way Mr. _____ makes me pronounce those words, and says it is the way they do at court—I've *hurd* him say so *manne* a time, pappa." (*The Columbia Magazine,* March, 1787)

On Pronouncing Dictionaries.

Custom, says a great writer, is the tyrant of fools: if so, how few, at this advanced age of the world, are wise! Fashions begin with the rich, and the poor follow on. It has been observed, that the wiser sort of people are the last to come into the fashions; but this we must not believe, when we see the literati contending for error. Dictionarians ought to be wise, as well as learned; but these, we find, are the first to stamp authority on error. They say duty is *djuty,* endure is *endjure,* tune is *tshune,* stone is *stan,* sky is *skei,* kind is *keind,* fortune is *fortshin,* tyrant is *tir-ant,* and a thousand more absurdities. Now where do these grammarians and dictionarians go for authority? Shakespeare is so antique, Addison so solemn, Pope so holy, and Dean so swift, that they will not copy after them—No: they can't *endjure* it; they don't think it their *djuty;* so they *keindly* took *skei* to the English theatre, as a brighter *skei,* in hopes of making their *fortshin*—Heard, they say, should be pronounced *hurd;* guide, *geide;* creature, *creetchur,* etc.

Neow, I advise these *keind* polishers of *ower* language, to go to brother Jonathan, for a *geide:* he'll *larn'*um to say *keow* for cow, *veow* for vow, *geal* for girl, *heouse* for house, and a grate many other rathur clever things, and he won't *ax'*um a *farding for't* nether. (*American Museum or Repository,* August 7, 1787)

A Letter on the Modern Mode of Pronunciation.

I have often wondered that the London dialect, or in other words, the Irish innovation, should ever have obtained the sanction of Lexicographers. Does the language of courts, and of diplomatic characters, possess any peculiar charms, that its verbage should be so greedily devoured? Is it the fate of our tongue, to be in part 'occluded', for every new coined term, that makes its way through the presidential glottis! Or because their lordships, at the court of St. James, have given countenance to the infraction upon the language, which I am condemning, ought their example to have weight with those who should regulate the literature of England and America? Believe me! it is very *unforchunate* that our language should be thus despoiled of its *beauchy* and masculine *feachures.* The chewing of words, I can excuse in those, who have been *edjucated* in the habit: but I feel *injignant,* when I see a person affectedly *churning* aside from his *natchural* mode, to follow the *jictates* of the u-mangling innovators. It affects me with *society* and disgust. It *woonds* my honor. I feel an *imporchunate,* I may almost say, an *inshuperable* disposition for a *juel*. The importance of exposing the impropriety of this usage, is enforced by considering that it might be extended to more *parchiculars* with as much reason as has justified its advances hitherto; that its progress will be marked with confusion, since a *multichood* of words are rendered similar in sound, which stand for different ideas; and that *creachures* or rather persons, the *furnichur* of whose names is composed of the sounds *habichurally* answering to the letters, du-tu & c. will, by the new *accenchuation* or pronunciation, be obliged to submit to a disgusting alteration of their wonted appellations. From the court and the stage, those corrupters of the language, this deviation from the true standard of pronunciation, has found its way to the pulpit and the university. I am not about to show how the perversion of language is attended by the perversion of sentiment; but should this supplication *'churn* us, and we shall be *churned'*, in its ascent from the sacred desk, reach the ears of that inspired writer, who denounced the 'turning the grace of God into lasciviousness', would he not likewise denounce the *churning* it into ridicule. (*The Literary Cabinet*, May, 1807)

Let's look at these three passages to see if we can determine exactly which features of pronunciation bothered the writers. Matters of pronunciation are hard to derive from the spelling of a single speaker, but the similarities among these three writers make us more confident of our evidence than if we had the views of only one writer.

1. The spelling *eow* for *ou* or *ow* is used by the first two writers to indicate a particular pronunciation of such words as *cow, gown, house, now, vow,* which they spell *keow, geyown, heowse, neow, veow.* This probably refers to the fronting and raising of the first part of the [āw] diphthong; i.e., instead of pronouncing the [ā] part of the diphthong like the [ā] in *father,* some speakers pronounced it like the [æ] or [ēə] in *man.* Americans today still vary in the way they pronounce [āw], and the fronted pronunciations are sometimes felt to be less prestigious just as the nonfronted are felt (by others) to be affected. Can you hear the difference in speakers from different parts of the country? Do you ever use (or have you heard others use) an exaggerated front pronunciation to make fun of hillbilly or rural speech? Or a very backed pronunciation to portray highly affected speech?

2. One of the most troublesome features with all the writers seems to be the palatalization of *t* to *s, d* to *j,* and *s* to *sh* when they are followed in the spelling by the letter *u.* Palatals are formed with the surface of the tongue near or against the hard palate ([y] as in *yet*). As a speaker pronounces the consonants *t, d,* and *s* before [yūw] he palatalizes because the tongue anticipates the palatal position for [ūw].

11

The critics of palatalization represent the *ch* pronunciation by *ch, tch,* or *tsh;* the *j* pronunciation by *j* or *dj.* Examples are *feachure, natchural, tshune,* for *feature, natural, tune; juel, endjure* for *duel, endure.* This refers to different changes affecting *t, d, n, s, l, r* before the sound [yūw] or often when unstressed, [yə]. Apparently the palatalization proceeded earlier and faster in British English when unstressed so that some Americans were still saying *natyure* when the British were already saying *nachure.* Also some British speakers had palatalization in stressed position whereas many Americans lost the [y] altogether. Thus for *tune,* the pronunciation *chune* of some British speakers differed from the pronunciations *tyune* or *toon* of American speakers. Pick out all the examples in the texts; in which instances do the "funny" spellings agree with your pronunciation? How else have you heard these words pronounced?

3. Other examples of palatalization also appear in these writers' examples: *t* or *d* before the high front vowel [īy] and *k* or *g* before the diphthong [āy]. These pronunciations represent local dialect features that have never become widespread in either British or American English. Pick out all the examples of these in the texts. Where have you heard pronunciations like these?

4. In the case of *woond,* the writer is reflecting the more common British pronunciation [ūw] in comparison with the usual American pronunciation at the time with the *ou* diphthong [āw]. Compare the way you pronounce a *wound* from a sword and the past tense of *wind.* Actually *woond* [āw] is the older pronunciation, and the regular change of Middle English *u* to Modern English *ou* (from [ūw] to [āw]) came late in this word and established itself more strongly in America. In 1789 Webster called *woond* a recent innovation (from England) and said: "*woond* is the softer pronunciation [and] should not be adopted; for the idea it conveys is extremely disagreeable, and much better represented by a harsh word." Which pronunciation won out?

5. The spellings *anne* and *manne* for *any* and *many* reflect the pronunciation of the first vowel as the short *a* in *man* instead of the short *e* in *men,* the usual American pronunciation then, as now. The short *a* pronunciation is still heard in Ireland and some parts of England and is occasionally recorded in the United States; it may be either the older pronunciation or a reinstatement based on spelling. These two words are the only instances in our modern spelling where the spelling *an* has the pronunciation in standard speech of *en.* But in early American English there were other examples, such as *hend* for *hand,* which have either disappeared or are restricted to local dialects. Have you

ever noticed any other cases of short vowels before nasals being pronounced differently from their spelling? (Clue: how do people pronounce *pen, hymn, thing?*)

6. Of the remaining "funny" spellings, some reflect real differences in pronunciation (e.g., hurd [hərd], heard [hīərd]), some just spelling differences that did not represent different pronunciations (e.g., *passed, past*); and some seem to be mistaken extensions of a pronunciation difference (e.g., *churn* for *turn* on the model of *chune* for *tune,* even though no one said *churn*). The vowels before *r* vary in pronunciation from one region to another in the English-speaking world, and the American who has the same vowel sound in p*er*son and w*or*d is surprised to hear a Scotsman pronounce them differently. In particular, the alternation of *er* and *ar* appears even in doublets as in *person* and *parson,* which are historically the same word. What British-American differences between *er* and *ar* pronunciations have you noticed? (Clue: *clerk* and *derby, darby* are examples.)

These samples of half-satirical, half-serious proposals for standardization should not mislead us into accepting what is today a prevalent folk notion: that standardization has been a national ideal since 1776. On the contrary, aside from some frequently quoted famous personalities, such as John Adams, many other Americans—both elite and nonelite—favored diversity in language in both dialects and styles, across users and uses. Individuals from various parts of the country and different social classes clung to their speech forms as part of their identities. In the words of one observer:

> . . . in all the states, there is but one language; yet come to vernacular dialects and hardly any rights will be more jealously guarded by a Virginian, a Pennsylvanian, or a Bostonian. In the polished inhabitant of New York and of South Carolina, we perceive a pride so admirably united with complacency that they reciprocally forbear to infringe the idiomatical peculiarities of each other. (Wilson, *A Volume for All Libraries,* 1814)

Uniformity and standardization would have to depend on models or standards; such a choice would have to be arbitrary, and those who followed it would have to submit to governmental or other institutional dictates for language control. United States citizens in the eighteenth century and first half of the nineteenth century preserved language differences that identified the user's geographical origin, socioeconomic status, etc., as well as reflected stylistic variations that depended on the uses of speech (business, storytelling, etc.). These

13

variations were regarded as inevitable and necessary; each had its special requirements and purposes.

4. The Beginnings: Grammar and Diction

Americans who regarded variation as an expected—and even worthy—characteristic of language use concurred with the opinion of Samuel Pegge, a prominent Londoner, whose notes on the "local dialect of London," or "Cockney," were published in 1807. This book was widely circulated in the United States; its view that different dialects should not only be recorded, but also recognized for their value to native speakers, no doubt influenced many Americans. Disturbed by proposals in England for a "standard," Pegge wrote: "Few people trouble themselves about the daily provincial-seeming jargon of their own County, because being superficially understood [by outsiders], it answers the purposes of the natives without farther investigation. . . ." (Note the similarity of Pegge's view to that of current linguists and sociolinguists concerned with language variation geared to user and use.) Pegge found several reasons to justify dialects: (1) they served the purposes of communication among their native speakers, (2) they appeared in earlier stages of the language, and (3) they were used in the writings of prominent authors.

Compare Pegge's list of London dialect items with those noted by the American writers reviewed above. Which forms are found in both American English and the London dialect? How many of these occur today in the United States? Are they attributed to geographical origin or socioeconomic status?

aggravate for *irritate*   *hisn, hern* for *his, hers*
kiver for *cover*   *ourn, yourn* for *ours, yours*
chimley for *chimney*   *t'other* for *the other*
somewheres for *somewhere*   *weal* for *veal*
taters for *potatoes*   *know'd* for *knew* and *known*
wonst for *once*   *seed* for *saw* and *seen*
sot for *sat*   *mought* for *might*
aks for *ask*   *learn* for *teach*
took for *taken*   *fit* for *fought*
rose for *risen*   *his-self* for *himself*
fell for *fallen*   *this here* for *that there*
wrote for *written*

Many of these you will recognize as shibboleths of today, words that often mark a speaker as uneducated or inexperienced with appropriate language models. Relatively few of these are pronunciation features: /l/ for /n/, /i/ for /ə/, /w/ for /v/, and a few more. (You will remember that the latter was recorded by one American writer as occurring in Philadelphia—*wine* for *vine;* this feature was common among Pennsylvania Dutch speakers as well as in the Cockney of Pegge's day.)

Most of the other items are either vocabulary choices (*aggravate* for *irritate*), nonstandard irregular forms of past participles, or nonstandard pronoun forms. In the United States, some of these same *kinds* of differences became designated as "gross grammatical blunders" to be avoided in both speaking and writing. An 1829 grammar lists the following: "I loves, you was, might I go today, he told you and I, the man what I saw at your house, I have not none, look beautiful." (Fletcher, *The Little Grammarian.*) You will note that though the same specific items are not identified, these "blunders" relate to verb forms and pronoun choices.

Which of the "blunders" of 1829 is regarded as nonstandard today? Are any in a state of transition from nonstandard to standard designation? Do you know anyone who says, "He invited you and I," "Just between you and I"? The example *look beautiful* is a particular case of confusion over whether adjectives or adverbs should follow verbs. Fletcher suggests that *looks beautifully* is correct, presumedly reasoning that *beautifully* modifies *looks.* Have you heard people who say "he feels badly (handsomely, poorly, beautifully)"?

Beyond these "gross" errors, other items were identified in American grammars written before the mid-nineteenth century as matters of choice according to language use. Specific recommendations were made for written and spoken styles and for different uses of language. "Super" standard English, for example, demanded precise vocabulary choice, particularly in the use of prepositions. The following "incorrect phrases" may seem ambiguous. As you work through this list (from Hull, *English Grammar,* 1829), try to write the "correct phrase."

This is not *as* good as that.
This is Mr. Brown *from* New York.
I shall be there *by* 4 o'clock.
He has a *good* many scholars.
I *guess* we can get tickets there.
I have been *to* Philadelphia.
Let me get *in* the stage.
Be you going?

The weather is *awful*.
Let me have the *balance*.
It feels *like* it has been burned.
That is a *mighty* big dog.
The weather is *muggy*.
I'd *calculate* it will be about 6:00.
The evidence has not *proven* that to be true.
I *reckon* we can go soon.
She's a *tidy* housekeeper.
They *ran into* a big storm.
I have *got* to go.
Don't *tarry* over breakfast.
That's an *ugly*-tempered horse.

You may generalize that most of these items were to be "corrected" through vocabulary choices (*imagine* should be substituted for *guess*, *terrible* for *awful*, *remainder* for *balance*, etc.) "Errors" here are not matters of verb agreement, choices between nominative and objective cases, or double negatives noted in the "gross blunders." Instead they are matters of choice related to style level, degree of formality, etc.

Many of the items noted above are today either accepted or in a state of flux, for example, the choice between *proved* and *proven*. Some grammar books still show the forms of the verb *to prove* as *prove, proved, proven;* others prefer *prove, proved, proved*. In 1829, Hull preferred *proved*, so the change had begun even then. Forms of the verb *to strike* are also in flux; do you say *struck* or *striked?* Choices among prepositions no doubt puzzled you most, since current American English usage allows much flexibility in the use of prepositions. The 1829 grammar recommended *of* New York, *at* 4 o'clock. Today shibboleths related to prepositions are fewer though some remain (e.g., *different from* or *than, between* vs. *among*), and some texts still advise against ending a formal written sentence with a preposition.

Compare the recommendations given above for expository writing with the following advice to graduates of a Female Academy in 1846. The speaker initially recommends avoiding *done* for *did, shew* for *showed, between you and I* for *between you and me*. He then warns:

> . . . great care and discretion should be employed in the use of the common abbreviations of the negative forms of the substantive and auxiliary verbs. *Can't, don't,* and *haven't,* are admissible in rapid conversation on trivial subjects. *Isn't* and *hasn't* are more harsh, yet tolerated by respectable usage. *Didn't, couldn't, wouldn't,* and *shouldn't,* make as unpleasant combinations of consonants as can well be uttered, and fall short but by one remove of those unutterable names of Polish gentlemen, which

sometimes excite our wonder in the columns of a newspaper. *Won't* for *will not,* and *ain't* for *is not* or *are not* are absolutely vulgar; and *ain't* for *has not* or *have not,* is utterly intolerable. (Peabody, address delivered before the Newburyport Female High School, December 9, 1846)

You will be surprised at this speaker's awareness of ranges of "correctness" for various uses of speech; the use of *ain't* could make one either vulgar or intolerable!

The primary reason for this relatively liberal approach to achieving "a standard English" before the mid-nineteenth century was the widespread belief that grammars should be written to reflect how language is really used; the language should not be shaped by rules imposed from external sources. Many grammarians expressed this view and tried to write rules of language—both specific and universal. Many of our early grammars were imported from England and used traditional Latin designations of parts of speech (*nouns, verbs,* etc.) and stated the rules of declension of nouns, conjugations of verbs, and methods of composing rhetoric and oratory only slightly adapted from the classics.

Numerous eighteenth- and early nineteenth-century grammars stressed that categories and rules of Latin should not be applied as universals for English. Instead, these grammarians claimed that English structure would reveal its own rules—not through Latin. Note the elaboration of this idea from the following passages:

Why are youth so dull at study, and so active at play? Might I be permitted to assign the reason, I would do it in these plain words, *the almost* total neglect of *exercising their Understandings* . . . they are drilled into the study of the first principles of language and of English grammar; [these] are soon committed to memory, but to the generality of school boys, they convey no meaning. . . . (Adams, *The Thorough Scholar,* 1803)

Grammar is founded on common sense. Every sentiment expressed by words exemplifies its rules, and the ignorant observe them, as well as the learned. The principles of grammar are the first abstract truths which a young mind can comprehend. Children discover their capacity for understanding the rules of grammar, by putting them in practice. It is indeed difficult to make young people attend to what passes in their own minds . . . grammar is nothing else than a delineation of those rules which we observe in every expression of thought by words. (Alexander, *The Rudiments of Latin and English Grammar,* 1812)

The real principles of speech are simple, beautiful, and extensive in their application, to a degree which must excite the admiration of every enlightened investigator. How could it be supposed that a nation of plain men could agree in the adoption and use of a form of speech, the essential rules of which should bear any considerable resemblance to the artificial, perplexing, contradictory, and impracticable systems taught in colleges and schools. (Cardell, *Essay on Language*, 1825)

These comments support three important generalizations:

- The grammar of the language is in the language itself—not in a set of rules derived from either philosophical categorizing or from another language, such as Latin.
- This grammar is learned by the child as he comes to speak his native tongue, yet the rules for these operations are too abstract for young people to be able to state or understand.
- Thus, the attempt to teach these rules through memorization and abstraction from the context of usage by the language learner is futile.

It was unnecessary to search outside the English language and its contexts of usage for rules by which to fix a standard. Moreover, "lessons" that depended on rote memory of rules and unrealistic learning situations offered little that would encourage students to accept grammar rules as anything more than ceremonial resolutions. One author reminded students:

We learn our mother tongue by hearing it, speaking it, reading it, and writing it. The truth will be found, that the laws of grammarians, like those of other potentates of this world, reach only to a few gross enormities, which are capable of being punished, because they are easily proved. With respect to the production of positive virtue, both these sorts of laws, are nearly, and certainly equally inefficacious. (Gray, *Elements of English Grammar*, 1818)

Grammarians, therefore, found it necessary to justify why the rules of grammar, either universal or specific, should be stated in the abstract, if native speakers could acquire these rules as they acquired the language. They laid out special claims for the purposes of grammar: "to exhibit all the peculiarities of our language, every principle which distinguishes it from the grammar of every other language" (Fowle, *The True English Grammar*, 1829). They also believed that left alone, languages would decay, and the decay would lead to the deterioration of the nation itself.

In soliciting publick patronage, it cannot be deemed improper to observe in this place; that all living languages, being in the nature of things variable, the style and pronunciation of one generation, without some rallying point, becomes scarcely intelligible to the succeeding. The establishment of such a point, is therefore greatly to be desired. . . . (Allison, *The American Standard,* 1815)

However, this *rallying point* had to be indigenous to the choices of United States citizens. Teachers in the United States could act as "a species of literary court" precisely *because* they could neither fix the national language nor enforce their own views of a standard.

> At this *Tribunal,* although there may be conflicting opinions, an author may obtain a decision, founded on the merits of his work, and the nation a verdict, compatible with their literary character and interest. . . . Where can stronger claims be laid to philological legislation than in a country distinguished for *freedom* and *power* of speech? No nation has been more distinguished for a love of liberal principles than this country. (Brown, *An American System of English Grammar,* 1825)

Teachers could neither fix nor enforce standards for the United States; however, learning the rules of the language would discipline the minds of the young and would open up to them the immense potentials of English as the national language of the United States. Moreover, conscientious grammarians would clarify rules of grammar that had been erroneously applied to English. One writer proposed, "He who liberates any important branch of Science from the encumbrance of long-received errours, and he who simplifies what mistaken custom had rendered intricate in learning, deserves well of his country" (Sherman, *The Philosophy of Language,* 1826). "Innovation and refinement in the science of grammar even led men to thank God and rejoice in this display of national spirit" (ibid.). During the first half of the nineteenth century, refining grammar and providing instruction to discipline the minds of the young were goals of American nationalism, because of the self-conscious awareness Americans had of their nation's unique position in world affairs. Founded on principles of freedom, which could be kept intact only by an informed, educated public, the United States had to view language as an instrument critical to national success as well as to individual knowledge and self-advancement.

> All that concerns our public happiness, our union and peace, within ourselves; all which tends to develop our resources, improve and perpetuate our institutions; all which may give us wealth, strength, and glory among nations, depends on the general course of instruction: that instruction, in a great degree, on the goodness of our national language, which is the instrument of all. . . .
> The principles of language, therefore, necessarily blend themselves with all our prime interests as a nation; and to those who are

prepared to enter on this investigation, it is a source of unceasing admiration, that while the great leading rules of speech are few and simple, the minor variations are endless. The relative changes of words, connected with the workings of thought, adapt themselves to every imaginable form of utterance, and run into each other by such nice graduations, as are hardly obvious to the keenest observations of philosophy. Instead of considering the study of language as the mere task of the schools, there is reason to believe that a better understanding of its elements will lead to great improvements in mental and physical researches. The structure of speech, as exhibited in different conditions of society, is an exhaustless store of practical facts and principles, which go far beyond all abstract reasoning, in teaching to man the great lesson 'Know thou thyself.' (Cardell, *Essay on Language,* 1825)

This quote sums up justifications for "grammar rules." First, there is a "specialness" to English which derives from its role as both a nationalistic symbol and a national tool. English in America is a national resource that serves the interests of the nation, because it serves individual citizens in a wide variety of ways. The grammarians argue that the search for the principles through which English revealed its "graduations" or "endless variations" is one benefiting the nation as well as the individual. Moreover, knowledge of "the structure of speech, as exhibited in different conditions of society," will lead to self-knowledge and intellectual advancement.

5. A New Prescriptivism

If you were asked to list four characteristics associated with the learning and use of SE in the history of American education, what would they be? What would your sources be for determining these characteristics? More than likely, you will remember specific stories your parents and grandparents have told about their study of grammar, and you will recall pictures from history textbooks that show a repressive atmosphere in classrooms of the nineteenth century. You may even remember specific admonishments they gave you to reinforce your use of SE. Consequently, you might list some of the following characteristics: SE is a national ideal; as a single standard, it has been revered across years of rote recitation of grammar rules and diagramming of sentences; *dialects, colloquialisms,* and *regionalisms* have been negatively viewed in American educational history. Learning SE is and has been a mark of individual achievement, a reflection of upwardly mobile aspirations, and a sign of self-respect.

The quotations from the nineteenth century cited earlier do not reflect these views of SE. The views of these grammarians seem "liberal" in contrast to those most frequently held by the "man in the street" today. Many grammarians of the first half of the nineteenth century were not willing to say with absolute certainty either what SE was or what learning SE would accomplish for the individual. They were aware of the contradiction inherent between the ideal of SE as established usage—a fixed standard—and the reality of diverse usage and the changing nature of language.

Most striking in their occasional expressions of uncertainty were such questions as: could or should a "standard" be taught to schoolchildren? Was any "established usage" stable, and if so, should it be inflicted on students through arbitrary rule learning? Fixing any standard for a tool that was intended to be used creatively seemed an unnatural contradiction.

> There was a time, before grammars were invented to clip the wings of fancy, and shackle the feet of genius, when it was considered more important to express a thought clearly and forcibly, than, as now, prettily and grammatically; when genius would as soon have stooped to accommodate itself to a rule of syntax as the eagle would to take lessons from the domestic goose; when grammarians were accustomed to *note* the movements of genius, and not prescribe rules for them. (Fowle, *The True English Grammar*, 1829)

For those who considered the contradictions in their task, the lot of the grammarian seemed a hard one indeed. Numerous texts began with an apology noting that grammars confused more than they helped (Fuller, *Grammatical Exercises*, 1822). Others argued against students taking too seriously the contents of grammar textbooks; instead, they sometimes selected quotations from the "great writers" such as Pope and Swift to show students that they should consider matter before manner when they judged the writing of others.

> Whoever thinks a faultless piece to see
> Thinks what neer was nor is nor eer shall be
> In every work regard the writers end
> Since none can compass more than they intend
> And if the means be just the conduct true
> Applause in spite of trivial faults is due
> As men of breeding sometimes men of wit
> To avoid great crimes must the less commit
> Neglect the rules each verbal critic says
> For not to know some trifles is a praise

Most critics fond of some subservient art
Still make the whole dependent on the part
(quoted in Greenleaf, *A Concise System of Grammatical
Punctuation,* 1822)

These contradictions reappear in the writings of those promoting language as a national and individual resource before the mid-nineteenth century. These debates derived largely from the assumption that if speakers aware of the dynamics of language could control it, they would benefit primarily both the nation and the language and only secondarily the individual. All citizens should, therefore, join in the quest for rules and the efforts to impart those rules more effectively to the nation's young. Native authors, the national literature, and creative citizens were expected to explore the full resources of English as a tool. The symbol of SE was recognized as something akin to ceremonial law, existing not to reflect society's actual usage, but to support the ideals of some of its groups.

After 1850, attitudes toward SE changed: the role of SE as an adaptable tool gave way to SE as a symbol. Educational institutions began to emphasize not only what language *could* do for individuals, but also what it *should* do for them. When Americans realized and became concerned over the diversities among our cultures and different degrees of literacy, educational institutions came to view themselves as "factories," established to turn out similar products. Learning theory emphasized "fixing" knowledge in students' minds through rote recitation and memory. A student who passed through the educational system and could demonstrate the skills he acquired there would find vocational opportunities. No longer could people improve themselves solely through a program of self-education. The increasing number of urban centers put shoulder-to-shoulder people with different qualities and social backgrounds. There was a growing need to bring into the political process diverse cultures and language groups. As immigration increased, especially of illiterates, educational and political leaders came to believe that the only way to govern this growing diversity was to impose linguistic and cultural uniformity.

The Civil War heightened regional consciousness and rivalry. The educated urban elite wanted to justify their differences from their "country cousins" who spoke the idiom of the farm and had, among other novelties in their pronunciation, "a strange confusion with regard to the use of the letter [sound] *r!*" (Marsh, *Lectures on the English Language,* 1865). Increasingly, the educational hierarchy came to associate sameness with national stability.

When a society rejects variation for sameness, it implies that one variety can be picked as the model for all. Among the factors that contributed to a decision about the "best" variety of language were geography and social class. Boston speech, eastern New Englanders' language, in general, carried more prestige than other varieties. SE came to be defined as the language spoken by people born in New England, educated in northern schools, and exposed to the lecture circuits and writings of the northern literary and intellectual elite.

Numerous social, economic, and educational factors helped determine the generalized notion of SE that evolved during the late nineteenth century. These factors are too complex and interrelated with a myriad of historical events to be related here. However, social historians will no doubt soon add language to the list of subjects such as women, religion, Blacks, and asylums, for which they have recently begun to trace the evolving, often contradictory, and imprecise attitudes of Americans.

American literary figures were held up in grammar books as authorities. But ironically, because of their artistic need for stylistic variation, they found it necessary to protect themselves against the establishment of a fixed standard. Edgar Allen Poe expressed disgust with what he viewed as inept grammarians who passed on ancient rules in "the art of speaking and writing the English language correctly." In his critical scrutiny of grammar, Poe recognized, however, the sharp division between tool and symbol: "English Grammar and the end contemplated by the English Grammar, are two matters sufficiently distinct. . . . The definition, therefore, which is applicable in the latter instance, cannot, in the former, be true" (*The Rationale of Verse,* Vol. 14:212–3). Poe seemed to recognize that for those with position and fame, grammar was one thing; for those without social position, grammar had to be "good grammar" displaying one's education.

Walt Whitman's praise of the varieties and variations in language is well known. Teachers and textbook writers found it hard to dispute Whitman's successful use of these varieties and must have smarted under his disparagement of their fixed standards in grammar instruction and usage. Whitman proposed:

> Language . . . is not an abstract construction of the learned or of dictionary-makers, but is something arising out of the work, needs, ties, joys, affections, tastes, of long generations of humanity, and has its bases broad and low, close to the ground. Its final decisions are made by the masses, people nearest to the concrete, having most to do with actual land and sea. (*Slang in America,* 1888:69)

Most grammarians could not accept this variety, because institutional and societal goals seemed to demand uniformity to support national unity. One grammarian termed "inconveniences resulting from the existence of local dialects . . . very serious obstacles to national progress, to the growth of a comprehensive and enlightened patriotism, to the creation of a popular literature, and to the diffusion of general culture'' (Marsh, *Lectures on the English Language,* 1865).

Grammar books challenged the notion that language could not be *fixed* by reiterating an old distinction that was, if not especially precise and clear, at least familiar, i.e., grammar was both an art and a science. The *art* of grammar taught *how* English should be spoken and written; the *science* of grammar taught ''why one form of speech should be used rather than another'' (York, *English Grammar,* 1864). As an *art,* grammar was subject to the changing judgments of literary critics and orators; however, as a *science,* grammar remained intact over the years, its laws seemingly immutable in their explanations of language structures. Some grammarians even went so far as to suggest that grammar as *art* also had a fixed quality. In the following quote, note this attitude and think about its implications for SE as a nationalistic symbol.

> Grammar is both a *science* and an *art.* As a *science,* it investigates the principles of language in general: as an *art,* it teaches the right method of applying these principles to a particular language, so as thereby to express our thoughts in a correct and proper manner, according to established usage. (Bullions, *An Analytical and Practical Grammar of the English Language,* 1864)

Note that this author does not seem to question (as did earlier grammarians) whether there is a single ''correct and proper manner'' or ''established usage.'' Moreover, he asserts that within the art of grammar, there is a ''right method.''

This moralistic tone runs through late nineteenth- and early twentieth-century grammars. The use of ''good grammar'' is a virtue associated with ''book study.'' As education and literacy expanded and the written norm became more and more widespread, the spreading universal language was to be uniform in both spoken and written forms. Textbooks emphasized the co-occurrence of SE with industry, good behavior, and moral character. Grammarians realized that memorizing rules was boring and often unrelated to actual language use, but industry and devotion of both pupil and teacher would ''win out'' and the prize would be SE. One well-known grammarian warned:

> Suffice it to say, that English is not a language which teaches itself by mere unreflecting usage. It can be mastered, in all its wealth, in all its power, only by conscious, persistent labor. . . .

> While . . . I would open to the humble and unschooled the freest access to all the rich treasures which English literature embodies, I would inculcate the importance of a careful study of genuine English, and a conscientious scrupulosity in its accurate use, upon all who in any manner occupy the position of teachers or leaders of the American mind, all whose habits, whose tastes, or whose vocations, lead them to speak oftener than to hear. (Marsh, *Lectures on the English Language,* 1865)

Some authors equated the "fixed rules of grammar" with "right," and some argued that "the mass of the people, therefore, sin against the genius of their Mother-tongue in good company . . ." (*How to Talk,* 1857).

Instead of noting stylistic and dialectal varieties and describing language as it is used, many grammarians after 1850 prescribed absolutes for all uses and users of language:

- Do not use *them* for *these, this here* for *this.*
- Do not use adverbs as adjectives (as in 'The country looks beautifully in June.')
- Select such prepositions as express the relations intended.
  During should be used when the event continues through all the period mentioned.
  In, at, or *within* is used when the event does not continue during the whole period.
  In or *at* is used before the names of countries, cities, and towns.
  Into should be used after verbs denoting entrance.
- Do not use *like* or *with* for *as, but* for *than, that* for *why,* or *without* for *unless.*

(Harvey, *A Practical Grammar of the English Language,* 1878)

Can you correct the following sentences according to the rules given above? Do you note a change in the rules about *look beautifully* from the 1829 grammar?

1. I will pay you sometime during next week.
2. He put the money in his pocket.
3. She was feeling delicately.
4. They live in houses like we do.
5. We ought to be industrious like our forefathers were.
6. The answer is the same with that book.
7. He reads for no other purpose but to pass away the time.
8. This is the reason that I stayed at home.
9. I shall not go without you go with me.
10. I will be there in the evening.

You will think that many of the above need no "correction." You would not judge someone who uttered some of these sentences as deficient in taste, morality, or wisdom. Texts of the late nineteenth century did, however, link these qualities with grammatical correctness. Knowledge of grammar was described as "discovery of truth" (Metcalf, *English Grammar for Common Schools,* 1894). Acquisition of "good grammar" promised to bring all manner of "good things":

> this science not only lays (or, at least, should lay) the foundation of all sound logic and all true eloquence—has the closest connection with correct thinking, as well as with the correct transmission of the products of thought from mind to mind—but serves as a natural and indispensable introduction to our courses of intellectual training, and the first step in a philosophical education: (How much may the future success of the young student depend, on the manner in which this first step is taken?) (Mulligan, *Exposition of the Grammatical Structure of the English Language,* 1860)

Grammar teaching was based on the rote memorization of rules and on parsing (and diagramming) sentences. The same rules and correct examples were repeated in grammar book after grammar book. Students were "invited" to correct sentences containing errors, to diagram correct sentences, and to apply the rules in their own writing. If these methods were not sufficient to make students aware of the possible errors that they could commit in spoken and written language, there were books filled with nothing but examples of "the demerits of incorrectness" (for example, Hodgson, *Errors in the Use of English,* 1882). The moral virtues of "good English" and examples of its use were provided in McGuffey readers, from which passages were memorized and recited. During the same period of instruction, students studied grammar and spelling; reciting rules and performing in spelling bees were popular activities. Consequently, students learned to "show off" their spelling skills on "hard words," rule recitation, and allusions to the classics and literary giants.

But students did not learn the language skills necessary for composing a successful letter in a style appropriate for a purpose and the relationship of writer and addressee. In 1865, the children in a one-room school in Oregon expressed their feelings about school to the teacher in a special letter-writing event. The following letter illustrates how one student spelled all the big words correctly, but confused the style appropriate to speaking and writing.

DEAR TEACHER
    As all the scholars are writing letters I will try to write one too, for I think it is a pretty good thing to learn to write letters, for if a

person has any friends he aught to write to them once in a while. Well I am sory that school is so near at a close but as circumstances is it will have to close.

Well the studies that I have is Reading Geography Arithmetic Writing and Spelling and I believe that I like Arithmetic the best and I would like to know whitch you think is best I think that Grammar would be an important study. I think that we have had a very good school here this winter and we have had a very good teacher. Well I think that I canot write any more at present.

This student's letter illustrates the schoolmaster's emphases on spelling, rote memory, and formal phrases. The fact that these emphases had changed little over the years is illustrated in the following letter, written by a parent of a child in the same school.

SIR

I am vary sorry to informe that in my opinion you have Shoed to me that you are unfit to keep a School, if you hit my boy in the face accidentley that will be different but if on purpos Sir you are unfit for the Buisness, you Seam to punish the Small Scholars to Set a Sample for the big wons that is Rong in the first place Sir Make your big class Set the Sample for the little ones Sir is the course you Sould do in My opinion Sir

I shall in forme the Superintendant in which this Scool has been commeced and how it Seames to go on[3]

From these two letters, can you select sentences in which the writer is "showing off?" What are the major types of errors? How did the parent mark the ends of the sentences? How can you tell that schoolmasters of that day did not emphasize the differences among language used for different styles, writing and speaking purposes, audiences, and topics?

Though students may not have been aware of how to produce the different styles necessary for daily living, they were keenly aware of the potential for social and economic achievement attached to language use. One young student in the frontier school of Oregon took the matter philosophically:

FRIENDS, TEACHER AND PARENTS:

Your friend Mr Charles Henry Hargadine, who now makes his appearance before you, would like to say something to please you, but I am not used to speaking, and I may not succeed. But I can say that I have determined to be *somebody* when I come to be a man. I don't think I can ever succeed to be tied down to a yard stick, or watch the

_____
3. David Tyack, "The Tribe and the Common School," *Call Number* (Spring 1966).

tiresome motions of a sawmill. I'll clime the ladder of fame. I may go away up, and then come down 'ker-spat'. But what of that, we are bound to have our ups and downs in this world any way[4]

"Good English" was a class marker, a step to success, and a way of avoiding "ker-spats." One grammar equated social class and grammar in this way:

> Good English is the English used by the best speakers and writers; and the use of such English is 'only a phase of good manners.' Bad English, that is, English unlike that which is used by well-informed and careful writers, produces in the mind of a well-informed reader an impression of vulgarity or ignorance similar to that which we get from seeing a person eat with his knife. It is with language as with clothes and conduct. Persons who wish to be classed as cultivated people must not only dress and act like cultivated people; they must also speak and write like them. A help toward this end is the study of grammar. (Buehler, *A Modern English Grammar,* 1900)

William Fowler, a prominent late nineteenth-century grammarian who wrote an English grammar for college students and professional men, warned: "unless men . . . bestow their attention upon the science and the laws of the language, they are in some danger, amid the excitements of professional life, of losing the delicacy of their taste and giving sanction to vulgarisms, or to what is worse." (*English Grammar,* 1887). Fowler expressed another concern uppermost in the minds of many Americans in the second half of the nineteenth century. In what was termed the "age of reading," more people were literate than ever before, and wide varieties of information were available. Conversations and other oral forms of communication—even public oratory—were declining in favor of newspapers and other written means of exchanging knowledge and opinion. This extension of writing into formerly oral areas of communication, such as public lectures, debate series, picnics, stump meetings, and conversation clubs, influenced the increasing drive for standardization by grammarians and like-minded citizens. Newspapers were urged to use "correct" language, and authors were reminded that "familiar idiomatic prose seems less attractive than in former times" (Moore, *American Eloquence,* 1857). Fowler put his concerns even more strongly:

> As our countrymen are spreading westward across the continent, and are brought into contact with other races, and adopt new modes of thought, there is some danger that, in the use of their liberty, they may break loose

---

4. Ibid.

from the laws of the English language, and become marked not one, but by a thousand Shibboleths. Now, in order to keep the la of a nation one, the leading men in the greater or smaller commun the editors of periodicals, and authors generally, should exercise the same guardian care over it which they do over the opinions which it is used to express. . . . (Fowler, *English Grammar,* 1887)

6. Changing Perspectives in the Twentieth Century

Many of these views have carried over in the techniques and tools for teaching grammar in twentieth-century schools. Moreover, the strong emphasis on assimilation and the role of "correct English" in that process encouraged the schools to maintain traditional methods of "teaching grammar." Immigrants, travelers, and all others uncommitted to a uniform English language were admonished: "a cleavage in the language now would mean to us a cleavage of the nation in its most vulnerable if not its most essential part."[5] In a time of national stress, which discouraged differences among groups, rules for uniform behavior in language (as in other areas of social life, such as drinking) became more institutionalized and uniform. Even "everyday English" for social settings such as clubs and other social gatherings should be learned from texts which stressed "Americanism from cover to cover" (Bolenius, *Advanced Lessons in Everyday English,* 1921). Others proposed that language texts and teachers could provide "development of the ethical and the aesthetic through language" (Kinard, et al., *Our Language,* Book I, 1927).

To be sure, linguistics was developing as a science during the late nineteenth and early twentieth centuries, and linguists often spoke out against the popular meaning of "grammar." W. D. Whitney of Yale wrote *Essentials of English Grammar for the Use of Schools* in 1877. He prefaced his work with the following summary of grammar and grammar teaching:

> That the leading object of the study of English grammar is to teach the correct use of English is, in my view, an error, and one which is gradually becoming removed, giving way to the sounder opinion that grammar is the reflective study of language, for a variety of purposes, of which correctness in writing is only one, and a secondary or subordinate one—by no means unimportant, but best attained when sought indirectly. . . .

5. Edward Steiner, *Nationalizing America* (New York: Revell, 1916), p. 102. During the second decade of this century, many books strongly promoted Americanism and the Americanization of all those who did not reflect American ideals of language and culture.

29

> It has been my constant endeavor to bear in mind the true position of the grammarian . . . he is simply a recorder and arranger of the usages of language, and in no manner or degree a lawgiver; hardly even an arbiter or critic. (Whitney, 1877)

During the twentieth century, linguists have continued to make the same points about definitions and uses of "grammar." However, these views have influenced very few textbooks or techniques of "grammar" teaching. In fact, until recently, attitudes toward SE as a symbol and a tool seem to have changed very little. Most teachers and texts have ignored the dynamic nature of language and prescribed criteria for language use without concern for setting or context. They have ignored contexts in which we learn language naturally, because their variety made it difficult to identify the process of acquiring SE.

In the past decade, this situation has changed. Today, many "grammars" are no longer prescriptive texts; they are descriptions of a language written in accordance with the "science of linguistics." What were formerly "grammar books" are now "language arts" books, reminding us of the how-and-why dichotomy of art/science which those who wrote about language in the mid-nineteenth century had recognized. Textbooks you may have used no doubt reflect in some ways this current distinction. What trends from linguistics and current emphases on cultural and ethnic pluralism in the United States do you see reflected in the following passage from a current text?

> Our premise is that all dialects of English, American or otherwise, are equally valuable, equally effective modes of communication. We believe that the standard English dialect is linguistically no better nor worse than any other dialect of English, and that 'standard' English is accepted as standard only for non-linguistic—historical, political, and sociological—reasons. Ideally, then, there should be no need to teach standard English at all, since speakers of various dialects of the same language can all communicate with one another if they want to. However, we do not live in an ideal society. Many students will find themselves at a disadvantage in a variety of situations, especially on the job market, if they do not have mastery of the standard dialect. (Gefvert, Raspa, Richards, *Key to American English,* 1975, preface)

These views should sound much more similar to those of grammarians of the early nineteenth century than to those of the post-1850 period.

Texts and techniques are beginning to reflect not only the attitudes of the early United States toward SE and grammar, but also those of today's linguists. However, most of the research on which these texts rely (and often continue to reuse) was done over a decade ago. It is very difficult for even relatively current linguistic research to influence texts and teacher-training techniques without a long period of "cultural lag." And even as the technical aspects (i.e., texts and teacher-training processes) have begun to catch up with current linguistic research, norms and ideals among the general population still show influence of late nineteenth-century views of how to acquire "good grammar." Many individuals in today's society also judge a person's social standing, character, and propensity for adherence to a series of mainstream values such as honesty, thrift, and hard work by his or her use of SE. No doubt, Edwin Newman reflected the attitudes of many parents demanding increased teaching of "basics" when he proposed: "Language is in decline . . . we would be better off if we spoke and wrote with exactness and grace, and if we preserved, rather than destroyed, the value of our language" (Newman, *Strictly Speaking,* 1974).

SE has evolved in its roles since the nation's founding, as have the sources and degrees of prescriptivisms associated with it. Initially, SE as a single norm was not considered either necessary or possible in a developing nation that was dependent on a flexible language for its exchange of information and free social expression. After the mid-nineteenth century, however, the increased demand for cultural uniformity extended to language. "Right," "proper," and "correct grammar" became linked in the American mind, which viewed the acquisition of SE as a semipatriotic goal that contributed to national strength and unity. What resulted is familiar: many citizens believe in SE as a symbol, i.e., they think it should be acquired, but they themselves either do not do so, or if they do, they often do not use SE with all listeners at all times. SE has thus remained an ideal—not a fixed, defined entity—precisely because it has met our cultural needs. The ideal of SE is just that—an ideal—not a static reality. As a symbol, SE could be held immutable and fixed; as a tool, it was recognized and used as a flexible, changing resource. Integral to SE is its dialogic quality, and its capabilities for being addressed by changing national, historical, and cultural perspectives.

Suggestions for Further Reading

Almost all books on American English include some discussion of the role of SE in the cultural life of the nation, especially in education. H. L. Mencken provides both substantive and humorous details on how a "standard" evolved in the editions and supplements to *The American Language* (1919–48, 3 volumes, 4th edition. New York: A. A. Knopf, volume 1 The American Language, 1936; volume 2, The American Language, Supplement

One, 1945; volume 3, The American Language, Supplement Two, 1948) C. Merton Babcock's reader, *The Ordeal of American English* (Boston: Houghton Mifflin, 1961), consists of primary sources (letters, official documents, and contributions to periodicals) reflecting evolving views of a "standard" American English. Students in History of English courses have since 1958 read with pleasure Albert Marckwardt's *American English* (New York: Oxford University Press, 1958). For a survey of changing attitudes toward SE, and especially its role in literature and national culture, articles in the journals *American Speech, American Literature,* and *American Quarterly* will be useful. Discussions of "grammar" and education found in *English Journal* and *College English* show the relationships that have developed in the twentieth century between the principles of linguistic science and educational guidelines given to grammar teachers.

Chapter 2

The Rise of
Standard English

Margaret Shaklee

Margaret Shaklee is a "philologist" in the English department at UCLA, teaching courses in the history of the language, Renaissance English, stylistics, and theoretical grammar. She is about to remand her title to the department and UCLA, and go off to do some field work in early childhood development.

Introduction: The Overlapping Features of Regional, Social, and Style Dialects

Like all languages, the English language varies—from time to time, from place to place, from class to class, from style to style, from speaker to speaker. Many factors contribute to this situation of variation, and one of the most interesting is that people use language to make and maintain social distinctions: a speaker may say "I don't have any money" rather than "I haven't any money" and identify himself as American rather than British; he may say "isn't" instead of "ain't" and identify himself with the American middle class, rather than with the lower class; he may use the word "indicate" when he is talking to his colleagues in business and "show" when he is talking to his wife and identify himself with a particular group of style choices within his class language. In each instance, he is choosing the "dialect" of a particular group. In this regard we can say that we all speak a dialect, or, perhaps more accurately, we all speak a variety of dialects, determined by where we live (regional dialect), which social group we identify with (sociolect), and who we are talking to (style levels or "dialects").

Dialects are usually maintained in contrast, although a speaker's choices among competing dialect characteristics may be made in varying degrees of self-consciousness. Regional dialects are often quite unselfconsciously maintained, especially by speakers who do not move out of a single dialect area. As people move more frequently from area to area, they become more conscious of contrasts and may then select

33

the characteristics of a single regional dialect or, as is increasingly the case with mobile Americans, may acquire a polyglot mixture of regional dialect characteristics.

Within any given regional dialect, the average speaker will identify himself most strongly with one class through its dialect and will quite likely consciously maintain that sociolect in contrast to one of another class, as, for example, the middle-class American who self-consciously avoids *ain't* in order not to be identified with the "lower" class. Most speakers will know of other class dialects and will maintain their sociolect in contrast, just as they maintain their class status in contrast. Style "dialects" are maintained perhaps most self-consciously, since a speaker constantly makes choices among several style variants, choices that depend on the degree of formality or intimacy of a speaking situation. Although the diagram in Figure 2.1 may oversimplify a complex situation with fuzzy and not always reliable distinctions, it offers a means of relating, conceptually, an individual speaker's dialect choices—his idiolect—to the language as a whole.

The average speaker of one language adopts the dialect of the region in which he lives; within that dialect, he speaks the dialect of the class with which he identifies; that sociolect comprises several style levels for use in various social situations.

This fairly neat description of dialect variation is complicated by

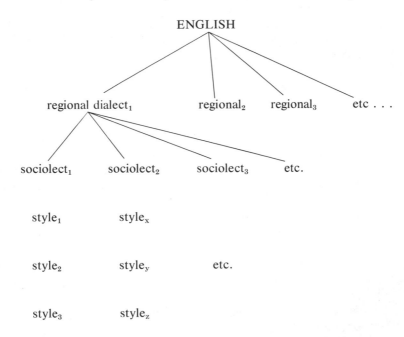

Figure 2.1. *Regional Dialects, Sociolects, and Style Dialects*

at least two factors: first, dialects share characteristics, and second, dialects vary in time. Dialects are dialects of a common language and not separate languages because they share a basic abstract structure (grammar) and much of their vocabulary. The characteristics that a dialect does not share with the other dialects of the same language constitute its hallmarks. A dialect will share some of its characteristics with neighboring dialects and is thus distinguished from it not by a set of exclusive features, but by a distinctive *combination* of features. We show schematically what happens in Figure 2.2. This scheme could be extended to include style dialects and idiolects; within a sociolect, style dialects manifest the same overlap of features.

The features of dialects overlap partly because dialects share ancestries, just as languages do. Dialects also share characteristics because they borrow from each other, especially from neighboring regional, class, and style dialects. Since a feature is added or replaced in the borrower dialect, this borrowing results in a change, a variation in time.

An example: regional dialects of American English differ as to the speakers' use of *pail* or *bucket;* recently a linguist, Hans Kurath, observed that in the *bucket* area the upper-class speakers are beginning to use *pail* as a style variant. Another instance: class dialects in American English have differed as to whether speakers use *ain't* or *isn't* and *am not;* again recently, the editors of the Merriam Webster dictionary have reported that upper-middle-class educated speakers are using the form *ain't* in the expression "ain't I?" in casual speaking situations. Again, the linguist William Labov has discovered that New York City speakers are changing their pronunciation of words like *fourth* from "fo-uth" to "forth"; they are reinstating the "r." Presumably they are imitating the midland dialect in America, and they are doing so most

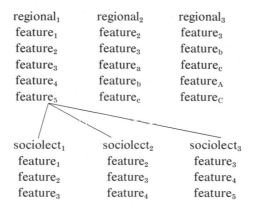

Figure 2.2. *Feature Overlap*

35

markedly at the most self-conscious and formal style levels. These examples illustrate not only that dialects borrow from each other, but that they borrow in a particular pattern: borrowing seems to begin at particular levels of style within a class dialect and at particular class levels within a regional dialect and then spreads to neighboring style and class dialects. A form borrowed from a relatively prestigious dialect (like the "r" in New York City or *pail* in the *bucket* area) is adopted first in the more formal and self-conscious levels of style. A form borrowed from a nonprestige sociolect (like *ain't*) appears first at the most casual levels of the sociolect of a higher class.

Local dialect borrowing changes a whole language when the borrowing is generalized to all speakers of that language. Such was the case with the pronouns *they, their,* and *them* in the Middle English period. Middle English speakers had inherited from Old English a pronoun case system in which the third-person pronouns were very similar in singular and plural: the singular was *hē, his,* and *him;* the plural was *hī, hira, him.* In the eleventh century, Danes who spoke a language closely related to Old English settled in northern England and eventually came to rule England for a time. Speakers of northern English dialects, in close contact with the Danes, adopted from them the pronouns *thai, there,* and *thaim* (they, their, them), partly to resolve the ambiguity of their own pronouns and partly because the Danes, as their rulers, spoke a more prestigious language. This change, which began as a regional borrowing in the northern English dialects, then spread to other dialects and eventually manifested itself in the language of all speakers. The change was motivated by ambiguity in the language itself (an internal imperative) and by the social prestige of the Scandinavian language (an external imperative). The following pages focus on external social pressure for change, but we need to keep in mind that internal structural pressures are also at work in almost all language change.

Sometimes large movements of people introduce language change quite radically by changing an entire social structure. Such was the case when the Danes ruled England in the first half of the eleventh century and when the French conquered England in the latter half of that century. In both cases, the foreign language—spoken by the upper class—exerted a tremendous influence on the English language, introducing not only new vocabularies, but also new syntactic and phonologic patterns. Such is also the case when large populations, seeking economic and social prosperity, move from country to city. Often, in fact, the lower class in an urban social structure will comprise outsiders or their descendents—e.g., the southern Black in New York City, the southern white in Chicago and Detroit, and the Chicano in Los Angeles. When a large, fairly homogeneous group with a common regional background constitutes a city's lower class, the characteristics of their regional dialect become the hallmarks of the urban lower-class dialect, often designated as "nonstandard," against which will play a notion of standard—the speech of the upper, established classes. Thus a nonstandard dialect may begin with characteristics of a regional dialect not indigenous to the city; as that regional dialect comes into the city, it becomes the sociolect of the lower class.

Let's use an extended illustration from modern English. *Ain't* used to be a regionalism of the South (and of a few "pocket" dialect areas elsewhere); it was a local form for *be + not* and *have + not*. It is still used by most southern speakers, although not in all contexts. At the end of the nineteenth century, when the South faced possible economic collapse, southerners flocked to the prosperous northern and midland cities, took jobs in factories, and were automatically members of the lowest social class. They brought with them their *ain't,* which the middle classes cited (along with *seen* for *saw, don't* for *doesn't,* and *they was* for *they were*) as a linguistic marker that excluded the speaker from membership in their group. If a southern speaker wanted to rise socially and economically, he had to change, among other things, his dialect, substituting the prestige forms of the negated *be* for his *ain't* (and changing other verb inflections). A characteristic of a regional dialect became a characteristic of a social dialect.

Out of this situation a national "standard" can develop when a nation institutionalizes language, begins to make self-conscious judgments of "correct" and "incorrect" usage, and begins to teach them to its children. Often the language described as "correct" is the sociolect of the economically powerful, as seems to be the case in American English. (Other nations, especially the self-consciously "emerging" ones, choose a national standard with other criteria in mind, e.g., the desire for a national unity through language.) The dialect characteristics of the South have become features of the lower-class dialect of American English because the southern laborer has settled in all American cities, particularly those of the Northeast and Midwest, where much of the economic power of the United States resides. In contrast, the characteristics of middle- and upper-class dialect of those areas have become the hallmarks of "standard" American English.

1. Regional and Social Variation in the Speech of Medieval England

Medieval England offers a much more simple, though forceful, demonstration of the way class mobility establishes a standard language. When William of Normandy came to England in 1066 to exercise a very doubtful right to the English throne, he found England to be a loose

37

political confederation of the surviving communities of seven Anglo-Saxon kingdoms. Because these communities were isolated topographically from each other, each community sustained a dialect of English quite different from that of its neighbors, although the dialects shared a common ancestry on the continent. William welded these groups into one nation by conquest and submission. He imposed on London, the city of his court, French culture and the French language, an imposition felt most keenly by the upper class and least and perhaps not at all by the common laborer. This culture remained in full force until 1204 when King John lost his claim to Normandy, and England and France reestablished their enmity. The eventual consequence of French withdrawal was room at the top for Englishmen and a general social upheaval that greatly increased the opportunity to move from class to class into social prosperity. At the same time and perhaps related to the exodus of the French, London began to draw a remarkably diverse population from all parts of England, speakers of widely divergent dialects, in search of economic prosperity. The maintenance of non-native French as an upper-class dialect and the emergence of a virtual Babel of country dialects in London set some people eventually worrying about a national standard of English. One such person was John of Trevisa, who discussed the problem in fairly complicated and interesting terms. Here is what he said, writing in southern England in 1385[1]:

	As *hyt* ys *y-knowe* houw meny maner people	*it/known*
	buth in this ylond, ther buth also of so meny people	*be*
	longages and tonges; notheles Walschmen and	
	Scottes, that buth *nowt y-melled* with other nacions,	*not/mixed*
5	holdeth wel ny *here* furste longage and speche, bote	*their*
	[yet] Scottes, that were som tyme confederat and	
	[lived] with the Pictes, drawe somwhat after here	
	speche. Bote the Flemmynges, that [live] in the	
	west side of Wales, *habbeth* y-left here strange speche	*have*
10	and speketh Saxonlych y-now. Also Englischmen,	
	[though] *hy* hadde fram the bygynnyng thre maner	*they*
	speche, Southeron, Northeron, and Myddel speche	
	(in the myddel of the lond), as hy come of thre	
	maner people of Germania, notheles, by commyxtion	
15	and *mellyng* furst with Danes and afterward	*mixing*
	with Normans, in menye the *contray*	*country's*

1. Joseph Rawson Lumby, ed., *Polychronicon Ranulphi Higden Monachi Cestrensis: Together with the English Translations of John of Trevisa and of an Unknown Writer of the Fifteenth Century,* 7 vols. (London: Longman, Green & Co., 1879), 1:8–10. Edited and reprinted in Fernand Mosse, *A Handbook of Middle English* (Baltimore: Johns Hopkins Press, 1954), pp. 286–87.

longage is *apeyred,* and som useth strange   *flawed*
wlaffyng, chyteryng, harryng and garrying,
grisbittyng. This apeyryng of the burth-tonge
20   ys bycause of *twey* thinges. On ys, for   *two*
chyldern in scole, *ayenes* the usage   *against*
and manere of al other nacions, buth compelled
for to leve here oune longage, and for to construe
here lessons and here thinges *a* Freynsch   *in*
25   and habbeth, *suthe* the Normans come furst into   *since*
Engelond. Also, gentilmen children buth y-tauyt for
to speke Freynsch fram tyme that *a* buth y-rokked   *they*
in here cradel . . . and *oplondysch* men wol lykne   *country*
hamsylf to gentilmen, and *fondeth* with grete bysynes   *try*
30   for to speke Freynsch for to be more y-told of.
     . . . Hyt semeth a gret wondur houw
Englysch, that ys the burth-tonge of Englysch-men
and here oune longage and tonge, ys so
dyvers of *soun* in this ylond. . . . for men of   *varied/*
35   the est with men of the west, as hyt were   *sound*
undur the same party of heven, acordeth more
in sounyng of speche than men of the north
with men of the south; therfore hyt ys that
Mercian, that buth men of myddel Engelond,
40   as hyt were parteners of the endes, undurstondeth betre the syde longages, Northeron
and Southeron, than Northeron and Southeron
undurstondeth eyther other.
     Al the longage of the Northumbres, and
45   specialych at York, ys so scharp, slyttyng
and frotying, and unschape, that we Southeron
men may that longage *unneth* undurstonde.   *hardly*
Y trow that that ys bycause that *a* buth ny   *I/think/they*
to strange men and aliens that speketh
50   strangelych, and also bycause that the kynges
of Engelond [liveth] alwey *fer* fram that   *far*
contray: For a buth more y-turned to the
south contray; and *yef* a goth to the north   *if*
contray, a goth with gret help and strengthe.
55   The cause why a buth more in the south contray
than in the north may be betre cornlond, more
people, more noble cytes, and more
profytable *havenes.*   *harbors*

Some background may help us understand John of Trevisa's (mostly correct) reasoning about the history of dialects in Middle English. In his first paragraph, he talks about the original dialect situation

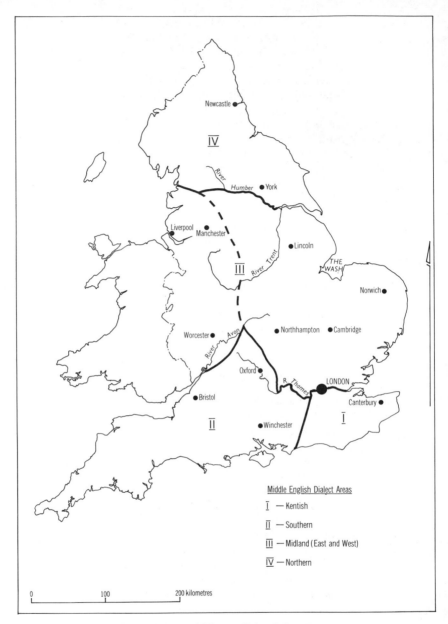

Figure 2.3. *Middle English Dialect Areas*

created by three Germanic tribes who settled the island in the fifth century. Angles settled north of the Thames, and their dialect is the ancestor of the Middle English midland dialect (see Figure 2.3). The group who settled north of the Humber River (Northumbria) developed a separate dialect when their "Anglish" mixed with the Danish of north coast settlers (line 14) in the ninth and eleventh centuries. Saxons settled south of the Thames, and their dialect is the ancestor of the southern dialect; Jutes settled in the southeast corner of the island, and their dialect is the precursor of Kentish in Middle English. On this side Trevisa speaks of a second "commyxtion," the Norman invasion in 1066. He dislikes the residual interest in French among the English nobility and in the schools, which he believes works to the detriment of the developmentof English.

In trying to puzzle out the choice of a "standard" English, Trevisa makes some observations about the sociology of language— the relationship between language and its speakers—and draws some tentative conclusions about what kinds of social phenomena influence change in language. He observes: (1) languages change through contact with other languages (14–19); (2) languages and dialects differ from region to region through the isolation of groups of speakers (44–52); (3) people who aspire to climb socially copy the language of their superiors (28–30); and (4) the upper classes reinforce "standard" through education (20–28). He makes two suggestions for a standard English that draw on important ideas of language change: at line 38, he suggests that midland English (Mercian) might act as a standard. Why? Strong hint: if languages change through contact, so must dialects; what is there about the midland dialect that would make it a likely choice? At line 48, he suggests that his own southern English might be a standard. Why? We will return to his two proposals to see with the advantage of hindsight what actually happened in Middle English when the upper class to which Trevisa belonged failed to impose a standard, and standard English "rose" quite without the constraints of grammarians and language legislation. The history of standard English witnesses the fact that it is natural for a complex social community to establish a standard among divergent dialects and to establish as standard the dialect of the economically powerful.

2. Variant Forms: Competition for a Place at the Top

Let's look at the dialects of Middle English and ask how a standard English was distilled out of Trevisa's three major dialects. First, his own dialect of southern English: there are five variants in his dialect that have become important to linguists in differentiating the three major Middle English dialects (southern, midland, and northern). Apart from matters of pronunciation (which are hard to derive from the spelling of a single speaker), Trevisa uses these grammatical forms:

1. *buth* (line 2 and through the text) is a dialectal form of *be,* third-person plural, present tense (we would use *are*). Old English expressed the copula with two verbs, *beon* and *wesan* (our modern conjugation of *be* is an amalgamation of the two):

	wesan			*beon*		
Ic eom	we ⎫		Ic beo	we ⎫	
thou eart	ye ⎬ sindon (are)	thou bist	ye ⎬ beo(n)
he is	hy ⎭		he be	hy ⎭	

The dialects of Middle English differed as to whether they expressed the copula with the first or with the second conjugation, that is, whether they used *am, is,* and *are* or forms of *be (be, beth, been).* Trevisa's *buth* is a variation of *beon* or *been* and displays in its inflection another characteristic of the southern dialect, which we will consider in a moment. In Trevisa's time, the dialects used the two forms to distinguish third-person singular and plural in the present. Trevisa uses *is* for singular (17, 20, etc.) and *be (buth)* for plural. The variants, then, are two: copula singular (*am* and *is,* or *be* and *beth*) and copula plural (*are* or *be, beth,* and *been*). A century later, dialects will distinguish the two forms for mood, rather than for number: *be* in subjunctive and *is/are* for indicative; subjunctive is used in surbordinate clauses, especially those of hypothesis *(whether, if)* and those beginning with *that* (this use survives, perhaps archaically, in modern English):

If this *be* treason, we are all traitors.

The teacher expects that we *be* quiet.

2. The inflection of the verb for third-person plural, present tense (the verb used with *they* and plural nouns as subject) is *-th* (as in *buth*); in line 5, *holdeth* is such a form (modern English has no inflection there now). Other dialects may use the variants *-n (holden)* and Ø *(hold);* Trevisa is not entirely consistent in his choice (see line 7).

3. The inflection of the verb for third-person singular present tense (the verb used with *he, she, it,* and singular nouns) is also *-th;* in line 31, *semeth* is such a form (modern English has *-s* there now: it *seems*). The dialects will differ as to whether they use *-th* or *-s*.

4. The forms of the third-person plural pronoun *(they, their,* and *them)* are *hy, here,* and *hem* (lines 5, 11, 29, etc.). The dialects vary as to whether or not *th* is the initial sound (these are actually two words,

not two pronunciations of a single word; we see here the competition between the Danish and the Old English forms we spoke of earlier— the ones with the *th* are of Danish origin). In Trevisa's time, the *h* often went unpronounced, so he sometimes uses *a,* meaning *hy* (line 27).

5. The past participle (the verb inflection used in constructing the perfect tense *has taken* and the passive *is taken*) is formed by prefixing *y-* to the infinitive verb; as in line 1, *y-knowe (known);* 4, *y-melled (melled);* 9, *y-left (left).* Middle English dialects differ as to whether they use this prefix or a suffix and infix inflection: *taken* and *risen* have the suffix *-en* (a variation is *-ed,* as in *rocked), left* and *taught* have an internal (infix) inflection in that the pronunciation of the internal vowel is changed. Trevisa often combines the two: *y-tauyt* (26), *y-rokked* (27), *y-told* (30); and occasionally uses only the suffix form: *apeyred* (17) and *compelled* (22).

In summary, Trevisa uses the forms shown in Table 2.1.

Now go back to the Trevisa passage and be more precise in a description of Trevisa's dialect: list all instances of the five (really six) items and decide in which items he uses more than one variant (he is then said to have a by-form in the alternative used less frequently). Be

Table 2.1. *Forms used by John of Trevisa, Southern England, 1385***

	Item	Trevisa	Alternate Form
1a.	copula singular, pres. tense indicative	he *is*	he *be*
1b.	copula plural, pres. tense indicative	they *be*	they *are*
2.	3rd-person plural indicative verb present tense	they hold*eth*	they hold (Ø) they hold*en*
3.	3rd-person singular indicative verb present tense	he us*eth*	he us*es*
4.	plural pronouns	hy here hem (ham)	they their them
5.	past participle	*y*-know	know*n*

*Spelling in Middle English was not fixed by any standard; therefore, *is* may also be spelled *ys* or *es,* *-eth* may be *-ith* or *-yth,* *-ed* may be *-yd* or *-id,* *be* may be *bi,* etc. Plan to see the inflectional form, not its peculiar spelling. In reading all of Middle English, one needs to sound out the words instead of depending on the look, or spelling, of the words.

careful in items 1a, 1b, 2, and 3 to count only regularly inflected verb forms. This means counting only the *first* verb in a verb phrase. Modals are irregular in having no inflection for third-person singular present tense and therefore should not be counted for item 3; they can, however, be counted for third-person plural present tense, where their inflection is regular (*will, can, must,* and *may* are modal verbs in modern English).

Compare Trevisa's choices with those of writers of the northern and the midland dialects. John Wyclif, although born in Yorkshire in northern England, studied at Oxford and lived there in the king's service for most of his life. His writing, then, is that of a midlander at about the same time as Trevisa's southern (1350). For the five items, list the choices Wyclif makes, noting primary and by-forms.

"Christ's Poverty"[2]

In the lif of Crist and His gospel, that is His
testament, with lif and techyng of His *postils,* oure   *apostles*
clerkis *schullen* not fynde but povert, mekenesse,   *shall*
gostly traveile, and dispisyng of worldly men for   *holy/work*
5   reprovyng of here synnes, and grete reward in
Hevene for here goode lif and trewe techyng, and
wilful sufforyng of deth. Therfore Jesus Crist was
pore in His lif, that He hadde no house of His
owene bi worldly title to reste His heed thereinne,
10   as He hymself seith in the gospel. And Seynt Petir
was so pore that he hadde neither silver ne gold to
geve a pore crokid man, as Petir witnesseth in the
bok of Apostlis Dedis. . . . And Jesus confermyng
this testament seide to His apostlis after His risyng
15   fro deth to life, "My Fadir sente me and I sende
yow,"—that is, to traveile, persecucion, and povert
and hunger and martirdom in this world, and not to
worldly pompe as clerkis usen now. Bi this it
semeth, that alle these worldly clerkis havyng
20   seculer lordischipe, with aray of worldly vanyte,
ben hugely cursed of God and man, for thei *doun*   *do*
ayenst the riytful testament of Crist and His postlis.   *against*

Next, look at the language of a northerner, Richard Rolle, born in Yorkshire and writing at about the same time (1350). List all instances of the five items, noting primary and by-forms.

---

2. H. E. Winn, ed., *Wyclif, Select English Writings* (London: Oxford University Press, 1929). Reprinted in Mossé, *A Handbook of Middle English,* p. 282.

The Bee and the Stork[3]

The bee has thre kyndis. *Ane* es, that *scho* es	*one/she*
never ydill and scho es *noghte* with thaym that will	*not*
noghte wyrke, bot castys thaym owte and puttes	
thaym awaye. Anothire es, that, when scho flyes,	
5 scho takes erthe in hyr *fette,* that scho be* noghte	*feet*
lyghtly *overheghede* in the ayere of wynde. The	*overcome*
thyrde es, that scho kepes clene and bryghte hire	
wyngez. Thus ryghtwyse men that *lufes* God are	*love*
never in ydyllness; for *owthyre* they *ere* in travayle,	*either/are*
10 *prayand*** or thynkande or *redande,* or othere gud	*praying/*
doande or with takand ydill mene and *schewand*	*reading/*
thaym worthy to be put fra the *ryste* of heven, for	*doing/*
thay will noghte travayle. Here thay take erthe,	*showing/*
that es, thay *halde* thamselfe vile and erthely, that	*rest/hold*
15 thay be* noghte blawen with the wynde of vanyte	
and of pryde. Thay kepe thaire wynges clene, that	
es the *twa* commandementes of charyte thay	*two*
fulfill in gud concyens; and thay hafe othere vertus	
unblendyde with the fylthe of syne and unclene	
20 luste.	
Arestotill sais that the bees are *feghtande*	*fighting*
agaynes hym that will drawe thaire hony fra thaym.	*against*
Swa sulde we do againes devells that *afforces* tham	*so/should/*
to [take] fra us the hony of poure lyfe and of grace.	*force*

---

*This is the subjunctive mood that we discussed above and should not be counted in item 1.

**The ending -*and(e)* is in modern English -*ing* and is a notable characteristic of northern Middle English.

If we compare even the limited data we have collected from only three speakers, we can see characteristics of regional dialects. Some characteristics are shared by two of the dialects but in every case by dialects that border one another. Such characteristics almost certainly moved from one dialect to the other through contact of the speakers. We can hypothesize which dialect had like forms by looking first for the dialect that uses the forms, or set of forms, most consistently. For example, we know that the midlanders adopted *they* from the northern dialect: the northern dialect has the complete set of plural pronouns in *th-,* and Rolle uses them consistently, while the midland dialect's pattern is primarily of the forms in *h-*. Again, like the northern dialect the midland dialect consistently uses the -*en* and infix past participial form; the southern dialect in Trevisa has a primary form in *y-* and a by-form

---

3. Hope Emily Allen, ed., *English Writings of Richard Rolle Hermit of Hampole* (Oxford: Clarendon Press, 1931). Reprinted in Mossé, *A Handbook of Middle English,* p. 231.

in *-en;* southern English probably adopted the form from midland speakers. Can you hypothesize how other correspondences might have come about? Now, compare the data for the three dialects and decide which dialect has the most forms that become standard English.

From the end of the sixteenth century, we have a statement that the speech of London (in the southern dialect area, bordering midland) has become something of a national standard. George Puttenham, the author of *The Arte of Poesie* (1589), advising young authors on the most acceptable style, says that at least for the class of gentlemen, the preferred dialect is that of London.[4] The young writer should *not:*

```
        take the termes of Northern-men, such as they use
        in dayly talke, whether they be noblemen or
        gentlemen, or of their best clarkes all is a matter;
        nor in effect any speach used beyond the river
5       Trent, though no man can deny but that theirs is
        the purer English Saxon at this day, yet it is not
        so Courtly nor so currant as our Southern English
        is, no more is the far Westerne mans speach; ye
        shall therefore take the usuall speach of the Court,
10      and that of London and the shires lying about
        London within LX myles, and not much above.
        I say not this but that in every shyre of England
        there be gentlemen and others that speake but
        specially write as good Southerne as we of Middle-
15      sex or Surry do, but not the common people of
        every shire, to whom the gentlemen, and also their
        learned clarkes do for the most part condescend. . . .
```

Add to your data, then, an ancestor of the dialect of Puttenham's London. Recall that London by the fourteenth century had probably taken on a dialect character unique from that of the surrounding southern dialect area, since it had become a center of commerce, attracting people from all over England. Here is the Mercers' petition to Parliament, written in the heart (and heat) of London life in 1386. List the forms of the five variants used by the writer. Which of the three Middle English dialects does it come closest to? Recall that Trevisa suggested two possible sources for a standard; if this dialect of London is a kind of "standard," does it bear out either of Trevisa's hypotheses?

---

4. *The Arte of Poesie*, 1589, reprint ed. (Menston, England: Scholar Press, 1968), Libre III, Cap IIII, pp. 120–21.

The Mercers' Petition to Parliament[5]

To the moost noble and Worthiest Lordes,
moost ryghtful and wysest conseille to owre life
Lorde the Kyng, compleynen, if it lyke to yow, the
folk of the Mercerye of London as a membre of

5   the same citee, of many wronges subtiles and also
open oppressions, y-do to hem by longe tyme here
bifore passed.
[Here is told a sad tale about Nichol Exton,
mayor of London, who apparently ran the city with
force and arms rather than with right reason and
democracy]
And yif in general [Nichol's] falseness were
ayeinsaide, as of us togydre of the Mercerye or   *opposed*

10   othere craftes, or ony conseille wolde have taken to
ayainstande it, or as tyme out of mynde hath *be*   *oppose/been*
used, wolden *companye* togydre, how lawful so it   *band*
were for owre nede or profite, were anon apeched
for arrysers ayeins the pees, and falsly many of us,

15   that yet standen endited. And we ben openlich
disclaundred, holden untrewe and traitours to owre
Kyng. For the same Nichol said bifor Mair, Alder-
men and owre craft bifor hem *gadred* in place of   *gathered*
recorde, that xx or xxx of us were worthy to be

20   drawen and hanged, the which thyng lyke to yowre
worthy lordship by an even Juge to be proved or
disproved, the whether that trowthe may shewe;
for trouthe amonges us of fewe or elles noman
many day dorst be shewed. And nought *oonlich*   *for many*

25   unshewed or hidde it hath be by man now, but also   *a day/only*
of bifore tyme the moost profitable poyntes of trewe
governaunce of the Citee, compiled togidre by longe
labour of discrete and wyse men, wyth-out conseille
of trewe men, or thei sholde nought be knowen *ne*   *nor*

30   contynued, in the tyme of Nichol Exton, Mair.

As a point of reference and comparison, go back to the language
of Puttenham on page 46, written two centuries after the Mercer's
petition and by then recognized as "standard," and pick out the forms
we have been looking at. How does the Mercer's language compare?
Where have Puttenham's "new" forms come from (which fourteenth-
century dialect)?

---

5. R. W. Chambers and M. W. Daunt, eds., *A Book of London English, 1384–1425*
(Oxford: Clarendon Press, 1931), pp. 33–37. Reprinted in Mossé, *A Handbook of Middle
English,* p. 283–85.

3. A Shift in Social Favor

Between the fourteenth and sixteenth centuries occurs one of the most important events in the "standardization" of English. William Caxton, living in the latter half of the fifteenth century, brought a printing press to England from the continent and printed virtually every manuscript he could lay hands on, including some of his own dubious scholarship. Caxton may have influenced the direction in which the language grew more than any other single man, for he set himself up as editor of the texts he printed and tried to settle the variant forms both of spelling and of grammar that came across his desk. Succeeding editors followed his policy, and thus a standard in printed language began to be developed. As a member of the rising middle class, Caxton was very conscious of the prestigious variants of his time and did not hesitate to feed them into the texts he printed. He virtually translated Trevisa's text of 1389; his edition of 1482 is presented on pages 50–51 with the relevant portion of Trevisa's original. What changes and corrections did he see fit to make? In the five forms we have been watching, which Middle English dialect is it most like? Supposing that Trevisa wrote his own notion of standard of the fourteenth century, what has happened to that dialect by the fifteenth century? Where did new forms come from?

Suppose the Mercers' petition (London dialect) were standard, as it is certainly its precursor, how does Caxton's standard of the fifteenth century compare? How, then, does Caxton compare with Puttenham in the sixteenth century? These three dialects are probably in direct linear relationship to one another.

Linguist John L. Fisher has recently suggested (see "Suggestions for Further Reading") that there were two standard dialects around London, one the standard spoken dialect of the city of London and the second a written standard—called "Chancery standard" by linguists—which was used by the court clerks in the Chancery, the seat of government at Westminster just outside the city. The Mercer's Petition (1386) is one of the earliest documents in Chancery standard. It was written a bit earlier than the height of Chancery standard, 1420–60, and is still close to the London dialect of its time. Around 1420, Chancery standard began to show more frequently the features of the emergent standard English, while the London dialect retained for a longer period of time its Middle English characteristics.

Written Chancery standard anticipated our modern written and spoken standard with its northern dialect characteristics (pronouns in *th-* and an *-ly* adverb ending instead of the southern *-lich*) along with southern (*-eth* third-person verb singular and *be/ben*) and midland (past participle in *-en*). It may be that features of northern dialects began to appear in southern writing at this time because many clerks in the government came from northern counties. London dialect, on the other hand, retained *her* and *hem* and an occasional *y-*.

Caxton probably adopted the current Chancery standard when he began to print in 1476, since he set up his press in Westminster instead of London and since Chancery standard had become the written language in which most businessmen (Caxton included) were schooled. (Caxton also took personal responsibility for the correctness of his printed language. He reported that he canvassed the best writers of the upper class for judgments on usage problems.) Chancery standard is a probable precursor of modern English standard. By the time of Puttenham (1589), London upper-class standard and Chancery standard were pretty much alike (the sixty-mile radius Puttenham spoke of included Westminster).

Now pull your data together for an intermediate hypothesis and a beginning on the question why. If standard English of the sixteenth century is that of London, as Puttenham says, but most of the forms of standard English belonged two centuries before that to the northern dialect, what had to have happened in the intervening centuries? Can you hypothesize from the following statistics as to how and why northern forms became standard in London? Here are some questions to help in interpretation.

Recall the discussion of *ain't:* who had economic power in England in the fourteenth century? the fifteenth century? the sixteenth century? What facts help you to decide? Is there evidence that these groups came to London? If England became involved in foreign trade for the first time, would there be a population shift? If so, from where to where? Who would be involved?

1. In the fourteenth century, the majority of the population of England lived south of the Humber River (see Figure 2.3); 85 percent was rural.
2. East Midland, the bulging area north of London, was the most densely populated, the least ravaged by the Black Death (1349–1400).
3. In the thirteenth and fourteenth centuries, East Midland became the economic center for the exportation of corn and wool.
4. In 1300, the officers of London city government came from the following regional backgrounds: from southern counties, thirty-eight aldermen and eighteen sheriffs; from midland counties (East Midland), ten aldermen and seven sheriffs; from northern counties, five aldermen and two sheriffs.
5. In 1365, the officers of London city government displayed this regional ancestry: from southern counties, thirty-two aldermen and seven sheriffs; from East Midland counties, thirty-three al-

John of Trevisa, 1385

As hyt ys y-knowe houw meny maner people
buth in this ylond, ther buth also of so meny people
longages and tonges; notheles Walschmen and
Scottes, that buth nowt y-melled with other nacions,
5   holdeth wel ny here furste longage and speche, bote
[yet] Scottes, that were som tyme confederat and
[lived] with the Pictes, drawe somwhat after here
speche. Bote the Flemmynges, that [live] in the
west side of Wales, habbeth y-left here strange speche
10   and speketh Saxonlych y-now. Also Englischmen,
[though] hy hadde fram the bygynnyng thre maner
speche, Southeron, Northeron, and Myddel speche
(in the myddel of the lond), as hy come of thre
maner people of Germania, notheles, by commyxtion
15   and mellyng furst with Danes and afterward
with Normans, in menye the contray
longage is apeyred, and som useth strange
wlaffyng, chyteryng, harryng and garrying,
grisbittyng. This apeyryng of the burth-tonge
20   ys bycause of twey thinges. On ys, for
chyldern in scole, ayenes the usage
and manere of al other nacions, buth compelled
for to leve here oune longage, and for to construe
here lessons and here thinges a Freynsch
25   and habbeth, suthe the Normans come furst into
Engelond. Also, gentilmen children buth y-tauyt for
to speke Freynsch fram tyme that a buth y-rokked
in here cradel . . . and oplondysch men wol lykne
hamsylf to gentilmen, and fondeth with grete bysynes
30   for to speke Freynsch for to be more y-told of.
. . . Hyt semeth a gret wondur houw
Englysch, that ys the burth-tonge of Englysch-men
and here oune longage and tonge, ys so
dyvers of soun in this ylond . . .

dermen and ten sheriffs; from northern counties, ten aldermen
and seven sheriffs.

6. In 1363, the Merchant Staple was located in the English-held city
of Calais, France, for the foreign trade of wool and other staples,
but not manufactured goods (the Staple was a protective regulat-
ing collective to enable English merchants to trade in foreign
markets).

7. Centers of production in the fifteenth century were Yorkshire
(north country) for woolens; the northern and west counties for

John of Trevisa edited by Caxton, 1482[6]

As it is knowen how many maner peple
ben in this Ilond ther ben also many
langages and tonges. Notheles Walshmen and
scottes that ben not *medled* with other nacions   *mixed*
5   kepe neygh yet theyr first langage and speche/ But
yet tho scottes that were somtyme confederate and
dwellyd with pyctes drawe somwhat after theyr
speche/ But the Flemynges that dwell in the
westside of wales have lefte her straunge speche
10   & speken lyke to saxons; also englyssmen
though they had from the begynnyng thre maner
speches Southern northern and myddel speche
in the myddel of the londe as they come of thre
maner of people of Germania. Netheles by commyxtion
15   and medlyng first with danes and afterward
with normans In many thynges the contrey
langage is appayred/ ffor some use straunge
wlaffyng chyteryng harryng garryng and
grisbytyng/ this appayryng of the langage
20   cometh of two thynges. One is by cause that
children that gon to schole
lerne to speke first englysshe/
& than ben compellid to constrewe
her lessons in Frenssh and that have
25   ben used syn the normans come into
Englond/ Also gentilmens childeren ben lerned and
taught from theyr youngthe to speke frenssh. . . .
And uplondyssh men will counterfete and likene
hem self to gentilmen and arn besy
30   to speke frensshe for to be more sette by.

It semeth a grete wonder that Englyssmen
have so grete dyversyte in theyr owne langage in
sowne and in spekyng of it/ which is all in
one ylond.

wool; the East Midlands for grain; and London, Norfolk, Essex, and Devon for shipping.

8. In 1486, Henry VII placed a higher duty on the export of wool than on that of woolen goods. In the fifteenth century, the export of woolens, England's primary manufacture, exceeded the export of wool (the primary agrarian concern).

9. In 1504, Parliament legislated ineffectively against enclosures (a

---

6. Mossé, *A Handbook of Middle English,* pp. 286–87.

movement by sheep farmers to enclose public pasture lands in order to graze sheep; the farmers tended also to reclaim the small farms of tenant farmers).

10. In 1548, Henry VIII issued a proclamation against enclosures.
11. In 1549, Kett's rebellion involved rural folk against the sheep farmers to prevent enclosures.
12. In 1550, the Enclosure Act permitted enclosures.
13. In 1550, broadsides, books, and pamphlets appeared against enclosures.
14. In 1560, grain was selling more profitably in England than wool; the government eased restrictions on the export of grain.

The changing fortunes of the London "standard" dialect reflected the shifts in economic power in England. In the fourteenth century, the East Midland area was the center of economic power: by the fifteenth century (Caxton), characteristics of that dialect were "standard," having replaced variants from the southern dialect (the regional dialect of London). In the fifteenth century, the center of wool production, the northern counties, became the center of economic power; by the sixteenth century (Puttenham), characteristics of northern dialect were "standard." Since standard English grew up in London, we have somehow to account for large (or at least prestigious) groups of speakers coming to London from these areas. Items 4 and 5 above suggest that they did, in fact, come, and won seats in not only national but local government.

What brought them south and eventually to London was probably England's development of international trade. In the thirteenth and fourteenth centuries, the East Midland area exported wool, which brought northerners (growers of sheep) into the Midland dialect area (and with them the *th-* pronoun forms and the inflection *-s* third-person singular). By the fifteenth century, London was the center of export, connecting the country with Calais on the continent. This eventually brought the economically powerful wool growers to London. At the end of the fifteenth century and through the sixteenth century, government legislation suggests that powerful lobbies were protecting the interests of sheep farmers. The last item (14) suggests that after the mid-sixteenth century, the center of economic power shifted south to the East Midland area and the growers of grain.

4. Social Dialects in London

As a final step in this problem, let's look at the structure of social dialects in London at the time of Caxton—in about the middle of the three-century span we have been considering—to get some idea of how the characteristics of the regional dialects (most especially the northern) might have made their way to "standard" status as part of the sociolect structure of London. If we posit the axiom that standard is the sociolect of the upper classes, then somehow certain characteristics of the northern dialect had to penetrate the prestige dialect. Such would happen if speakers of the northern regional dialect in the fourteenth and fifteenth centuries became members of the upper class and retained in their speech the characteristics of northern dialect found in Puttenham's speech in the sixteenth century. That is, if they *and* their dialect found places at the top of the social structure. If we posit further what we hypothesized earlier—that newcomers to a city usually find their initial social place in the lower ranks of society (as with the southern migration to the northern cities in America)—then we should find northern dialect characteristics working their way up through social ranks with the speakers.

The "rise of standard English," which we have been tracing from the middle of the fourteenth through the sixteenth centuries, parallels two unprecedented developments in England's social history: rapid and radical changes in the complexion of the social classes, especially of London, and the "rise" of the middle class, the second of which is, of course, a function of the first. At the outset of the fourteenth century, the society of London was rigidly structured. The nobility formed the upper class, which was usually an inherited status, although occasionally a man could be appointed to rank. The upper class was a minority, but they wielded almost all the power and owned most of the land, the source of economic power. The great mass of people in London were skilled or unskilled laborers who dealt locally. A few of the citizens were businessmen, and some of them were elevated slightly in rank by becoming government officials. Goods were manufactured in the private home, although the skilled laborers had founded craft guilds to protect themselves from exploitation by government officials (the Mercers' petition is written by one such group).

By the end of the fourteenth century, membership in the various classes in London had become more fluid. The primary cause was a series of disastrous plagues (the so-called Black Plague), which killed 30–40 percent of the population of England and much of the city population. The large labor force, tied by tradition and economic necessity to country manors in feudal servitude to nobility there, was greatly reduced. As a consequence of their smaller numbers and great demand, their labor became a commodity that they could sell, and there is ample evidence through the next century that they descended on the cities in overwhelming numbers, many of them bringing with them skills that enabled them to start cottage businesses of their own. Many from this group established themselves socially within a few generations, thus

53

swelling the "middle class" of businessmen. A second event reduced the ranks of the nobility: the Hundred Years' War drew the nobility onto the battlefields of France through the century. By 1362, Piers Plowman, a fictitious character, complained that soapsellers were being made knights.

By the outset of the fifteenth century, Henry VII was self-consciously trying to win the support of the middle class by giving offices of state and household and all of the council seats to businessmen of London (these positions were formerly given only to nobility). Although for a while the middle class held this strong political sway, the upper class and rank of nobility still held social power. Consequently many lower-class members aspired to the economic (and perhaps political) status of the middle class, while many in the middle class sought the social status of the upper-class ranks.

From the second half of the fifteenth century, we have the letters of two families whose businesses kept them close to London and whose correspondence serves as a model of the social dialects of two classes of London. In the context of London society, both seemed to be socially ambitious, although they stood at different social levels. The Pastons were an upper-middle-class family, whose home was Norfolk (East Midland); the Cely family was middle- or lower-middle-class and came from Essex (southeast of London).

At least three criteria are important in defining social class in fifteenth-century England: title, and with that one's admission to court circles; the source of one's monetary income (active participation in the trade market or independent wealth, usually derived from land holdings); and the kinds of marriages one could and did make. In order to rise out of one's class, one usually sought: (1) to use a nonprestigious commercial career to earn enough money, (2) to buy land that yielded a suitable income either directly through such profit-making pastimes as sheep raising or indirectly through rents, and (3) to bestow enough dowry on both sons and daughters to allow them to marry into prestigious families close to the court circle. The Celys stood at level 1: they were in the wool trade at Calais and London and although they owned one estate, it was not prosperous enough to bring a livable income. The Pastons initially stood at level 2 and finally advanced somewhere near level 3; they made a precarious living off the rents on several pieces of land; John Paston II became engaged to (although he did not marry) Ann Haute, a cousin to the queen, and he was knighted on the field at the Battle of Stoke.

The following are letters of John Paston II and his mother Margaret Paston and of Richard Cely and his brother George. Use the five criteria we have established in the Middle English dialects and differentiate the language of the two families. Watch out for the use of *be:* it is now being used to differentiate subjunctive from indicative mood in the copula (go back to the beginning of Section 2 for review), as well as singular and plural. Since *be* is consistently used by all speakers in the subjunctive, consider the usage in singular and plural indicative only. Also, there are many more periphrastic verb constructions, especially the progressive ("is going") and multiple structures like Margaret Paston's "they have be wronged" where she intends the past participle of *be,* not thc form we have been looking at. Many speakers got confused as the verb phrase became more complex, and they weren't sure how many verbs in the phrase received inflections. Of the two family *cum* social dialects, which is closer to the standard of the day (Caxton)? Which is closer to modern standard English? Which is more "northern"?

John Paston II to brother John III, 1475[7]

. . . I purpose to come to London warde . . . fore
to appoynt wyth the Kynge and my lorde for suche
retynwe as I sholde have now in theese *werrys* into   *retinue/wars*
Frawnce. Wherffore I praye yow in Norffolk and
5   other places [commune] wyth suche as ye thynk
lykly fore yow and me that are dysposyd to take wagys
in gentylmennys howsys and *ellys where* so that we   *elsewhere*
may be the moore redy whan that nede is. Neverthe-
lesse at thys *owre* I wolde be gladde to have wyth   *hour*
10   me dayly iii ore iiii more than I have suche as
weere lykly . . .
    I praye yow sende me som tydyngys suche
as ye heere, and howgh that my brother Edmonde
doth, for as for tydyngys heere, theere be but fewe
15   *saffe* that the assege lastyth stylle by the Duke of   *save*
Burgoyn affoore Nuse and the Emperore hathe
besegyd also, not ferre from thense, a castell and an
other town in lyke wise wherin the Dukys men
been. And also the Frenshe Kynge, men seye, is
20   comyn nyghe to the water off Somme wyth iiii
sperys, and some men *trowe* that he woll at the day   *believe*
off brekyng off trewes, or ellys byffoore, sette uppon
the Dukys contreys heere. When I heere moore I
shall sende yow moore tydyngys. The Kyngys
25   Imbassatorys, Sir Thomas Mongomere and the
Master off the Rollys, be comyng homwardys from
Nuse, and as for me I thynke that I shold be seke
but iff I see it.

---

7. Norman O. Davis, ed., *Paston Letters and Papers of the Fifteenth Century,* vol. 1 (Oxford: Clarendon, 1971), p. 482.

Margaret Paston to her husband John I, 1462[8]

Pepyll of this contre begynyth to wax wyld and
it is seyd her that my lord of Clarans and the *Dwek* *Duke*
of Suthfolk and serteyn *jwgys* wyth hem schold come *judges*
down and syt on syche pepyl as be noysyd ryotous
5 in thys contre. And also it is seyd her that ther is
retournyd a newe *rescwe* up-on that that was *do* at *rescue/done*
the last [shire]. I suppose swyche talkyng comyth of
false schrewys that wold mak a *rwmor* in this contre. *rumor*
The pepyll seyth her that they had *levyr* go up *rather*
10 *hole* to the Kyng and compleyne of sich fals schrewys *all*
as they have be wrongyd by a-for than they schold
be compleynyd of wyth-owt cause and be hangyd
at ther owne *dorys*. In good feyth men *fer* sor her of *doors/fear*
a common rysyng but if a better remedy may be had
15 to [appease] the people in hast, and that ther be sent
swyche downe to take a rewyll as the pepyll hath a
fantsy in that wole be indeferent. They love not in no
wyse the Dwke of Sowthfolk nor hys modyr. . . . The
peopyll feryth *hem* myche the mor to be hurt be-cause *them*
20 that ye and my cosyn Barney come not home. They
sey they wot well it is not well wyth yow, and if it
be not well wyth yow, they sey they wot well they
that wole do yow wronge wole sone do them wronge,
and that makyth them all-most mad.

Richard Cely the Younger, 1480[9]

hyt ys so that Syr Tomas Mongehowmbre ys comyng *it*
to Calleys *wharde* and so he *whyll consent* Tomers *ward/will/*
for to *fete* my lady. I pray you at hys comyng *send/fetch*
whate apon hym and thanke hym for us for he has *wait*
5 beyn howr spessyall good master in thys mater and
has promysyd me to *contenew* and labord for us *continue*
and *thorrow* hys labor I am cwm in [acquaintance] *through*
of dyvars *whorschylfull* men . . . I pray yow make *worshipful*
hym good *scheyr* for he has beyn good *cellysstor* for *cheer/*
10 ws and he bryngys yow a letter frome me. *solicitor*
        Syr I undyrstond by yowr letter that aull
the *whowlschypys* ar cwm to Calles savyng vii *wool ships*
quere of ii be spent. I *trwste* to God that the *where/trust*
Crystower of Rayname be cwm to Calleys by this
15 and as for howre matter of indittemente *whe* be thore *we*
and have howr *swepsedyas* undyr sele of *hoffes* of *subsidies/*

8. Ibid., p. 279.

9. Henry Elliot Malden, ed. for the Royal Historical Society, *The Cely Papers* (London: Longman, Green, & Co., 1900), pp. 49–50. The material from this volume has been re-edited by the author.

my loorde of Essex. . . . Petter recommend hym   *office*
owto yow and thankys yow of yowr grette cheyr at
Calleys. He has hys *deyd* of my loord and as for *whar*   *deed/war*
20   betwene ws and Frawns I can thynke ye schayl have
noyn; ther goys *hover* inbasette schorttely. What   *none/over*
they ar I connott tell. I wndyrstonde . . . that ye
hawhe sowlde . . . Cottysowlde *fellys* and thay ar in   *have/fells*
to Hollonde in safete as he *whryttes* to me. Thankyd   *(sheepskins)/*
25   be Jhesu and as for tydynges I *can* none.   *writes/know*
        The kynge the quehyn and the prynse lyes
at Eltam and I pwrpos to departe into Cottysowlde
the ix day of thys monthe.

George Cely, 1480[10]

As of any tydynges her *y* con none wrytt yow as *zett*   *I/yet*
ther ys but y cannot hawe the trewthe ther of; there
has ben an veryaunsse betwne the Dwukes men of
whar and his *Allmaynes* and ther ys many of his   *war/*
5   Allmanys slayne and therfor he takes grett *ceffle* fur   *Germans/*
ther ys dyvars of his jentyllmen stollyn away therfor   *care*
and some ar comyn to Callez and *hone* of them ys   *one*
sent to owr soveren lorde the kynge and some ben
Frenche men when that the Frenche kynge has
10   gottyn lattly dyvars of the best men of what the dewke
hade wherof he makes hym now bowllde.

The characteristics of the northern regional dialect of the fourteenth century are now the hallmarks of the lower-middle-class dialect
(Cely family) of London; by the end of the sixteenth century, most of
them will appear in the "standard" dialect, as we saw in Puttenham's
speech. Still later than the sixteenth century, the *-s* third-person singular verb inflection will finally appear in standard, having worked its way
down from the north and up through the ranks of the sociolect structure
of London. Here in the fifteenth century, in the middle of the "rise" of
standard English, we have the sociolect configuration shown in Table
2.2 (using Caxton as a "norm" ranking above the Pastons).

Where Trevisa used *hy, her,* and *hem,* Caxton uses two of the
three northern forms. Both the Pastons and Celys use the northern
forms, although the Pastons (Margaret, line 19) have a by-form in *hem.*
The northern forms are established in the middle-class sociolects, but
won't appear in the "standard" in full panoply for a century yet. *Are,*
another northern form, found most consistently in the lower-middle-
class sociolect, is the primary form in the upper-middle class (with *be* a
by-form), but is only a by-form in the "standard" of Caxton; frequency

---

10. Ibid., p. 52.

Table 2.2. *Fifteenth-Century Sociolects*

Item	Caxton	Paston	Cely
3rd-person plural pronoun	they	they	they
	their	their	their
	hem	them (hem)	them
be pres. singular	is	is (be)	is (be)
pres. plural	be (are)	are (be)	are
3rd-person plural verb	-en (∅)	∅ (-en)	-es
3rd-person singular verb	-th	-th	-s
past participle	-en	-en	-en

would indicate that it is working its way gradually into the upper-class sociolect. The third-person singular verb inflection also shows the lower Cely class with the northern form, eventually to be standard English, while the upper classes have the "old" standard form. In third-person plural verb inflection, a slightly different pattern is occurring, as Caxton seems to be archaic in his usage, the Pastons reflecting what will be standard, while the Celys again have a northern form, which, in this case, will not "make it" to standard English.

Most of the northern forms seem to be working their way up from the bottom, probably moving up into the upper-class sociolect as speakers of the dialect move into the upper class. Two forms, though, are not moving; one will and the other will not. What is happening to hold these two back at the end of the fifteenth century? If we hypothesize that speakers of the "correct" language—that represented by Caxton and to a lesser extent the Pastons—were formerly members of the lower classes (Caxton certainly was), then we might hypothesize that they began with the dialect of the Celys and corrected their dialect toward some social norm of prestige as they moved up in rank. The dialect characteristics which they retained were apparently not identified as class markers—the third-person plural pronouns and *are* seem to have been neutral, neither prestigious nor stigmatized. One form, though, was prestigious, to such an extent that the rising middle-class man adopted the form wholesale in place of his old form: the *-th* third-person singular verb ending. Another form was apparently stigmatized as "lower class," and the rising speaker dropped the form from his dialect: the *-s* third-person plural verb ending (there seems to be no "norm" here, since the Pastons and Caxton so definitely differ; therefore, the rising speaker did not drop the form for a prestigious one, as with third-person singular). The stigmatized item will never make it into "standard" or upper-class sociolect, but the *-th* inflection for third-person singular is giving way to the *-s* by the time of Shakespeare a century later (although it is debated well into the next century, as we will see).

Possibly, the third-person singular -*s* is the *ain't* of the fifteenth century. Just as *ain't* is now moving into the casual styles of the upper-middle-class speakers, so this -*s* will gain status as more middle-class comers begin to use the form in their casual speech. (We have some evidence that the form was used by Shakespeare's characters for casual situations, and it appears in the casual speech of Ben Jonson's middle-class characters.) *Has* and *does* are still out of vogue in the seventeenth century, although other -*s* inflections are acceptable.

5. Prestige Styles as a Force for Linguistic Change

We need not go completely by conjecture, though, about what might have been prestigious language in the fifteenth century. If a speaker tries more self-consciously to use "correct" or prestigious forms when he is talking to a superior than when he is speaking more casually, then we should be able to judge levels of prestige by looking at style levels. Here is a letter from the youngest Cely brother William to his oldest brother George (with whom he might be more formal). He uses traits of "standard" English that his brother Richard the younger does not use in a more casual situation (see "Richard Cely the Younger, 1480" above). What are they? Compare his letter to that of Robert Eryk, a favor-seeker to George. With what variants is he trying to impress George?

William Cely to his brother George, 1482[11]

Plese hit yowre mastarschypp to understond that
John Dalton and I have spoken to master *leff-*
tenaunte for payment of yowre warranttes and he   *lieutenant*
sayth we schall have payment within v or vi days,
5   but he sayth we can nott hawe all at thys tyme and
we desyryd to hawe them there sett upon yowre
bylles of costom and subsede and he sayth hit may
nott be for ther be moo soo don than may be
perfformed for the whych they shall bryng yn
10   sterlyng mony yn to the collectors again and nawe
her payment owte of the tressery. Syr plese hyt   *their*
yow to *wytt* her be many Hollanders butt they *bye*   *know/buy*
noo noder felles of [anyone] but London and
contrey felles.

---

11. Ibid., p. 96.

Robert Eryk, 1482[12]

Ser yf hyt plessith yow to *wete* that my mastras   *know*
your moder & my masters both your bredurn my
emer Wylliam Maryen & all your houssold faryn   *superior*
well & my mastres is in gud *heell* thankyd be Jhesu *health*
5   & mery, God kepe her long soo. Also Ser pleseth
hyt yow to wyt that my emer and I be agreed that
I schold have xl *li* that schold be delivyred by   *pounds*
yow . . . Ser I perpose to be at Brygges mart yf I
may & els I prey yow that hyt may be redy when
10   I come *fer* I tryste to have hyt redy as my em   *for*
tellyth me when so I come.

We must be very tentative in drawing conclusions about correct and incorrect language in the fifteenth century because we have no one's word on the subject. When grammarians began to talk about language at the beginning of the seventeenth century, in fact, they gave little attention to variation and "correctness." They referred to peculiar forms in London English as "antiquities" or forms from regional dialects (most grammarians felt that anything outside of London was "country"). Alexander Gil, in *Logonomia Anglica* (1619), entitles one chapter "Dialecti" and includes in it several forms that he heard in London but which are not *au courant*. By the end of the century, Christopher Cooper calls the same forms "De Barbera dialecti" and refers to them not only as regional but "incorrect." Gil's generosity toward people who spoke something different from Puttenham's court language had disappeared by the end of the century, when grammarians were prescribing the correct language for getting ahead in London society, and standard English had risen to consciousness.

Here are some of the grammarians' conclusions about the forms we have been watching:

1. Gil cites "Have ye y-do?" as "western" dialect.
2. Ben Jonson (*The English Grammar,* 1623) cites the *-en* third-person plural verb inflection as "now archaic."
3. *be* shows a divided situation: all grammarians agree that it is the correct form in subjunctive. Paul Greaves (*Grammatica Anglicana,* 1594) and others after him describe *be* in present-tense indicative mood as "vulgair." Jonson cites the use of this form as correct for the plural only (1623).
4. Most grammarians find the *-s* third-person singular present-tense verb inflection an acceptable alternate form for the *-th,* except in *doth* and *hath.* Gil says in 1619 that *does* and *has* are incorrect

---

12. Ibid., p. 94.

forms (he calls them "dialect"), but Cooper, a half-century later (1685), says they arc alternate forms for *doth* and *hath* (no comment on correctness).

Because the grammarians choose to comment on the correctness of just these forms, we may hypothesize that people were conscious of variant forms and were worried about which was socially correct and that they looked to grammarians—educators—to show the way. But we can see that they are describing—codifying—the tail end of a changing standard. Indeed, the standard they describe will eventually change, although some of the later grammarians thought that if they could write it down thoroughly enough and teach it rigorously enough, they could establish a language that would never change. As we fret about *lie* and *lay, hanged* and *hung, though he be* and *though he is, if I were* and *if I was,* we are tangling with some of those rules meant to correct our language into stability. The rules really don't work, though, in this last quarter of the twentieth century, and the gap between rule and actual usage points to a still-changing "standard" English.

Suggestions for Further Reading

This chapter has combined several approaches to language and dialects, so the following suggestions will each take you further into one aspect of the problem. For a very general overview discussion, Otto Jespersen's *Mankind, Nation, and Individual* (London: G. Allen, 1946) is helpful. Most apropos the study are its immediate antecedents in Henry Cecil Wyld, *A History of Modern Colloquial English* (Oxford: Blackwell, 1953), especially Chapters 3 and 4, and E. J. Dobson, "Early Modern Standard English," *Transactions of the Philological Society* (1955), 25–54. The seminal study of language change as a function of social-class structure is William Labov's *The Social Stratification of English in New York City* (Washington, D. C.: Center for Applied Linguistics, 1966); also helpful and more accessible by Labov is "The Social Motivation of a Sound Change," *Word,* XIX (1963), 273–309, reprinted in Labov, *Sociolinguistic Patterns* (Philadelphia: University of Pennsylvania, 1972), 1–42. The relationship between social and regional dialect is presented by Hans Kurath in "Interrelations between Regional and Social Dialects," *Proceedings of the Ninth International Congress of Linguists,* ed. H. Lunt (The Hague: Mouton, 1964). Background studies in the language of the Middle Ages and the early Renaissance include Fernand Mosse's *A Handbook of Middle English* (Baltimore: Johns Hopkins, 1953) and more detailed studies in Samuel Moore, Sanford Brown Meech, and Harold Whitehall, "Middle English Dialect Characteristics and Dialect Boundaries," *Essays and Studies in English and Comparative Literature* (Ann Arbor: University of Michigan, 1935) and M. L.

Samuels, "Some Applications of Middle English Dialectology," *English Studies,* 44 (1963), 81–94. A good overview of language attitudes in the period is presented in Basil Cottle, *The Triumph of English, 1350–1400* (London: Blandford Press, 1969) and Richard Foster Jones, *The Triumph of the English Language* (Oxford: Clarendon Press, 1953). Finally, the most recent and provocative word on the subject is John L. Fisher, "Chancery and the Emergence of Standard Written English in the Fifteenth Century," *Speculum,* 52 (1977), 870–99.

Chapter 3

English Orthography

"They spell it Vinci and pronounce it Vinchy;
foreigners always spell better than they pronounce."
Mark Twain *Innocents Abroad*

Wayne O'Neil

*Wayne O'Neil writes of himself: "I work at MIT, where I teach courses
in linguistics and in the politics of education. My research follows
along these same divided lines. My current work in linguistics is
concerned with the effects of literacy on language change and
development—phylogeny, not ontogeny. My work in education is not
so easily summarized, so I'll simply give a bibliographic reference to
deal with that part: W. O'Neil in the* Radical Teacher, *numbers 2, 5,
8, 11. In my spare time I build yurts and edit radical periodicals and
bicycle wherever there are roads."*

Introduction

In this chapter we concern ourselves with the rational foundations of
modern English spelling. But we deal as well with (1) the origins of
English spelling, when the rational principle underlying the modern
system appears to have been absent, and (2) the developments in the
system, its evolution from an irrational system (or—more accurately—rational by a different principle) to its present state. This, then,
is the order of our orthographic business: the present, the beginnings,
and the passage from past to present.

1. Some Principles of Writing

There are several ways we can write the words of a language. For
example, without paying attention to the sounds of the words, we could
invent a set of symbols, one for each word of the language and related

to the words in any arbitrary fashion—that is, not necessarily pictures of the thing or state or action represented. Or we could seek to represent the sounds of the language directly, breaking the stream of speech up into syllables—representing each syllable with a symbol—or breaking it into individual segments of sound, with a symbol for each separate sound. Regardless of the kinds of symbols we decided upon—a set of *logograms* ($, ¢, &, etc.), a *syllabary,* or an *alphabet,* we would have to establish some conventions for ordering the symbols. We could begin, say, in the lower right-hand corner of a writing space, arranging the symbols in a way corresponding to their order in real speaking time, move leftward to the left edge of the writing space, up one line, rightward to the right edge of the writing space, up one line, and leftward, etc.—*boustrophedon,* as the Greeks said, the way the ox plows the field. Many other possibilities for ordering the symbols suggest themselves.

Now representing the stream of speech as segments of sound, either syllables or smaller units that make up syllables, seems more apt for writing languages down, for such systems require a small set of symbols and a simple set of conditions on their combination. A logography does well enough for some "languages" of limited expressiveness, for example, the "language" of symbolic logic, but it is out of the question for a natural language. A syllabary, moreover, works nicely for a language, say, like Japanese, which has a quite simple syllabic structure. Its syllabary needs just fifty characters. But if the syllabic structure of a language is complex, perhaps even unclear, a syllabary can be a burden. It is for languages of this sort that an alphabetic system can work well. English is such a language. It is written alphabetically.

From this discussion we must not infer that each language gets the writing system it deserves. Arabic writing, in which the short vowels are not written because they are perfectly predictable from context, works imperfectly for Persian, a non-Arabic language, in which the short vowels are *not* predictable from context. Thus Persian *r-ft-n* stands unclearly for both *raftan,* "go" and *roftan,* "sweep."[1]

Let us turn now to the alphabetic representations of English words. How complete are these representations? How accurate are they? What principles of completeness and accuracy are there? We

---

1. I have, of course, transliterated the Arabic form of the letters into their Roman equivalents and reordered them so that they run from left to right rather than right to left, as in Arabic writing.

In the text, I have employed various clarifying conventions in the citation of forms: spelled forms are italicized, phonological representations of all sorts are enclosed in square brackets, and double quotes are used to indicate the meaning of a word or form. Thus Old English *mearh* = [mæərx] = "horse." However, in the inset examples I have not used these conventions unless clarification of reference is necessary.

begin our inquiry simply: consider, for example, the following words and in particular the *p*'s in them.

(1)   pet, spit, append, tapper, sip, papaya

In them we find the letter *p* in several different positions, which we can describe in at least two ways: on the one hand we can say the *p*'s occur word initially, in second position following either a vowel or *s,* intervocalically, that is between vowels, and word finally; and on the other hand we can say the *p*'s fall either at the beginning of a stressed or accented syllable (where we define 'stressed' as the relative prominence or loudness of a syllable over its neighboring syllables) or at the beginning of an unstressed syllable. Question: does *p* represent exactly the same sound in each of these positions? If you think not, what are the differences from position to position, as nearly as you can describe them?

In the phonetics of English, when the sound [p] opens a stressed or accented syllable as in *pet* and *append,* but not in *tapper,* it is aspirated; that is, along with its other characteristics, we pronounce it with a slight puff of air. This is not true of [p] when it begins an unstressed syllable as in *tapper* or the first syllable of *papaya,* or when it follows [s] as in *spit.* Word finally, [p] is often swallowed, unreleased, and unexploded, and if not exploded then certainly not aspirated. You are supposed to be able to blow out lighted matches on pronouncing *pa* but not with *spit* or *sip*—unless (as you can) you explode the final [p] of *sip.*

These phonetic details, which are also true of [t] and [k], are not, of course, written into our spellings of these and similar words. Phoneticians, for reasons of their own, have developed ways of indicating the differences: [pʰ] for the aspirated one, [p⁻] for an unexploded or imploded one, and [p] for the neutral one, and they spell our examples in their alphabet (the International Phonetic Alphabet) in the following way, in which ´ above a vowel indicates the position of stress:

(2)   [pʰét⁻], [spít⁻], [əpʰénd], [tʰǽpər], [síp⁻], [pəpʰáyə]
      pet   spit   append   tapper   sip   papaya

Why do you think that these quite striking differences in the actual phonetics of the various [p]'s are not, "of course," represented in the orthography?

Let us proceed, then, with the following working hypothesis—one that naturally suggests itself: excluded from the alphabetic representations of English words are all and only predictable phonetic facts. Thus we do not need to represent the various [p]'s with different or modified symbols, for the position of [p] in the word both in its relationship to stress and to the other sounds of the word is enough to indicate the exact range of phonetic shapes it can assume: *p* will do to represent them all.

As stated, our working hypothesis suggests a straightforward way to look for evidence that would confirm or disconfirm it: can you predict what is omitted and what is included in alphabetic representations? That would at least be a beginning. For example, it is not predictable whether an English word will begin with a voiced or voiceless consonant; therefore we must distinctly represent the initial sounds of *bin* and *pin, din* and *tin, van* and *fan,* etc., sounds that except for their voicing are in most other respects the same.

2. English: Some Special Rules

Let us turn now from these rather simple matters to a quite complicated example of something that is omitted from spelling. The most obvious difference between, say, a dictionary's phonological representation of English words and their spelling is that a dictionary clearly indicates stress or accent (which we have defined as the relative prominence in loudness of one syllable—centered in the vowel of the syllable—over another). Does the fact that we omit stress from our writing system confirm or disconfirm our working hypothesis?

Now if you know Spanish, or a similar language, you will remember that there whenever stress is not predictable from the phonological structure of the word, i.e., whenever the general (and quite simple) stress rule of Spanish fails to predict where stress occurs, stress is marked in the spelling: e.g., *romántico,* where the stress rule predicts **romantíco.* (The * means that the word is not well-formed if pronounced this way in Spanish.) The Spanish stress rule simply stated says to look to the last syllable of the word; if it ends in a consonant other than *n* or *s,* stress the final syllable (the ultima); if the ultima is not so stressed, stress the syllable second from the end (the penult). All violations of the rule(s) must be indicated as such with an acute accent mark over the syllables that do receive stress, since they are *not* predictable by the rule(s). There are similar rules for Latin and for many other languages in which there is stress. Thus stress in general is not written into the spelling of words in these languages. What about English: is there a prediction for stress or not? Is stress excluded from the orthography on principle or through oversight?

Consider the following sets of words (all of them nouns) in

which we mark stress (primary or main stress only) with a 1 over the relevant syllable:

$$
\begin{array}{ll}
\textbf{(3) a.} & \overset{1}{\text{macaroon,}} \ \overset{1}{\text{smithereens,}} \ \overset{1}{\text{baboon,}} \ \overset{1}{\text{Kalamazoo}} \ldots \\
\textbf{b.} & \overset{1}{\text{bin,}} \ \overset{1}{\text{bean,}} \ \overset{1}{\text{cat,}} \ \overset{1}{\text{Kate}} \ldots
\end{array}
$$

(3) a. macaroon, smithereens, baboon, Kalamazoo . . .
    b. bin, bean, cat, Kate . . .

(4) a. horizon, aroma, corona, hiatus . . .
    b. agenda, synopsis, asbestos, utensil . . .

(5)   merit, bandit, measles, image . . .

(6)   elephant, rhinoceros, venison, America . . .

In (3) the stress is on the last syllable or only syllable; in (4) and (5) on the next to last; and in (6) it is on the syllable third from the end (the antepenult). Would a better spelling system include these accent marks, or are they predictably placed? Taking care not to be misled by the spelling and paying close attention to their pronunciation, can you work out a prediction for the stress in these sets of words?

How does this one match yours?

(7) a. Check the ultima: if it contains a long vowel or if it is the only syllable, place the stress there.

b. If stress has not been placed on the ultima, look to the penult: if the penult is strong, i.e., if it consists of either a long vowel (followed by any number of consonants), of a short vowel followed by at least two consonants,[2] or if there are only two syllables, place the stress on the penult.

c. If neither of these conditions holds, place the stress on the antepenult.

O.K.—(7) certainly predicts well enough the stress facts of (3) through (6), but what about the following?

---

2. We refer to the numbers of sounds, not letters. Thus *ph* = [f]. To simplify somewhat: long vowel sounds occur in the words *pool, pole, pale, peel, pile,* where for all but the first, the sound of the vowel is the name of its vowel (and we do get the letter *u* representing its name in words like *cue, due,* etc.). Short vowel sounds occur in words such as *pull, Paul, pot, pell, pill.* Most long vowels are phonetically complex, made up of not only a vowel but also an off-glide; in an off-glide the tongue moves as the vowel is pronounced. Short vowels are shorter in duration than long vowels and generally simple, made up of just the phonetic vowel segment.

(8) maȧintain, erȧase, carėen, cajȯle . . .

(9) torment, usurp, cavort, adapt . . .

(10) astonish, edit, cancel, consider . . .

Our prediction (7), as we have formulated it, gives us rather peculiar results when applied to the words of (8)–(10). It handles (8) correctly, doesn't it? But for (9) and (10) it assigns stress as follows: *torment, *usurp, etc., and *astonish, *consider, etc. What is there to say? Do we have or want two somewhat overlapping predictions? Are there any differences between the words in (3)–(6) and those in (8)–(10) on which the stress differences might depend?

There is a clear grammatical difference: (3)–(6) are nouns, as we noted when we presented them; (8)–(10) are verbs. There is possibly a prediction for verbs and a slightly different and overlapping one for nouns. What about adjectives?

(11) obscene, remote, discreet, inane, obsolete . . .

(12) absurd, corrupt, robust, overt . . .

(13) solid, fantastic, vulgar, common . . .

Do we need a new prediction for adjectives?

Now, you should notice a very important difference between the complication of what we have now said about the predictability of Spanish stress and that of English. Reread the section on Spanish stress and then state the difference—if you can.

In English, then, we have a rule for verbs and adjectives and a slightly different and overlapping one for nouns. Stress is thus predictable and properly omitted from the spelling; but in order to predict correctly, we must know the part of speech—the lexical category to which the word belongs. The spelling does not, of course, provide this information. Thus before we can correctly predict stress we must bring that knowledge to bear on the spelled forms.

Are there any other problems? Well, just sticking to a consideration of simple nouns will soon force a whole lot of them to the surface. Consider the following nouns:

(14) silo, hindu, chianti, albino, broccoli . . .

Where does the noun rule (7) predict that stress will fall on the words of (14)?

Of course, it is obvious that the predictions are all wrong. In **silo, *albino,* etc., the final vowels are long. Is it simply that our rule fails for these words, or is there some deeper generalization that we are missing? On the assumption that (7) is worth saving as a generalization, let us consider more closely the words of (14); for it is here that we can see for the first time in this discussion the way in which spelling aligns itself with our predictions and reflects the deeper generalizations previously just hinted at.

Look at the spellings in earlier examples of stressed long vowels. Are these spelled in the same way as the long vowels of (14)? If not, how do they differ, and is that difference consistent in some interesting way: *hindu* and *Kalamazoo, broccoli* and *smithereens,* etc.? Or look at the verbs ending in long vowels: *maintain, erase, cajole,* etc. How do the spellings of the long vowels, in apparent violation of the noun rule (7), differ in spelling from those in accord with it? (Note also spellings like *résumé*—now often and confusingly *resume.*)

Clearly, the words in (14) are spelled as if they contained short final vowels. If we were to take the spellings as representing abstractions distinct from the obvious phonetic manifestations of the given words, abstractions upon which our predictions or generalizations operated in some orderly way, we could see how *silo,* etc., would then directly represent that abstraction: *silo → sílo → sílō.* First by a rule that assigns stress, i.e. (7), and then by a rule that lengthens word-final vowels. For in English a word-final vowel (unless it is *a*) *must* be long, and therefore it need only be marked long or written long when that fact is crucial to the correct assignment of stress (as in *Kalamazóo*). Otherwise, if the length is totally predictable, why write it? This means that the distinction between long and short vowels is neutralized in the actual pronunciation of English, while for the purpose of stress assignment it is crucially distinct at an abstract level. As is often true in cases of this sort, where there is a crucial distinction between 'actual' and 'abstract,' spelling captures the abstract level.

Notice that all of this supports our working hypothesis: a spelling will not represent what is predictable. The words of (14), which began as counterexamples to the hypothesis in general and to (7) in particular, have turned out to support both.

There are, of course, spellings that do not measure up to the generalizations: *wíndow,* for example, has a final unstressed long vowel spelled as if it were abstractly long, as if it should be stressed. Our hypothesis specifies a condition of spelling optimality which will not be met always and everywhere. In short, there are exceptions—a partial explanation of which we return to belów.

If everything that has emerged so far is correct, or at least tending toward correctness, then it is clear in fact that spellings generally represent abstract forms in which appears only that which we can predict. Now you may wonder if this is useful for a reader who knows the language in a mature way as opposed to a reader who knows the language as a foreigner or as a child. In order to answer this question, let us consider some data in which, on the one hand, the same sound under the same conditions of stress and syllable structure is spelled in several different ways and in which, on the other hand, the same word is always spelled the same regardless of its differing pronunciations in different grammatical contexts. These are really two perspectives on the same general problem.

Consider, first, the following:

(15)   final syllable [əC]: móral, sólemn, cívil, pérson . . .[3]

where in each typical case we have a [əC] sequence with a different vowel symbol: *a, e, i, o.* Can you see any reason for this?

In the old days, schoolteachers used to tell students learning the higher reaches of spelling or having difficulty with it to pronounce the vowel symbols with their 'full' values. Cleverer teachers told them to try to think of related or derived words in which the 'full' values emerged. Try it; where possible fill in the blanks with the words in (15) and mark the stress on the resulting words:

(16)   _____ + ity

_____ + ify

Notice that the *n* of *solemn* is also realized in derived words, cf. *sign-signal, bomb-bombard, gnostic-agnostic,* etc.

Next, consider the following type of alternation:

(17)   telegraph, telegraphic, telegraphy . . .

Here we must introduce a notion that you are probably familiar with from ordinary dictionary entries: secondary stress. For example, if we utter *baby* and *sitter* in isolation, each word would have primary or

---

3. [ə] (schwa) is the vowel onto which all vowels in English collapse in unstressed position. A variant of schwa is the higher [ɨ] (barred *i*), the variation depending generally on the phonetic surroundings. Thus *person* is more accurately [pərsɨn]. C = any number of consonants.

1-stress on its first syllable. But when we put them together in a compound word *babysitter,* the first part of the word will have 1-stress on its first syllable, but the first syllable of *sitter* will be less prominently stressed than it is in isolation and less strongly stressed than the first syllable of *baby* in the compound. In fact, it has secondary or 2-stress: the first syllable of the compound is now more heavily stressed than the third, which is in its turn more heavily stressed than either the second or fourth syllables of the word. The stress on the compound is in these terms *bábysìtter.*

With these facts in mind, mark the stresses (primary *and* secondary) on the words of (17); try also to represent the vowels of these words. In this connection, ponder also the following typical alternations:

(18)   reject (verb), reject (noun), rejection . . .

Consider not only the stress variations, but also the vowel *and* consonant variations. Are these isolated triples? Are there any generalizations not spelled out, any way of predicting the differences between and among these sets of words?

In some sense, writing is edited speech. There are spaces between words where there are no pauses in speaking: [áyskrīym] = *ice cream* = *I scream,* etc. There is invariance of basic word representation where there is predictable variation in speaking: thus *telegraph-* for [télǝgrǽf], [tèlǝgrǽf + ik], and [tǝlégrǝf + īy]; *reject-* for [rīyjékt] or [rǝjékt] (verb), [rīyjèkt] (noun), and [rīyjékšǝn] or [rǝjékšǝn]; *solemn-* for [sáləm], [solémn + ǝtīy], [sáləmnàyz] *(solemnize);* etc.

What about unpredictable variation? It is spelled out if the segment involved is changed in a way that is unexpected. Then we spell the plurals of *mouse, foot,* and *ox* as *mice, feet,* and *oxen,* the past forms of *sing, drive,* and *ride* as *sang, drove,* and *rode;* and the past forms of *keep, weep,* and *lose* as *kept, wept,* and *lost.* If, however, a segment fails to undergo an expected change, it is generally not spelled out. Thus the vowel before *-ity* is generally shortened in English: *sublimity (sublime), insanity (insane), obscenity (obscene),* etc. But in *obesity* the expected does not happen, and yet the orthography does not signal it. Notice it is not necessary that things be done in this way. We could spell *feet *foots* and simply understand that *foot + s = feet* or that *sing + ed = sang,* etc. The problem of *obesity* could be solved by spelling it **obeesity.* It is not obvious why such solutions to irregularity are not employed.

71

3. The Principle of Abstract Representation

The editing principle is clear: spell out what is unpredictable and/or irregular. The spelling of English, of all spelling, is largely optimal in this sense. There are certainly spellings that fall short (near or far) of this ideal, optimal condition. But to emphasize the *enough*'s, the *through*'s, the *though*'s, the *knight*'s, and the *right*'s is to lose sight of the real virtues of English orthography.

But what is the virtue of having a writing system that is optimal in the sense just defined? Or to put the question the other way around, what difficulties would follow if the spelling system always spelled out what general rules about phonological and grammatical structure predict? Say we were to write the items in the left-hand column of (19) in a new way (that of the right-hand column):

(19)		
ice cream, I scream	āyskrīym [1]	
the food	ðəfūwd [1]	
moral	morəl [1]	
solemn	sāləm [1]	
solemnity	səlemnətīy [1]	
person	pərsən [1]	
personify	pərsānəfāy [1]	
telegraph	teləgræf [1] [2]	
telegraphy	təlegrəfīy [1]	
telegraphic	teləgræfik [2] [1]	
reject	rəjĕkt [1]	
reject	rīyjĕkt [1] [2]	
rejection	rīyjĕkšən [1]	

Have we gained or lost? What have we gained? What lost?

Respelling closer to phonetic ground is on the one hand a lot like removing the spaces betweenthewordsastheyareprintednormally. It would undo part of the system that helps us understand what we read. Just think of what is involved when we understand what is said to us: first of all it is necessary to somehow enrich the signal that we have received, to beef it up enough so that we can interpret it. For much of what we hear or utter is in a technical sense degraded and mixed up with irrelevant side noises, etc. We must then analyze the utterance into its constituent words and phrases, figure out the meanings that the words of the utterance have in relationship to one another, and so on—until we can associate a meaning with the sounds that we have heard.

Now if writing were simply a narrowly drawn record of speech, not only would there generally be no spaces between the words, but also the letters themselves would be half-formed, as if typed with a typewriter whose characters were encrusted with dirt or as if set with type from a font of broken type slugs. Thus, apparently simple things like spacing and punctuation do some of the work for readers that they would have to do for themselves in listening. In this respect, the written word and paragraph and page are like very slow and measured speech.

Standard spelling—abstracted as it is away from the surface phonetics—is a boon for another reason: for the spelling system strives to preserve the identity (and thus the meaning relationships) of words regardless of their various positions. The general principle seems to be this: always spell the word or stem or root the same, regardless of what prefixes, suffixes, endings, etc. are associated with it; if we reflected those accidental properties of a word in our spelling, it would lead to total confusion. To repeat: to a large extent, our spelling system avoids representing the accidental and concentrates on the fixed substance from which the accidental follows. All this can be seen in the words that we have been looking at in the previous paragraphs.

Thus the written word represents speech at a level abstracted severely away from phonetic reality, at a level which does, however, have psychological reality. Thus we feel there to be a [t] in [rīyjekšən]¹ because at some level this [š] derives from [t]. We do not feel the [t] because of the spelling of the word; rather it is in the spelling because of that felt sense of it, because it is psychologically real.

Notice that this alternation of [t] with [š] is not a phenomenon restricted to just these three words. Matters can be even more complex: consider, for example, the *t* of *create* in the series *create, creation, creature*. The *t* is always there psychologically because we understand all three words to contain the verb *create*. In fact, the meanings of the three are closely related, and the alternation of the *t* sound can be accounted for in terms of general (and predictable) phonological processes.⁴

---

4. See Sapir, "The Psychological Reality of the Phoneme" in Mandelbaum; also O'Neil, "Our Collective Phonological Illusions: Young and Old" in Kavanagh and Mattingly. (See the Suggestions for Further Reading for full references.)

It is because orthography operates as this abstract level that we can understand what we read faster than we can understand what we hear. We are able to read much faster than that, in fact.[5]

The abstractions that spelled words represent are not, however, part of everyone's knowledge: children hover close to phonetic ground as they try to learn the abstractions and the generalizations of the language. Foreign-language speakers learning English, or sometimes even those who have already learned it, are simply dealing with it through the medium (the rules and abstractions) of their native languages. So the standard orthography does offer some difficulty for these people. Attempts at spelling reform (often justified the way the metric system is: i.e., that it would be easier for children to learn and use) fail because in fact standard spelling works extremely well for the vast majority of the speakers of the language: the mature, native speakers. For it is they who have internalized the phonological representations that the spelled forms more or less capture.

This suggests that within a language these abstractions will not differ significantly from dialect to dialect. And it is in fact a claim, an empirical one borne out by a certain amount of evidence, that these abstractions stand above dialect differences: thus the spelling system would be supradialectal, a system that relates directly to all dialects. Dialects will differ phonologically in the rules that relate underlying phonological representations to surface phonetic ones. But they will not differ significantly in their underlying phonological representations, and standard spelling will work for them all.

For example, there are dialects in which the word-final distinction between [f] and [θ] is eliminated in favor of [f]: instead of *mouth* there is *mouf*. And there are dialects in which there is no contrast in stressed syllables and after dental consonants between [yūw] and [ūw], for example, there is no [dyūw] *(due)* contrasting with [dūw] *(do),* [nyūw] *(new)* versus [nūwn] *(noon),* [tyūwn] *(tune)* versus [tūwl] *(tool),* etc. But these surface neutralizations do not necessarily disturb the underlying contrasts. For example, a speaker may not say [kấntənyū̆wətīy] *(continuity),* but the y-glide will be there when the syllable in question is not under stress: [kəntínyūw] *(continue).* Compare also [nūwtrəl] *(neutral)* with [nyūwtrəlāyzḗyšən] *(neutralization).*

If then we want to indicate exactly the way in which English is pronounced in a given regional or social dialect, we *cannot* depend on the standard orthography; for it gives us only the underlying represen-

---

5. See Bower and Bever in Levin and Williams (see Suggestions for Further Reading). I do not allude to speed reading here, for it is simply a higher-level form of scanning.

tations common to all dialects of the language. Thus whether we want to represent exactly the way English is pronounced among, say, the Brahmin of Boston or the citizens of Charleston, S.C., among the seraphim of Los Angeles or the goyim of Kenosha, Wisconsin, we must depart rather sharply from standard orthography and resort to either the International Phonetic Alphabet (and thus risk being understood by no one but the phoneticians) or to more impressionistic devices. Unfortunately, and this is a comment on the severe stratification of our society, the assumption that standard orthography reflects "proper" speech leads to dialect spelling being reserved usually for the speech of the poor and the illiterate.

4. Variation Through Time and Place

Let us now turn to variations in English spelling from place to place and from time to time. English was not always spelled as consistently as it is today; indeed it is not now spelled the same everywhere. But the differences between now and then and here and there (between modern English and, say, Chaucer's English; or between the United States and England (and the Commonwealth nations generally) are either trivial or simply reflect the phonology of an earlier period. In any event, these differences do not graze the general principles that we have discussed above. Consider, for example, the following differences between American and British spelling:

(20)   U.S.   U.K.

a. honor . . .   honour . . .

b. center . . .   centre . . .

c. criticize . . . criticise . . .

The type (20a.) in British spelling simply reflects the abstract phonological representation of an earlier period in the language, from the time of the Middle English of Chaucer, say, when words of this sort were pronounced with a long final vowel and stressed on that final syllable. For example (from Chaucer's *Knight's Tale*, lines 1139–41—where the metrical pattern clearly indicates where the stresses and rimes are to fall):

(21) "It nere," quod he, "to thee no greet honour
        x /   x / x / x / x /

75

For to be false, ne for to be traitour
x x x /   x x x / x /

To me, that am thy cosyn and thy brother. . . .''
x / x /   x / x /   x / x

("It would be," said he, "no great honor for you to be
either false or a traitor to me who am your cousin and
brother. . . .")

In a system like an orthographic one whose development is
determined only in part by its primary connection to another system
(i.e., phonology) and which is also under the control of such forces as
tradition, it is not surprising to find examples of striking incongruity at
the primary level, not surprising to find -*our*'s long after what they
represented has changed pronunciation. Thus do we also account for
the -*ow* of *window* by noting that the word was originally a compound:
wind + *aug* ("wind-eye"—the latter part in the form borrowed from
Old Norse). The spelling presumably preserves that of a time when the
word was still felt to be a compound, when there was still secondary
stress on the second element in the compound word.

Residual also are the various spellings of the sound [īy]. Consider just these two:

(22)   read–reed, meat–meet, feat–feet

The spelling in *a* derives from a period in English when there were in
fact contrasting sounds in these words: long [æ] as opposed to long [e]
(where the first of these sounds was very much like that of modern
English *had;* the second like that of *cape*). Chaucer would not rime
such pairs. [mǣt], for example, was spelled *meat* because its vowel had
some of the characteristics of both *e* and *a*. These phonological distinctions later collapsed, but the spelling contrast has remained. There is a
similar explanation for load–lode = [lōwd]. And the many *gh*'s of English spelling remain from a time when these letters in combination
represented a consonantal sound [x], as in German *ich* "I" or Scots
loch. The *gh* spelling for some reason remains as a fossil in our present
orthographic system, a reminder of the former Germanic "glory" of
the English language.

For a long time the Chicago *Tribune* made war on these spelling
archaisms, a war which it could never win; but it did not recognize this
fact and thus did not give up the struggle until quite recently, retaining
only the terrain of *tho* and *thru*. It is generally the fate of spelling
reformers to lose; from the medieval English didactic poet Orm (or as

he would have it: Orrm), to the twentieth-century didactic playwright George Bernard Shaw—who continued the fight for orthographic reform from beyond the grave, leaving in his will money to be spent for developing a new English orthography.[6] For in their zeal the reformers lump together the archaic and the structural. For example, such *Tribune* spellings as *fotograf* are counterintuitive: alternative ways of spelling the same underlying sound often serve to mark off the separate parts of the vocabulary from one another: to distinguish the words that can enter into certain kinds of alternation and derivation from those that enter into others. For example given *photo-graph,* we suspect a possible *photo-meter.* Given *-graph* we dismiss a possible plural **graves* (*wife–wives,* etc.). If a spelling reform grates against something psychologically real, it is bound to meet with resistance. Spelling reform that works in accord with what is psychologically real is generally acceptable. Noah Webster, who saw it as his duty to reform American spelling and bring it in line with phonological reality, was at least successful in getting rid of the *our*'s in *honour, colour,* etc.

Let us now turn to (20b.). Here there is no past difference in pronunciation involved, merely a difference in spelling conventions: where to place the *e.* But what, in fact, does the *e* represent?

If you found it difficult to answer the question, it is because the *e* is being used not to represent any particular vowel sound. It is used there diacritically to indicate the vowel (vocalic and syllabic) quality of the *r.* In British spelling the *e* is found after the *r;* in American spelling it is found before the *r.* But notice that if two principles of orthography come into conflict, we become British in our spelling: *acre,* not **acer.* For the *e* is often used to predict something of the quality of the preceding consonant: refer to *stag–stage* and the discussion below. Which of these ways is consistent with the general way of spelling out such specifications?

Clearly the British way is, for it seems always to be the case in English spelling that diacritics of this sort refer back rather than ahead. Regardless of how it is done, though, notice that the *e* must be dropped in related words in which the *r* is not syllabic:

(23) center/re–central
meter/re–metric(al)
theater/re–theatrical

Turn now to (20c.)—*ize ~ ise*—instances in which a particular diacritic value of *e* is used more extensively in British than in American

6. See G. B. Shaw, *Androcles and the Lion–The Shaw Alphabet Edition.* Baltimore: Penguin Books, 1962.

spelling. (Note also *defense–defence*.) In *muse, raise, bathe* (as opposed to *bath*, etc.) what work is the *e* doing?

Thus in addition to indicating the length (or quality) of the preceding vowel (as in *bath–bathe*), the *e* can also mark the voiced character of the preceding consonant. If then *bathe*, for example, were taken as representing the underlying phonological form of the word, there would have to be phonological generalizations in English that accounted for the lengthened vowel in *bathe* (as opposed to the short vowel in *bath*) and the voiced consonant. Insofar as these exist—and they do—the spellings *bathe*, etc. conform to the general principle(s) discussed above. However, there is no phonological justification for deriving the [z] of *ise/ize* from an underlying [s]. Insofar, then, as British (or American) spelling does not represent the underlying state of things, it is nonoptimal.

It should be clear by now what the orthography of modern English and of its earlier periods is like, the nature of the principles that determine what is included in and excluded from orthographic representations. This principle seems natural enough; thus it is extremely surprising to find that in the earliest English writing, that of Old English (ca. 700–1000 A.D.), the general principle is often and obviously not followed. For example, in Old English the word for "day" was *dæg* (pronounced [dæɣ], where [ɣ] is the sound that you may have heard in Modern German *sagen,* "say"; it is the voiced counterpart of [x] as in German *ich* or Scots *loch*). In Old English the system of inflectional endings was quite complex in comparison with that of the modern language. In order to express the various relationships that words could bear to one another (which in the modern language is more often done by position and/or in prepositional phrases), Old English employed a variety of inflectional endings. We find, then, the following endings added to words like *dæg:*

(24)		*Singular*	*Plural*
	Nom./Acc.	-Ø	-as
	Genitive	-es	-a
	Dative	-e	-um

And when added, the character of the vowels of the endings often affected the stressed vowels in the word and the final consonant of its stem. Thus instead of:

(25)	dæg	dægas
	dæges	dæga
	dæge	dægum

78

we get:

(26)   dæg   dagas
          dæġcs   daga
          dæġe   dagum

That is, when the vowel of the inflection is a back vowel ([u] or [ā]), the vowel of the stem is also back ([ā], approximately the vowel sound of *hot, pod,* etc.). When the vowel of the inflection is a front vowel ([e]), then so is the vowel of the stem ([æ], the vowel sound of *cat, pan,* etc.). The stem-final consonant, *g,* is front (or palatalized)—here indicated by placing a dot above the consonant, *ġ.* This contrast is like that between the [k]'s of *cool* and *keep*—the [k] of *keep* is made with the tongue more advanced in the mouth.

    Now, the curious thing about these alternations is that the vowel alternation between [æ] and [a] is spelled out. Thus we find the following spelling in Old English (*g* = [ɤ]): *dæg, dæges, dæge, dagas, daga, dagum.*

    And so it goes for very many predictable alternations in Old English phonology: because the alternations are captured in the orthography, the form of the basic stem changes with different inflections.

    Take, for another example, the stem *tæl-,* "number." It, like *dæg,* turns up *tal-* in its noun paradigm. In (27) and (28) we give the forms in their Old English spelling:

(27)

	Singular	*Plural*
Nom./Acc.	tæl	talu
Genitive	tæles	tala
Dative	tæle	talum

(*Tæl* has its Nom./Acc. plural in -*u* because it is grammatically neuter, different from *dæg,* which is grammatically masculine.) And in the denominative verb *tellan,* "to count," the stem *tæl-* turns up *tel-, tell-,* and *teal-:*

(28)

		Present	*Past*
Singular	1st person	tell-e	teal-d-e
	2nd person	tel-est	teal-d-est
	3rd person	tel-eth	teal-d-e
Plural	all persons	tell-ath	teal-d-on

And in the paradigm of *mearh* [mæərx], "horse" (modern English *mare*), consider the *h* (= [x]), which is predictably deleted when it falls between vocalic sounds—say between an [r] and a vowel:

(29)		Singular	Plural
	Nom./Acc.	mearh	mearas
	Genitive	meares	meara
	Dative	meare	mearum

Notice, again, that what is perfectly predictable is spelled out.

Now if all of this is predictable from the phonological structure of the words (and so far as we can tell it is), why is it written out in Old English spellings? Are we to imagine that Old Englishmen were different in their powers of abstraction from us moderns? For doing what Old Englishmen did would be like writing our *create, creation, creature* as *create, creashion, creechure*. And this would amount to ignoring the core common to all three words and the predictable alternations that take place in its pronunciation. Such spelling might be easier for foreigners, but it would place an unnecessary burden on people who already knew the language in the way native speakers know their native language.

The explanation of this violation of the general principle governing orthographies lies, I believe, in the origins of English orthography. Consequently, we have to present a bit of the history of English writing habits.

When the Germanic tribes (the Angles, the Saxons, and the Jutes), who were to become the English, started taking over Britain in the middle of the fifth century A.D., they brought with them an alphabetic writing system: the runes. It was a writing system common to all the Germanic peoples, one that originated in Mediterranean Europe sometime in the very earliest years of the Christian era. Because of their pagan associations, runes did not thrive in England after its conversion to Christianity began toward the very end of the sixth century A.D. Indeed, it had not prospered much as a writing system prior to that time, for it was only used epigraphically—thus its quite sharp and angular lines:

ᚠᛁᛋᚳ · ᚠᛚᚩᛞᚢᚾ · ᚠ ᚾᚠᚠᚷ ᚠᛗᚱᛉ
f i s c . f l o d u . a h o f o n f e r g

ᚾᛉ ᛒᛗᚱᛁᛉ
e n b e r i g

(30) "The flood lifted up the fish on to the cliff-bank."

The Anglo-Saxons were, then, essentially illiterate except for some few who could cast runes. Then the Church came bearing Roman letters from two directions: Rome and Ireland. For at the time of the conversion of the English, the Roman church was essentially divided between these two centers of learning and tradition. Being good missionaries, the Romans and the Irish began to set down the gospel in the local language and in an orthography of their own devising in order to teach and develop an indigenous clergy. So the first non-runic writers of English were probably foreigners, *not* native speakers of the language. Nothing remains from the earliest English writing, but we can reconstruct enough about it to understand that the Irish way of writing English won out over the Roman. In all matters of the church, the Romans won the day but in this one matter of converting the English, the Irish prevailed calligraphically and orthographically.

Now it is likely or at least reasonable to speculate, that the peculiarities of early Old English orthography exist because it was not devised by native speakers. For which of them could write? The system was probably put together by people whose grasp of English was that of a foreigner—there are contemporary complaints that the missionaries didn't know well enough the language of the people they were trying to convert. Their own languages and ways of writing them down stood between them and their self-assigned task of working up an orthography for Old English. It is thus not surprising that they should write down the phonological surface of the language: these foreigners did not know its phonological abstractions. Their own ways of spelling (in particular Irish ways) account for such spellings as *secean,* "to seek"; *adwæscean,* "to quench"; etc. The *e* following *c* and *sc* indicate that the consonants are palatalized, being pronounced *ch* and *sh,* respectively; the *e* is not to be pronounced. This was an ordinary orthographic practice of the Irish. Their superficial knowledge of the language accounts for the surface spellings discussed above.

Now when the native speakers of the language began to use the orthography for themselves and some of the respect for the tradition had worn off, the beleagured native scribes (the bearers of that tradition) often could not remember where, for example, to put *a* and where *æ;* for them to consistently write down what was entirely predictable was difficult. Thus in later manuscripts we begin to find *æ*'s where earlier we would have found *a*'s and vice-versa:

(31) a.   hwælas   "whales"
         hwales   "Whale's"

    b.   dægas   "days"
         dage   "day" (*dat. sing.*)

And so it was for a host of violations of the general orthographic principle whereby what is generally predictable is not written out.

The orthographic tradition began to break down in the direction of not representing what was predictable. But exactly how things would have sorted themselves out we shall never know, for the complex inflectional and derivational system of Old English began to come apart under the burden of the language contact with the Scandinavians in the east and the north of England and later (following the Norman Conquest) with the French.

But in any case the later variety of English—Middle English— that emerges from these contacts is written in a way that conforms to our general orthographic principle. Thus Middle English spelling does not represent such predictable alternations as that between long and short vowels, for example, in *kepen,* "to keep" (pronounced—more or less—as we would a spelling like *capen*) and *kepte,* "kept" (pronounced like modern English *kept* with the addition of a final [ə]). Where this alternation is irregular in modern English we spell it out: *keep/kept, feel/felt,* etc.But in Middle English, where this alternation is perfectly regular, the spelling does not indicate the alternation. This is exactly what we are led to expect by our general principle.

However, it is also true that earlier English spelled the same sound in different ways. For example, during the Middle English period, we find the first sound of "she" spelled here *sch,* there *sh,* and other places ʒ*h.* Yet these did not represent different sounds, because different parts of the country developed separate traditions as to which symbols would indicate which sounds. The disruption caused by the Norman Conquest contributed to parochial spelling traditions for English, for it was no longer the language of state and church. These separations began to coalesce after the anglicization of the Norman conquerors, a process that quickened with the advent of printing in the late fifteenth century. The wider the expected audience for a given piece of writing, the more necessary it was to have a common orthography.

These are, however, matters of form—(shall we write the initial sound of *think* with þ or with *th*) not substance. After the earliest periods of English writing, no one thought of violating the general orthographic principle, probably because this principle is the one naturally obeyed by native speakers of a language trying to write it down. Thus, except for a few crabbed reformers, people have been pretty much content with the standard English orthography. For it captures a psychologically real and vital level of the phonology of the language. We can thus appropriately reduce the general principle to the following aphorism: don't put your orthography where your mouth is; put it where your head is.*

Suggestions for Further Reading

Readers who wish to pursue some of the topics and issues raised in this chapter can turn to the following essays and books which in their turn will lead them to further sources of information. The central point of this chapter is dealt with in some detail by Noam Chomsky in H. Levin and J. Williams, eds., *Basic Studies in Reading* (New York: Basic Books, 1970) and by Carol Chomsky in her "Reading, Writing, Phonology," *Harvard Educational Review* 40: 287–309 (1970). The Levin and Williams volume also contains other valuable essays, including T. G. Bever and T. G. Bower, "How to Read without Listening," mentioned in footnote 5.

There is additional discussion of these matters, some of it of a more technical nature, in J. F. Kavanagh and I. G. Mattingly, eds., *Language by Ear and by Eye: The Relationships between Speech and Reading* (Cambridge: MIT Press, 1972). See, especially, the essays by E. S. Klima ("How Alphabets Might Reflect Language"), W. O'Neil ("Our Collective Phonological Illusions"), and S. E. Martin ("Nonalphabetic Writing Systems: Some Observations"). For further discussion of the psychological phenomenon, see E. Sapir, "The Psychological Reality of the Phoneme" in his *Selected Writings,* D. G. Mandelbaum, ed. (Berkeley: University of California Press, 1949).

There is no good or modern work on the history of English orthography, or on its origins. The history of writing has, however, been well done: see, especially, I. J. Gelb, *A Study of Writing* (Chicago: The University of Chicago Press, 1952) and D. Diringer, *Writing* (New York: Praeger, 1962). For more analytic approaches see W. Haas, ed., *Writing without Letters* (Manchester: Manchester University Press, 1976).

---

*Work on this project was supported by grants to the Massachusetts Institute of Technology from the National Institute of Mental Health, #MH 13390-09 and to the Center for Applied Linguistics from the National Science Foundation.

The New
Generation

Chapter 4

How Pablo Says
"Love" and "Stove"

Timothy Shopen

Timothy Shopen teaches descriptive and applied linguistics at the Australian National University. He has recently begun a study of children who speak an Australian Aboriginal language to see what the structure and use of their language reveals of how their community is maintaining itself within the larger English-speaking society.

1. Child Language: Imitation vs. Original Creation

This is about the speech of a two-year-old boy learning English. His name is Pablo. What he does is not unusual. If you are surprised by what is recorded here, you probably haven't been spending much time with two-year-old children lately.

One of the great questions bearing on the nature of the human mind is how children learn languages. All children of normal intelligence do it with no special teaching, mainly within the first six years of life and sometimes not just with one, but with several languages. A child's biological parents do not give him an advantage in learning any particular language; a Vietnamese child adopted by an English-speaking family, or a child born of English-speaking parents adopted by a Vietnamese family, will learn the language of the community just as easily as all other children do. And yet in all languages, sounds are put together to form words, and words to form phrases, clauses, sentences, and discourses in exceedingly complex ways; and the number of utterances in a language is potentially infinite!

We must recognize that there are important characteristics shared by all languages which, it would appear, any infant is prepared to develop just out of the genetic specifications that make him human. These genetically shaped aspects of language do not have to be learned in full; they lie latent when life begins. But a child will not develop language unless he or she grows up in a natural, language-using community. It remains for the child to observe and master all those characteristics that make a particular language unique; in the case of English, this means everything that makes English different from Vietnamese, or from any other human language, actual or potential, including Turkish, Arabic, Zulu, Basque, Welsh, German, French, Spanish, Russian, Chinese, Hawaiian, or Navajo—and that is quite a lot!

There is an age-old debate over how children learn languages, over how much a child develops the ability to speak his language by imitating the older people around him, and how much he does so by creating original generalizations of his own. Only the first idea is compatible with strict stimulus-response theory of the sort originated by Pavlov, where an external stimulus causes behavior. The adult language used in the presence of the child would be the stimulus, and what the child does with language would be the response. The second idea is supported to the extent that there are regularities in the speech of the child that are different from those of the adult, not just "mistakes."

The regularities of child speech, the regular 'errors,' may yet be viewed as a transition stage on the way to adult speech, a development caused by external 'reinforcement.' Here there is the idea that the closer the child comes to behaving like an adult, the more the older people around him will approve and thereby reinforce his development in that direction. External factors certainly influence child behavior, but the question remains how original patterns of child speech take shape in the first place; moreover, if 'reinforcement' were the primary motivating force, the most obvious pattern would be for each new stage to differ from the one before it only by small increments, with the direction of change always toward the adult standard. There are, however, innovations by children so original that the path to the adult standard looks much more like an irregular zig zag than a straight line, and the matter of when the child changes from one stage to another does seem to have little relation to the amount of reinforcement he has been receiving. These are some of the reasons why the internal workings of the child's mind must be viewed as so important in the learning process.

Something like imitation is part—but only just part—of the process of acquiring a language. The child has to learn which combinations of sound features make a difference for meaning in the speech of the adults around him. In English, voicing is distinctive at the end of words, but not in Vietnamese: to an English speaker, the English words *mid* and *mit* sound different from each other because he notices the vocal cords vibrating at the end of the first, but not the second; Vietnamese has a word *mit,* but Vietnamese *d* never occurs at the end of a word. On the other hand, Vietnamese is a tone language while English is not. There are five words *co* in Vietnamese whose pronunciations differ only in the pitch contour or melody of the word: they mean "to contract" (as with a muscle), "to have," "grass," "stork," and "to rub"; and though they may sound the same to an English speaker, they each sound different to Vietnamese speakers just because of their pitch contours.

The child also has to recognize the meanings adults associate with particular sequences of sounds. The four-legged animals that provide people with milk and beef are called *cow* in English, but are referred to as *bò* (with a low-falling tone) in Vietnamese. The English word *cow* might evoke several meanings in Vietnamese. If *cow* could be mistaken for the Vietnamese word *cao* it would mean "to be tall," and if for *khao,* it would mean "to honor someone with a feast." Imitation is part of what it means to sound like an English speaker, but as we will demonstrate with data taken from two-year-old Pablo, there is much more going on.

Like all children, Pablo is trying out a lot of expressions that are different from what he hears adults say. To express the same idea, he has recently said all of the following, some with an air of playful experimentation:

John's back hurts.
John back hurts.
Back hurts John.
John hurts back.
John hurt backs.

He is striving to develop principles of maximum generality. This can be seen in his vocabulary. When he was eight months old, he made up the word "dahdee" (not "Daddy"). He used it often in commands or requests. It meant either "Take it from me" (said while offering something to someone), or "Give it to me." He used this word for four months. About the same time, he learned to say "hot" and attached an interesting meaning to it: he would say "Hot!" to refer to objects that emitted just light as well as ones emitting heat. When he was fifteen months old he took the name of the first dog he knew, "Mab," and extended it to refer to all dogs. "Mab" remained his word for dog for six months until he started saying the adult word (which he pronounced "goggie"). During the same period, Pablo frequently heard an adult friend named "Miles" play the fiddle. Pablo first used the name for just that person, but once again changed a proper noun into a common one and made it his word for music. The word "miles" has meant music for him from the time he was sixteen months old until now when he is just past his second birthday.

The changes that occur in word meanings as a child learns a language are not unlike those in the history of language; both the similarities and the differences are of interest. In Pablo's *miles,* "music" we have an instance of *metonomy,* the taking of the part for the whole. Compare an example in American English, the evolution of one of the meanings of the word *date:* from the time for a social engagement it came to mean the social engagement itself; from a word meaning a person who played music, *miles* came to mean the music itself. Here is a clear similarity.

Metaphor as a means of semantic change in early childhood may be virtually nonexistent or it may be everywhere. A live metaphor is one where there is a conscious misapplication of meaning as in "That man is a camel." The sentence cannot be literally true so it must be understood metaphorically: the man *resembles* a camel in some salient respect; for instance, he can go a long time without water or he can survive well in a desert. If some time from now people refer to a certain kind of person as a "camel" without thinking of the original four-legged animal, then this would be an instance of metaphor leading to semantic change. There is nothing to indicate that Pablo has so far made any metaphors. To the author he has always appeared to be adopting a new *convention* for the meaning of a word when he has extended it to a new part of the world; one reason for this belief is that once he has made a new extension of a word meaning, he has typically used it often, as if practicing it. By this interpretation we have a difference from adult behavior. Another difference concerns *narrowing.* *Stool* is a word from Anglo-Saxon that used to mean anything for one person to sit on; when the word *chair* was borrowed from French, the meaning for *stool* narrowed to the one we know today. Instances of original meanings by narrowing in Pablo's speech, not just narrowing to adult meanings, have been rare or nonexistent.

In Pablo's *mab,* "dog" we see an instance of the most prevalent kind of semantic change for him, *widening,* the taking of the name for some particular member (or members) of a set and extending it to the set as a whole. Compare what happened to the word *bird* in the history of English: it originally meant just "little bird." Widening always amounts to simplifying a definition: we can see this in the change Pablo made with his meaning for the word "cow." When he was eighteen months old, he was using this word and the word "horse" the way adults do, but then he dropped "horse" and used "cow" to refer to both horses and cows, in real life or in pictures, and soon for zebras, elephants, hippos, and other large animals as well. From using "cow" to talk about the kind of large four-legged animal that gives milk, he left out particular restrictions such as "gives milk," simplifying the definition to apply to any large four-legged animal. Now at age two, he has separate names for most of these animals with pretty much the adult meanings. Metonomy, metaphor, narrowing, and widening are the four ways that word meanings change in adult language, and in Pablo's speech widening has stood out from all the others. When he learned "knee" he soon applied it to elbows as well as knees. At age two he uses "taxi" to refer to taxis, police cars, and ambulances (cars with lights on top). He uses "clock" for scales with circular dials as well as for clocks. "Close the door!" means to either open the door or close it. "Up!" means either "Pick me up!" or "Put me down!"

If we keep in mind that the essence of widening is simplifying definitions, the removal of restrictions on membership, then we can see it in other areas of the grammar besides meaning. He recently extended the use of the determiner "this" to that of an adverb: "Is Mommy this?" he asked, meaning "Is Mommy here?" The meaning of "this" and "here" are essentially the same; the widening in this case concerned parts of speech, the widening of the part of speech 'adverb' to allow *this*, a word which in adult speech is used only as a determiner or a pronoun.

Children older than Pablo are noted for the way they 'overgeneralize' rules of morphology. This is another kind of widening: there is a removal of the restriction that regular rules not be applied to certain 'irregular' forms. They apply the regular rule of plural formation to say *foots*, and the regular rule for the past to say *swimmed*. They say *gooder* instead of *better* and *goodest* instead of *best*. One might think that this widening is because the children haven't yet learned the restrictions on the regular rules, but it is not so simple. Remember that Pablo first used "cow" and "horse" the way adults do, and then he did the widening. Compare morphology. A common sequence is for a child to say an irregular form like *broke* the way adults do, but then regularize this by saying *broked!* A child will often go from *two foot* to *two foots*, from there to *two feet* (the adult form), but then to *two feets* and even *two feetses* before finally settling on *two feet* once and for all. For those who want to explain a child's progress entirely in terms of external stimuli and reinforcement, sequences such as the ones just described with *broked* and *feetses* present a problem on two counts: first, adults don't say these forms, so there is no immediate 'stimulus,' and second, the sequence makes the child appear to take a step backwards.

Advocates of reinforcement theory must explain overgeneralizations such as *feetses* in the following manner: the child is being reinforced for putting the plural ending -*s* on words elsewhere, *bugs, lights*, etc., so he feels encouraged to put it everywhere; if he can put it twice as he does in *feetses*, all the better! But for the child to identify *feet* and *bug* as 'same' (as he must have to have created *feets* or *feetses*), is not just an *over*generalization, it is an *original* generalization: "*feet* is the same kind of word as *bug*, so if I gain approval by

91

adding -*s* to *bug,* then I ought to gain approval by adding it to *feet* as well." The child's *feets* or *feetses* is distinctly different from adult speech because adults do not view *feet* as the 'same' as *bug* in the relevant respect. *Feetses* is not just a "mistake," and it cannot be explained simply as a 'response'; it is an independent act by members of a new generation recreating a language.

Pablo's longest utterances at this point are four words long, usually shorter. He concentrates on the words that carry the most information and tends not to produce the other words an adult would use. His "Mommy guitar!" means "I want Mommy to play the guitar!" He finds ways of naming objects he doesn't know the adult word for. When he found an old cheese grater in the woods, he said "Look! For cheese!" Similarly, he will refer to something belonging to his mother that he doesn't know the name for with the expression "for Mommy" (if he knows the word he will usually say "Mommy's shoe," "Mommy's pillow," etc.); he doesn't know the name for the coffee pot filter, but he refers to that object as "for coffee." He calls firewood "for fire." He pointed to a picture of an electric skillet in a newspaper ad and said "Look! For pancakes!"

On a visit to a farm, he took his father to a shed where some forty-year-old halters and harnesses were hanging. "Look!" he said, "Horse!" Then he moved his hands and said "Neck!" He meant something like "These halters and harnesses are for horses! They wear them around their necks!" We can see the child learning how to name the parts of his ideas with words, and then put the words together to form larger units of communication. Now we will examine how he puts sounds together to form words.

2. Pronunciation

This section is on Pablo's pronunciation. What Pablo does that differs from adults is what most attracts people's attention. Sometimes, there is no perceivable pattern to the differences, as when Pablo insists on saying *tummel* for "tunnel." Here one might be tempted to say that he is just making "mistakes." But more often than not, his innovations are highly systematic; if you know how he pronounces some words, you can predict how he will pronounce others. You can write 'transfer rules,' rules that describe how to change adult pronunciation to Pablo's. Rules of this sort are a good first step in finding out how the child perceives the sound structure of his language, and in turn how he produces it.

2.1   "Love" and "Stove"

2.1.1   Words Beginning with S
Consider the following data:

Adults	Pablo	Adults	Pablo
sun	sun	snake	nake
see	see	stop	top
sick	sick	sky	ky
spoon	poon	swing	wing

(a) How does Pablo's pronunciation differ from an adult's? What rule describes the change from the adult pronunciation to Pablo's?

State the rule in the most straightforward way possible, for example, "Remove the s sound when it is followed by a consonant sound." If you are familiar with the notation for phonological rules, you can say the same thing with symbols, "s → ∅ / __C." However you state the rule, you want to make sure it is a true generalization, that it accounts for *all* and *only* the forms that Pablo produced: here that means leaving unchanged all the words where [s] is followed by a vowel sound in adult speech, *sun, see,* and *sick,* and changing the pronunciation of all the adult words where [s] is followed by a consonant, *spoon, snake, stop, sky,* and *swing.* By saying "Remove the s sound when it is followed by a consonant sound," you call for just the right changes and no more.

(b) Any interesting generalization will make predictions about new data, and if you have a chance to collect that data you will have a means of testing the generalization. Predict how Pablo would pronounce the words *spill, scooter, scene,* and *psych* (assuming he had the inclination to say them!). Give three more words beginning with the sound [s] you can predict Pablo would pronounce the way adults do, and three more where he would differ in the same manner as with "snake, stop, sky, and swing."

(c) Discuss what this data demonstrates about aspects of linguistic structures that are part of the child's language. What categories does the rule you have written in (a) refer to? If your rule has mentioned a category 'consonant,' as opposed to 'vowel,' doesn't this demonstrate a systematic distinction being made by the child? Doesn't this show that Pablo can tell the difference between the 'first sound' and the 'second sound' of a word? This is an abstract distinction in that there is no clear physical or acoustical cut-off point between one 'sound' and another in the stream of speech. The stream of speech is, as the name implies, a continuous flow.

The notion *widening* that we used in the discussion of word meanings is useful here too when we think of the way sounds are used to signal meanings. Adults use the sound [w] to begin the word meaning "wing," but not the one meaning "swing"; Pablo has removed the limits on the set of words beginning with [w] so that it can include the one meaning "swing" as well as "wing"; similarly, you can say that the class of words beginning with the sound [n] is widened to include the word meaning "snake" and so on. The explanation for this widening would appear to lie entirely in the area of sound structure, the principle of not having two consonant sounds together at the beginning of a word.

2.1.2 Words that End in Consonants

Adults	Pablo	Adults	Pablo
bed	bet	tub	tup
wet	wet	soap	soap
egg	eck	bus	bus
rake	rake	buzz	bus

(a) What is the difference between the adult pronunciation and Pablo's? Find the rule that describes the change from the adult pronunciation to Pablo's. The important feature here is 'voicing.' A word of explanation: notice that if you prolong the last sound of *buzz* and say *zzzzzz* . . . you can feel your vocal cords vibrating; you do not feel that vibration if you prolong the last sound of *bus* and say *ssssss*. . . . Hold your thumb and forefinger on your larynx (adam's apple) and alternate *zzzzzz* . . . *sssss* . . . *zzzzzz* . . . *sssss* . . . and feel for the vibrations with your fingers. [z] is a 'voiced' sound, and [s] is 'voiceless.'

Now consider the following additional data:

Adults	Pablo	Adults	Pablo
man	man	girl	girl
door	door	boy	boy

(b) Should you modify the rule you made up in (a) in any way? State a more complete rule.

(c) Predict how Pablo will pronounce *fuss, fuzz, back, bag, ball,* and *bear.*

(d) Discuss what this data demonstrates about aspects of sound structure in Pablo's language. First, notice that Pablo produces the [b],

[d], and [g] at the beginning of words *(boy, door, girl)*, but that something has happened to them at the end of words.

There is more to say about the sounds Pablo changes at the end of words, and it concerns what kind of sound they are. (2.1.1) showed a distinction between vowels and consonants; here the data reveals a distinction between different kinds of consonants. What is the difference between [b], [d], [g], [v], and [z] on the one hand, and [n], [r], [l], and [y] on the other? An immediate observation is that the first set of sounds are voiced sounds that have corresponding voiceless sounds. If you devoice [b] you get [p], and similarly [d] corresponds to [t], [g] to [k], [v] to [f], and [z] to [s]. While [n], [r], [l], and [y] on the other hand are among the English sounds where there are no voiceless counterparts.

The sounds [b], [d], [g], [v], and [z] and their voiceless counterparts [p], [t], [k], [f], and [s] are 'obstruents,' so called because the air flow being pushed up from the lungs is obstructed: with [b], [d], [g], [p], [t], [k] the air flow is stopped completely by the lips or the tongue, and with [v], [z], [f], and [s] the tongue slows down the stream of air causing a noisy turbulence or friction. All sounds in a language which are not obstruents are called 'sonorants': with sonorants the air stream always has an unimpeded channel, through either the mouth or the nose, or both. Because the unimpeded air flow of sonorants makes it easy for the vocal cords to vibrate, these sounds tend to be voiced and not voiceless in languages throughout the world: it is rare to have voiceless nasal sounds like [m] or [n], voiceless vowels or voiceless [l] or [r]. Here is why Pablo does not pronounce *man, door, girl* or *boy* on the same original pattern as he does *bed, egg, tub* and *buzz*.

Pablo is *widening* pronunciation over the adult system in the sense of simplifying the constraints on the class of words that end with voiceless obstruents. Adults make obstruents voiceless at the end of words to communicate one set of meanings "bet, bus," etc., but not for another set of meanings "bed, buzz," etc. Pablo has simplified the limits of the first set of meanings so that it includes "bed" and "buzz" along with "bet" and "bus." We should ask why he has done the widening in this direction instead of the other way around. The answer seems to lie once again in the universal characteristics of languages, and here with another fact about how sounds for any language are produced physically. Obstruction of the air flow that takes place in sounds such as [p], [t], [k], [f], and [s] makes voicing a difficult gesture, and so there are many languages that have just the voiceless obstruents [p], [t], [k], [f], [s], etc. and not their voiced counterparts [b], [d], [g], [v], and [z]. It is easier to make a voiceless obstruent than a voiced one. Pablo has both the voiced and voiceless ones at the beginnings of words, but in word-final position he has come up with a system simplified, not surprisingly, in the direction of many of the world's languages.

2.1.3 The f Sound

Adults	Pablo
laugh [læf]	lap [læp]
off [ɔf]	op [ɔp]
coffee [kɔfīy]	coppee [kɔpīy]

Write the rule that characterizes Pablo's production of the words he is learning from adults.

2.1.4 Grand Finale

(a) Given all you know of Pablo's speech, what will his pronunciation of *love* be?

(b) What will his pronunciation of *stove* be?

(c) Let us shift ahead in time three months. Pablo now says *laugh, off,* and *coffee* essentially the same way as adults do. The rest of his sound system as analyzed here has not yet changed. Now how will he pronounce *love* and *stove?* The answer is given at the end of the chapter.

2.2 More on Pablo's Consonant System

2.2.1 Aspiration

(a) See if you can find a distinction in your speech between the [t] in *top* and the [t] in *stop*. Compare also the sound [k] in *care* as opposed to the one in *scare* and the [p] in *pan* as opposed to the one in *span*. There is a systematic difference in adult dialects of English. (Put your hand in front of your mouth so that you can feel the breath come out as you say these words—better still, watch what happens to a match flame or a piece of paper in front of your mouth as you pronounce them.) Write the rule that expresses this regular variation in the pronunciation of the [p], [t], and [k] sounds in adult speech.

(b) Given the characteristics of adult pronunciation of the sounds [p], [t], and [k], consider the following question: might Pablo pronounce the adult words *top* and *stop* differently from each other? If so, how? The answer is given at the end of the chapter.

2.2.2 *More Words Beginning with Consonant Clusters*
Here is some additional data that shows more of Pablo's treatment of groups of consonants:

Adults	Pablo
truck	sometimes *tuck,* sometimes *chuck*
Brownie	Bownie
plane	sometimes *pane,* sometimes *bane*
broken	boken
crack	kack
clay	kay

(a) What principle appears to be operating here? Can it be stated in such a way so as not to conflict with the rule you formulated in 2.1.1? Write the best rule you can for this data: you may ignore for the moment the variants *chuck* for "truck" and *bane* for "plane." (These have to do with additional principles. To formulate them we would need additional data.)

(b) The principle that Pablo is following in this data is notably different from the one illustrated in 2.1. Why should "stop" be pronounced *top,* while "truck" is pronounced *tuck?* In words like "stop," the first sound of the word is dropped; in words like "truck," the second sound is. Pablo almost always reduces a group of two consonants at the beginning of a word to just one; however, which one of the two he deletes depends on what kinds of consonants they are. It is the sounds [r] and [l] that get deleted from second position. It would appear that there is a hierarchy among different kinds of consonants here. We can say that when Pablo simplifies a consonant cluster he preserves the "strongest" consonants and omits the "weakest." In respect to this notion of "strength," you might try to rank the consonants.

(c) How do you suppose Pablo says the word "slip"? Does he follow the principle formulated in 2.1 and say *lip,* or does he do something analogous to what he does in "plane" and say *sip?* Discuss the reasons for your hypothesis. The answer is given at the end of the chapter. Note that you can formulate your hypothesis in terms of the notion of "strength" just discussed. Which consonant appears the "weaker" and therefore most likely to be omitted? What does the strength hierarchy look like now for all consonants seen so far?

(d) Consider the way you pronounce the words "cute," "beautiful," "twig," and "quack." They all begin with consonant clusters, the sounds [ky], [by], [tw], and [kw]. Without [y] as the second sound of "cute," that word would be pronounced the same as "coot." If you guessed that Pablo doesn't pronounce most of these words the same way adults do, you are right. He simplifies most of the consonant clusters. But which consonant does he leave out? What Pablo actually does is reported at the end of this exercise, but before you peek there, write down your best guess as to which consonant he leaves out, the first or the second, and your reasons for the choice you have made. If he follows a pattern like the one with "stop" and leaves off the first consonant, then "beautiful" will be pronounced *you-tiful* and "twig" *wig* (actually *wick*). If he follows a pattern like the one with words like "truck" and deletes the second sound then "beautiful" will be *bootiful* and "twig," *tig* (actually *tick*). The answer you give hinges on what you think the "strength" of the sounds [y] and [w] is as opposed to sounds like [k], [t], and [b].

There is information about sound change in present-day adult English that is relevant to your answer here. At one time all speakers of English had something close to the following pronunciations with a [y] sound occurring after a consonant and before the vowel sound [ūw]:

(a.)		(b.)		(c.)	
pew	[pyūw]	tune	[tyūwn]	cue	[kyūw]
abuse	[abyūws]	Tuesday	[tyūwzdīy]	cute	[kyūwt]
few	[fyūw]	dew	[dyūw]	cube	[kyūwb]
view	[vyūw]	suit	[syūwt]	acute	[əkyūwt]
mute	[myūwt]	new	[nyūw]	argue	[argyūw]

While this pronunciation is largely maintained in Great Britain, most American English speakers have dropped the [y] sound in one of these groups, group (b), where the consonant preceding the [y] sound has an alveolar point of articulation (where the tongue makes contact with the gum ridge behind the upper teeth). They say [tūwn, tūwzdīy, dūw, sūwt] and [nūw] for the words in (b). How do you pronounce these words? Do you say "dew" the same as "do"? Would you expect the innovations that Pablo is introducing to be related to the ones going on historically in English as spoken by adults? If you think so, then the data presented here would be a reason for guessing that Pablo drops the [y] and the [w] sound in words like "beautiful" and "twig."

2.2.3 A Medial Cluster: How Pablo Says "Taxi"
So far we have just seen cases where Pablo simplifies consonant clusters at the beginning of words. The following data illustrates how he

will tolerate the cluster [ks] at the end of an expression, but not in the middle before a vowel. Notice that the letter *x* represents the sound sequence [ks] in the adult pronunciation of these words:

Adults		Pablo	
tacks	[tæks]	tacks	[tæks]
taxi	[tæksīy]	tackicks	[tækiks]
fix	[fiks]	fix	[fiks]
fix it	[fiksit]	fickicks	[fikiks]
box	[bāks]	box	[bāks]
boxes	[bāksəz]	bockicks	[bākiks]

He does the same thing with *fox-foxes* as he does with *box-boxes*. To describe the innovative principle Pablo is using here, see if you can state the transfer rule that summarizes the changes from the adult pronunciation to Pablo's in this data. This is a challenging assignment.

3. Answers

3.1 Answers to Sections 2.1.4 and 2.2.1
Pablo said [ləp] for *love* and [tōwp] for *stove* until he got the [f] sound, then he said [ləf] and [tōwf]. The adult pronunciation is [ləv] and [stōwv]. Note that adults have no aspiration for the [t] of "stove," i.e., they do *not* say [st^{h}ōwv], but Pablo said [t^{h}ōwp]; the same holds for all the voiceless stop sounds that occur after [s] in adult speech, the [k] sound of *sky,* the [p] sound of *spoon,* etc. Pablo makes pairs of words like *top* and *stop* sound exactly the same, i.e. here both [t^{h}āp]. Children somewhat older than Pablo, however, have been reported to pronounce "stop" [tāp] (no aspiration) and "top" [t^{h}āp] (aspiration).

3.2 Answers to Section 2.2.2, c and d.
c. Pablo said *lip* for "slip," *low* for "slow," etc., and by a combination of two processes, *slide* sounded exactly like *light*.

d. At the time this data was collected, Pablo was doing the following:

Adults		Pablo	
cute	[kyūwt]	coot	[kūwt]
beautiful	[byūwdifəl]	bootiful	[būwdifəl]
twig	[twig]	tick	[tik]
quack	[kwæk]	quack	[kwæk]

Whereas he deleted the semi-vowel sounds [y] and [w] in the first three words, he was pronouncing the words "quack" and "quick" the way adults do. Somehow it was more acceptable to him to pronounce the cluster [kw] than [tw], [by], or [ky].

Note that there is a plausible explanation here. Of the four combinations of sounds, [kw], [tw], [by], and [ky], only [kw] occurs in a general range of contexts; the others are in one respect or another special in their distribution. [tw] as well as [dw] appear only at the beginning of a limited number of words: these are words such as *twin, twain, Dwight,* and *Dwain;* they are uncommon and they seem slightly foreign. [ky] is more common, and like [kw] it can occur in clusters with [s]: we have the sequence of sounds [sky] in *scue, obscure,* and *rescue.* But [by] and [ky] come only before the vowel sound [ūw], the one in *boot* and *coot:* that is the vowel sound that follows [sky] in *scue, obscure,* and *rescue,* and the one after [ky] and [by] in *cute, cue, cure, beauty, abuse, rebuke,* and so forth. [kw] on the other hand occurs before virtually all vowel sounds except the high back ones [ūw] and [u], the ones in *boot* and *put* respectively, and the vowel sounds most similar to [w] phonetically. Note the range of vowel sounds following [kw] in the words *queen, quick, quake, quest, quack, quite, quandary, quartz,* and *quote,* as well as the vowel sounds following [skw] in *squeak, squib, square, squander,* and *squawk.* In sum, the only way in which either of the two 'glide' sounds [w] or [y] occurs freely following another consonant is in the combination [kw].

This would be motivation enough for Pablo to adapt himself to [kw] earlier than to the other three combinations. We can speculate further, however, that from a psychological point of view [kw] is not a combination of sounds but a single unit in the sound system of English; in other words, it would be reasonable to say that English has two [k] sounds, the one in *kick,* and the one that occurs with extra lip rounding in *quick.* It is possible that many speakers of English perceive the sounds this way, not just Pablo. The *ch* of *chew,* which Pablo says the way adults do, is usually analyzed as a single distinctive sound [č] even though from a physical point of view it can be seen as a combination of the [t] sound of *two* and the [š] sound of *shoe;* just so, we could adopt the notation [kʷ] as a single symbol and say that there is no consonant cluster in *quack* ([kʷæk]). From this point of view we could say without exception that before vowels Pablo always simplifies the consonant clusters of adult speech to single consonants; there is no change in the pronunciation of *quack* because it does not contain a consonant cluster.

4. Postscript

The author is grateful for all that he has learned about language from the person who provided the data for this chapter, his son Pablo Sasha Shopen, born June 14, 1971.

Pablo lived in the U.S. (in Indiana and then Virginia) until he was four. Then he moved to Australia. He has made some notable innovations adjusting to an Australian standard. In words such as *writer,* most Americans produce a kind of 'tap' *d* sound instead of a *t,* and they do so invariably (whatever the speech style: formal, informal, etc.). The same happens with the *t*'s of *water, little, dirty,* etc. Many Americans make no distinction in the pronunciation of the words *rider* and *writer.* (You might note that the generalization here has to do with several factors, and one of them is stress. Thus, the tap *d* will occur in *wríter,* but never in *attáin.*) Australians vary between the use of both *t* and the tap *d* in words like *writer* when speaking casually, and the use of just *t* when speaking carefully or formally. Pablo picked up on this *t* as a marker for good speech in his new community, but for a period of six months produced it in a quite original way. His pronunciation for some of the words was variable, but he tended strongly to put a clear *t* sound not only in *water, letter, better, little, bottle, cattle, dirty,* etc., the way Australians do, but also in place of the *d*'s in words such as *ladder, Daddy, already, rider,* and *noodle!* This is something he hasn't heard anyone do. Most original was his extension of this pattern to the word *Sydney* [sitnīy].

This is an overgeneralization (and hypercorrection) of classic dimensions and presents the same philosophical problem discussed at the beginning of the chapter. The new model Pablo was exposed to had many occurrences of the *t* pronunciation for words like *water, little,* and *dirty,* but there was zero frequency of *t* pronunciations for words like *ladder* and *noodle.* *

Suggestions for Further Reading

There is a large and interesting literature on language development in children, and fortunately some excellent and recently prepared pedagogical and review works are available which people can start with as they begin

---

*The author owes thanks to a number of people for important criticisms and suggestions on earlier drafts of this chapter; they are Courtney Cazden, Charles A. Ferguson, James Fidelholtz, Victoria Fromkin, Jean Berko Gleason, Shirley Brice Heath, Muriel Saville Troike, and Arnold Zwicky.

101

reading in the field. Two textbooks and two review articles will be recommended here. A wealth of further bibliographical references will be found in those works. There is the textbook on child language by Dale (1976) and the textbook in psycholinguistics by Clark and Clark (1977), which contains ample discussion of language development in children. Lois Bloom (1975) has written a review article concerning all but phonology in child language, while Ferguson and Garnica (1975) have done a review article on the phonological development of children.

Bloom, Lois. "Language Development Review." In *Review of Child Development Research,* vol. 4, edited by F. Horowitz, E. Hetherington, S. Scarr-Salapatek, and G. Siegel. Chicago: University of Chicago Press, 1975.

Clark, Herbert H., and Clark, Eve V., *Psychology and Language: An Introduction to Psycholinguistics.* New York: Harcourt Brace Jovanovich, Inc., 1977.

Dale, Philip S. *Language Development: Structure and Function,* 2d ed. New York: Holt, Rinehart and Winston, 1976.

Ferguson, Charles A., and Garnica, Olga K. "Theories of Phonological Development." In *Foundations of Language Development: A Multidisciplinary Approach,* vol. 1, edited by E. H. Lenneberg and E. Lenneberg, pp. 153–80. New York: Academic Press, 1975.

An Afterword

How English Speakers Say "Finger" and "Sing"

Timothy Shopen

The simplification of consonant clusters, so characteristic of the language studied in this chapter, takes place in the history of languages all over the world. Successive generations recreating a language are continually simplifying consonant clusters, but of course other processes often create new clusters, as when a vowel is dropped between two consonants. When a change takes place in the history of a language, it is usually the case that there is variable pronunciation for a while where different norms will coexist, often in the speech of individual speakers. Here is an interesting instance from the history of English, a process still going on today.

Notice what is happening to the pronunciation of the voiced stops [b], [d], and [g] in the following English dialects:

A. A dialect spoken by our ancestors:

Point of Articulation	Position in word			
	Medial		*Word Final*	
Labial	lumber	[ləmbər]	bomb	[bāmb]
	ramble	[ræmbəl]	dumb	[dəmb]
	robber	[rābər]	throb	[θrāb]
	able	[ēybəl]	lobe	[lōwb]
Alveolar	wonder	[wəndər]	bend	[bend]
	handle	[hændəl]	find	[fāynd]
	saddle	[sædəl]	bad	[bæd]
	spider	[spāydər]	feed	[fīyd]
Velar	finger	[fiŋger]	sing	[siŋg]
	angle	[æŋgəl]	long	[lɔ̄ŋg]
	bugle	[byūwgəl]	bug	[bəg]
	logger	[lɔ̄gər]	rag	[ræg]

B.   The present day 'standard' dialect:

Position in word

Point of Articulation	Medial		Word Final	
Labial	lumber	[ləmbər]	bomb	[bām]
	ramble	[ræmbəl]	dumb	[dəm]
	robber	[rābər]	throb	[θrāb]
	able	[ēybəl]	lobe	[lōwb]
Alveolar	wonder	[wəndər]	bend	[bend]
	handle	[hændəl]	find	[fāynd]
	saddle	[sædəl]	bad	[bæd]
	spider	[spāydər]	feed	[fīyd]
Velar	finger	[fiŋgər]	sing	[siŋ]
	angle	[æŋgəl]	long	[lɔŋ]
	bugle	[byūwgəl]	bug	[bəg]
	logger	[lɔgər]	rag	[ræg]

1.   What is the difference between dialects A and B? What rule has operated historically?

2.   Consider the words *bombard* and *longer*. If you accept that these words contain *bomb* and *long* within them, then you can also understand them to have retained an earlier pronunciation of those smaller words. *Younger* gives evidence for an earlier pronunciation of *young*. These words are relevant to any generalization you may have arrived at in (1). Look for more evidence of this sort.

   In fact, when you look further at contemporary evidence for a historical process, you often find that an initial generalization is too simple and needs more articulation and qualification. Individual words have a character of their own: some will hold on to an earlier pronunciation longer than others. Some changes have affected all the vocabulary of a language, others only one word.

   Sometimes you can find regularities for small groups of words that have some clear defining characteristic. Most speakers retain a stop after a nasal in *longer* and *younger,* not in *singer* or *ringer,* but the -*er* endings are not the same, they mean different things. A language can have different 'boundaries' between the units of meaning that come together to form larger words with distinct pronunciations associated with them: this can reflect different stages in the history of the language and varying degrees of tightness in the way parts of words are held together. We can say that the comparative suffix -*er* that occurs in *longer* and *younger* regularly has one kind of boundary with the stem it follows, and the -*er* of *singer* and *ringer* ("one that does") has another.

The notion of boundaries can be used to account for the fact that most speakers pronounce a [g] for *strong* in *stronger,* but not in *strongly.* But it doesn't stop there. While you can say that a particular boundary produces a consistent effect on the NS sequence (Nasal plus Stop) in *longer, younger,* and *stronger,* you should also allow for the fact that the earlier [b] of *dumb* has not been retained in *dumber.*

3. The reader could profitably seek more data here, more instances where words used to end in an NS sequence and now retain just N, but where these same words are part of larger words where the S might still be retained. The full picture is rich with the marks of a long and varied history. Child language presents more regular patterns.

   As opposed to [b] and [g], [d] has been more stable in NS sequences, but even here there are exceptions. One concerns the word *hand* (where you usually hear a [d]), and *handkerchief* (where you usually do not). And that is not the only exception.[1]

C. Another widespread present day dialect:

Point of Articulation	Position in word			
	Medial		*Word Final*	
Labial	lumber	[ləmər]	bomb	[bām]
	ramble	[ræməl]	dumb	[dəm]
	robber	[rābər]	throb	[θrāb]
	able	[ēybəl]	lobe	[lōwb]
Alveolar	wonder	[wənər]	bend	[ben]
	handle	[hænəl]	find	[fāyn]
	saddle	[sædəl]	bad	[bæd]
	spider	[spāydər]	feed	[fīyd]
Velar	finger	[fiŋər]	sing	[siŋ]
	angle	[æŋəl]	long	[lɔ̄ŋ]
	bugle	[byūwgəl]	bug	[bəg]
	logger	[lɔ̄gər]	rag	[ræg]

4. What is the difference between dialects A and C? Again, what rule has operated historically?
5. What is the difference between dialects B and C? In which of these two dialects is the historical process exemplified here most fully developed?
6. Write down additional words that would have pronunciations in dialect A that are distinctive in the same way as the examples in this problem. Do the same for dialect C. Do you share any of the traits of these dialects? Have you heard people who do? If you can present examples you have heard, tell where and from what people.

---

1. An excellent place to look for more data relevant to this problem is in Otto Jespersen, *A Modern English Grammar,* Volume I, Sounds and Spellings. London: George Allen and Unwin, Ltd., 1961.

Chapter 5

Creative Spelling by Young Children

Charles Read

Charles Read works at the University of Wisconsin, Madison, where he teaches applied linguistics, primarily in the Department of English, and conducts research on children's language development. Being a former teacher of English in high school and the father of two children (who obligingly developed their own spelling), Read is especially interested in applying his research to language development in the schools.

Introduction

"Creative spelling"—somehow the phrase seems anomalous. Like "creative table manners," it suggests an activity which is at best mildly antisocial. Except perhaps in our facetious moments, we adults do not "create" spellings; either we *know* a spelling, or we *construct* it by putting together familiar parts, or we simply *look it up*. We are strengthened in this attitude by the frequent assertion that English spelling is peculiarly archaic and unreliable. Because of this view of spelling as conventional, we do not think of children's spelling as developing in the way that, say, their drawing develops—in stages, from earless heads to stick figures to more elaborate representations. A child doesn't learn "how to" spell, it seems; he or she merely memorizes an assortment of words along with a few handy rhymes expressing maxims which are, as often as not, inapplicable. Of course, children, like the rest of us, make mistakes in spelling; indeed, except for a few dazzling spell-down champions, they make more than their share of mistakes. But we tend to consider these mistakes "creative" only in an ironic sense of the word that might also include eating Jello with your fingers.

Against this unpromising background, this chapter will present some evidence and a line of reasoning that suggest there is a truly creative component to young children's spelling, and that because it develops systematically, we can consider certain nonstandard spellings more advanced than other, equally nonstandard, ones.

When we approach a topic like children's early spelling, we might first seek out some evidence, collecting and sorting examples of children's spelling; on the other hand, we might begin by speculating about the conditions of the problem, asking ourselves questions like: What does a child know before he begins to spell? What does he have to know in order to spell? What kinds of standard spellings are there? What characteristics of sounds and spellings are likely to be "easiest," that is, most accessible to children? Much has been written about these two ways of approaching a scientific problem. Fundamentally it seems to catch us in a circle from which we cannot escape; we can't even collect evidence, let alone "sort" it, without some concept of what we are looking for, and yet we can't speculate effectively without some notion of what the evidence is like. Because of this tangle, about the best we can say is that scientists really begin in both ways, seemingly at once. The scientific study of any subject is known for its quest for data—the years spent in a library or laboratory—but a good scholar looks for the evidence that he or she suspects will be meaningful. One uses what one knows, even if it is nothing more than a hunch.

Take a moment now to think about the problem that confronts a five- or six-year-old who wishes to spell a message. Put yourself in his place: suppose that you know the names and shapes of the letters of the alphabet. Suppose also that you have learned to spell your name, and that in this process, or by asking about familiar signs, such as "stop," you have grasped the notion that "B" spells [b], as in *Bob,* or that "S"spells [s], as in *stop.* Now suppose that you want to spell a message and that you are sufficiently independent to attempt this task without simply asking your big sister how to spell each word. Would you be able to identify the sounds in every word, or even count them? (Many children have difficulty with this step.) Would you be able to match the sounds with letters? How would you do it? What sounds would be easy to spell? Which ones would be difficult?

Now let us look at a little (presorted) data. Figures 5.1 to 5.4 present some messages from first-graders.[1] Even though the spelling is nonstandard, you will find that you can figure out the message if you assume that it makes sense and fits with its context.

Alberto, the author of Figure 5.1, is a native speaker of Spanish in a multigrade primary classroom in San Diego. His message displays two common characteristics of children's creative spelling:

- There is a mixture of standard and nonstandard spellings (I, TO, A vs. LIK, RID, BOT).

---

1. Figure 5.1, by Alberto Hernandez, is used with the permission of the *Harvard Graduate School of Education Association Bulletin* and Dr. Courtney Cazden. Figures 5.2 and 5.4 are used with the permission of Dr. Carol Chomsky. Figure 5.3 is reprinted from Dr. Chomsky's chapter in Resnick and Weaver, eds., *The Theory and Practice of Early Reading, volume 2* (Hillsdale, N.J.: Lawrence Erlbaum Associates, 1979), with permission of the author and publisher.

Figure 5.1

- The nonstandard spellings often involve using a letter to represent the sound that is its name (the use of *I* and *O* in LIK, RID, and BOT).

In addition, we may note how fortunate it is that these messages appear in a context of words and pictures. Out of context, we might interpret, say, LIKT as *licked* or RID as *rid,* but when we consider the entire context, it is difficult to find more than one plausible interpretation for Alberto's message. This fact is crucial to saying anything about spelling, of course.

A secondary observation we might make about Alberto's message is that it is not unusual to find that children do not separate words with a space. Is this because they simply do not know, or follow, the convention, or could it be that they do not always know what is to count as a word—where words begin and end? I won't pursue this question here, but you might want to think about what kind of evidence would count. Also, if you were attentive, you noted that I did not include ON as one of Alberto's standard spellings. In fact, there is evidence from other writings of his that he uses ON to represent *in,* a puzzling fact.

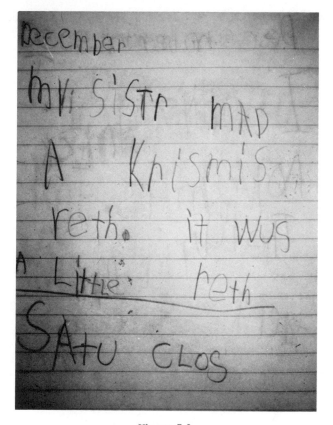

Figure 5.2

Figure 5.2 supports our two basic inferences from Alberto's message; in MAD and RETH we see additional examples of what we will call "letter-name spellings." Here, however, there are suggestions of two more characteristics that we will see in children's spelling:

- The use of standard spellings in nonstandard places (*K* to represent the [k] sound in KRISMIS).
- The nonrepresentation, or omission, of some sounds.

SATU CLOS is actually an instance of both of these. The first-grade writer uses *U* to represent the [ə] at the end of *Santa,* perhaps because she has learned that *u* spells "uh." More puzzling, perhaps, is her apparent omission of the [n] in *Santa.*

Figures 5.3 and 5.4 show pages from a book created by another first-grader. He employed an idea that has yet to occur to even the most *avant-garde* adult publisher, as far as I know: a book whose *shape*

109

Figure 5.3

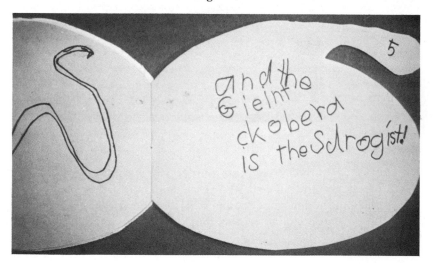

Figure 5.4

indicates its subject-matter; it was, of course, a book of snakes. Again we see some confirmation, in SNACK, INDEA, and FET, of our hypothesis about letter-name spelling. CKOBERA is an excellent example of the nonstandard use of standard spellings; *ck* as a representation of [k] is perfectly standard, but it is restricted to the ends of simple morphemes, like *truck*. This first-grader knows one of the ways of standard spelling, but he doesn't yet know the restriction. (Notice how important it is for a teacher to realize that the spelling is only mis-applied, not wrong.) Finally, we see in LOGIST and SDROGIST two more examples of what we saw in SATU CLOS—the omission of a nasal sound; indeed it is the same letter that is missing, although a different sound is involved. We will come back to these examples; at this point, they merely suggest to us that two different children have produced similar nonstandard spellings. The *D* of SDROGIST will not look so strange to you if you know that the [t] which it represents is in fact not identical to the [t] of *tong*. In one important respect it is like a [d]. We might consider this an example of a nonstandard grouping of sounds reflected in children's spelling—but with a phonetic basis.

Overall, Figures 5.1 to 5.4 suggest that the apparent errors in young children's spelling are not quite as random as they may at first appear. What we have seen so far indicates that children use several different strategies at once in order to improvise spellings: the letter-name strategy; the unrestricted use of standard spellings (in nonstandard positions); certain omissions, which may be regular; and a phonetic regrouping. Together, these strategies account for nearly all of the nonstandard spellings in these examples. From such a small sample, we cannot reach any general conclusions, but certainly our first hypothesis must be that what appear to be puzzling errors actually may have some reasonable basis, or at least regularity. In other words, young spellers behave more like people who are using general principles, extending them to new instances, than like people who search for "the" spelling of a word, but who happen to be afflicted with poor memories.

At this point, an investigator might well ask him/herself, "where do I start collecting evidence?" "Where did these examples come from?" "Under what circumstances do children produce the kinds of spellings that might reveal their strategies, as opposed to no spelling at all or completely standard spelling?" Are there any other kinds of evidence that might test our hypotheses? A layman looking at these examples often asks, "How come these children produced original spelling? Weren't they worried about whether or not it was right? And if they weren't worried, weren't their parents or teachers worried? What happens if we let children grow up with a do-it-yourself attitude about spelling? Surely you aren't suggesting that we should *all* spell in this fashion?"

No, I am not suggesting that adults should spell in this fashion; standard (and standardized) English spelling has some important virtues. In this chapter, I am not primarily concerned with whether or not children's original spelling is good; I am interested in developing an explanation for why it takes the particular forms that it does. But in fact, I do believe that children develop a healthier attitude toward

111

spelling—and even reading and writing generally—when they are encouraged to write messages in their own way. Figures 5.1 to 5.4 were created by children in primary-grade classrooms with teachers who gave them that kind of encouragement. In addition, I have a large collection of spellings that young children have done in their homes, with parents who also allowed them to do their own spelling. These parents and teachers were indeed concerned that the children eventually learn standard spelling, but at this early stage they placed a higher value on allowing children to produce a written message fluently and freely. They answered the children's questions about spelling, of course, but they tried not to suggest that the children should ask them about every unfamiliar word. A few of these children are now well on their way to adulthood, and the minimum that one can say is that their spelling is at least as good as most people's. Their spelling has developed, just as their other cognitive abilities have developed, toward progressively more adult forms.

There seem to be two conditions necessary for children to create their own spellings. One is a child who is sufficiently interested in writing messages (and most children are, at some stage) and sufficiently confident and independent of adult advice. The other is a teacher or parent who encourages and appreciates the child's efforts, and who answers questions in a normally helpful way without placing undue emphasis on standard spelling. One finds such spelling in some homes and in quite a few classrooms; the encouragement of a child's own spelling is traditional in Montessori classes, for instance.

As a result, the evidence to be presented here comes from two basic sources; the large collection of children's spelling done at home and samples of spelling from schools, including samples of first-graders' apparent errors on spelling tests. Some of the children who created spelling at home began as early as age three-and-one-half; some of them, indeed, produced messages in considerable quantity. They wrote stories; invitations to playmates (who could not read); a series of conciliatory notes to an irate parent; a letter to a relative, describing what it is like to be sick in bed with little to do; and a get-well card to a sick mother. All in all, the children discovered most of the honest uses of written communication and found that it broadened and brightened their lives. Surely that is a more basic lesson than learning that SDROGIST is spelled with a *t* and an *n* and an *e*.

No doubt you can imagine other strategies that might account for the spelling so far, alternatives to some of those that I proposed. This situation is the usual one in linguistics, where one can almost always construct competing hypotheses about the same data. To the extent that our description goes beyond reporting the data and strives for generality, it allows room for alternative descriptions, and we find ourselves needing evidence from other sources to help choose between these descriptions. A good investigator is particularly concerned with finding corroborative evidence.

In this case, the evidence from first-grade spelling errors provides a check on the conclusions we might draw from the younger children's original spelling. Among other things, it guards against the possibility that the children who made up spellings at home were unique in their strategies. In addition, I have tested some of the less obvious generalizations in a quasi-experimental fashion. Consider, for example, the *D* in SDROGIST; I suggested that the young writer unknowingly grouped the phonetic segment in question with [d], rather than with [t], and that he had a good phonetic basis for doing so. This is an hypothesis, and there are, of course, alternatives—with just one example like this, our first guess might be that he simply made a mistake, in the sense that he did not print the letter that he intended. What is more, it is a *mentalistic* hypothesis, in that it dares to suggest what went on in the writer's mind—a controversial kind of explanation. To test such hypotheses, I have interviewed kindergarten and first-grade children (one at a time) in game-like situations, in which I tried to elicit their judgments of similarity and dissimilarity among various speech sounds. As you might imagine, it is not easy to design these games to be meaningful to the child and meaningful, in a different sense, to the investigation. But notice that in such a case, we really have three kinds of evidence: the spelling, the phonetic facts, and the experimental judgments. If evidence from three different kinds of sources all supports one hypothesis, it usually excludes most alternative hypotheses at the same time. As we now look at more intricate examples, we will consider all these kinds of evidence.

1. Spellings of [e]

Our next example is part of a letter written by a boy about four years old:

> HOW R YOU WAN YOU GAD I CHANS
> SAND IS OL I LADR
> RAD R YOU TACEG CAR IV
> YORSALF

Once again there are some standard spellings, HOW and YOU, and there is one instance of letter-name spelling of vowels; TACEG repre-

113

sents *taking*. We also see the rebus-like device of using a letter to represent the entire syllable that is its name: *R* represents *are*. But the rest of the letter includes more complex relations between spelling and sound. With the help of the boy's parents, I interpret the message as follows:

HOW R YOU WAN YOU GAD I CHANS
How are you? When you get a chance,

SAND IS OL I LADR
send us all a letter.

RAD R YOU TACEG CAR IV
Red, are you taking care of

YORSALF
yourself?

There are two large classes of unexplained spellings; one of them involves the vowel [e].

WAN	(when)	LADR	(letter)
GAD	(get)	RAD	(Red)
SAND	(send)	YORSALF	(yourself)

Obviously, in each instance, the vowel in question is spelled *A*. This spelling is interesting, if only for its regularity in this message. The regularity becomes more striking when we find that this spelling of [e] is common, not only in this boy's spelling generally, but also in that of other children. Table 5.1 presents some examples, drawn from the spelling of more than thirty children.

The fact that quite a few children, independently of each other, produced a spelling that they surely did not learn from adults naturally prompts us to ask why they came up with this particular spelling. The first fact that we must notice is that this is a vowel that does not occur as the name of a letter, unlike [ēy], [īy], [āy], and so on. The vowel [e] does occur in letter-names, but always together with other sounds, as in the names of *f, l, m, n, s,* and *x*. If the children simply looked for a letter whose name contained this sound, they might have used any or

Table 5.1. *Spellings of [e] with A*

PAN	pen	TADDEBAR	teddy bear	SHALF	shelf
FALL	fell	PRTAND	pretend	DAVL	devil
LAFFT	left	RAKRD	record (n.)	ANE	any
MAS	mess	ALLS	else	ALRVATA	elevator

all of these letters to represent [e]. In fact, they did not do so. Rather, they analyzed these letter-names in the opposite way, using F to represent [f] and so on. Since these are also standard spellings, they are not surprising. But the fact that the children looked elsewhere for the spelling of [e] becomes all the more interesting.

One possible explanation, and one which researchers must always consider, is that this is simply random performance. Like the old remark about monkeys and typewriters, perhaps if you take enough spellings from enough children, you can find examples of anything. And there *are* seemingly random events in children's spelling, like Alberto's use of *ON* to represent *in*. So let us look at a table of all the spellings of [e] from a collection of over 2,500 words spelled by young children. Table 5.2 shows the spellings, arranged (vertically) in order of frequency and (horizontally) according to the age of the child.

We see that *A* is the most frequent spelling for the children younger than six years. For children of unknown age and those older than six, it is less frequent than *E,* the standard spelling, but it is still far more frequent than any others. While *A* and *E* occur about 42 percent of the time overall, most other spellings occur less than 1 percent of the time.

Moreover, the next two spellings of [e], namely *I* (5 percent) and omission (5 percent), occur mainly in special circumstances. *I* occurs mostly in words where the sound [e] precedes a nasal sound, as in *pen*. It is well known that in this context [e] tends to sound like [i], and in some dialects, the vowel of *pen* is indistinguishable from that of *pin*.

Table 5.2. *The Frequency of Spellings for the Sound* [e]

Age:	Under 6		Unknown		6 or Over		All	
Spelling	Freq.	Pct.	Freq.	Pct.	Freq.	Pct.	Freq.	Pct.
A	96	49.7	32	34.0	63	38.7	191	42.4
E	72	37.3	40	42.6	80	49.1	192	42.7
I	11	5.7	6	6.4	8	4.9	25	5.6
(omit)	9	4.7	10	10.6	5	3.1	24	5.3
EE	2	1.0	2	2.1	1	0.6	5	1.1
AE	1	0.5	0	0.0	0	0.0	1	0.2
AI	1	0.5	0	0.0	0	0.0	1	0.2
EU	1	0.5	0	0.0	0	0.0	1	0.2
O	0	0.0	0	0.0	1	0.6	1	0.2
U	0	0.0	1	1.1	1	0.6	2	0.4
EI	0	0.0	1	1.1	0	0.0	1	0.2
EY	0	0.0	0	0.0	2	1.2	2	0.4
EA	0	0.0	1	1.1	2	1.2	3	0.7
EAR	0	0.0	1	1.1	0	0.0	1	0.2
Totals	193	100.0	94	100.0	163	100.0	450	100.0

115

Thus the spelling *I* makes sense in this environment. Furthermore, there are explanations for most of the omissions, the fourth most frequent spelling of [e]. Of these omissions, about 60 percent occur in syllables containing [ef], [el], [em], [en], and [es]; that is, syllables containing the *names* of the letters *F, L, M, N,* and *S.* In these cases, the children simply use those letters to represent the letters' names; for instance, in PNSUL (pencil), it seems that *N* represents its own name, [en]. Another 30 percent of the omissions of [e] are from words such as *very* and *there* in which [e] is affected by the following [r]. This vowel is not identical to that of *bet,* and it is not surprising that children tend to omit it. With these observations, then, we can account for most instances of *I* or omission, leaving *A* as the only unexplained nonstandard spelling that occurs more than 1 percent of the time, and it occurs far more often than all the others combined. Some of the other spellings, such as *EA,* are actually infrequent standard spellings (for instance, *bread*), and we may well regard spellings like *U* and *O* as random performance, but surely there must be some reason for the great frequency of *A.*

We are left, then, with the following situation: the use of *A* to represent [e] is very common, particularly with young children. It is nonstandard, so the children could not have learned it from literate adults. It is common in the spelling of many different children with different dialects, and it occurs in a variety of contexts, so it probably does not represent a dialectal peculiarity of pronunciation. It is far more frequent than every other nonstandard spelling, so much so that it certainly is not merely random spelling. We can understand, at least in part, why children have to *create* a spelling for this particular vowel (it does not match a letter-name), but we have not explained why they use *A.*

At this point we have proposed what is known in linguistics as an observational generalization, or a generalization at the observational level of adequacy. A real, or valid, observational generalization is no small matter; it summarizes what we take to be a significant fact in our data. A good deal of labor went into collecting, sorting, and tabulating the data which we have worked on and into identifying the interesting fact, as opposed to any number of other true statements that we might have made about the data. In this respect, this example is fairly typical of many cases in the study of language, although perhaps it seems unusually easy to spot the significant fact here, once the data are displayed properly.

But even this step is not so trivial as it may appear. There have, of course, been many studies of children's spelling "errors," including those of children in the early grades. These studies typically categorized misspellings as *omissions, substitutions,* and *insertions.* You can see that as long as all 'substitutions' are grouped together, the generalization which we have arrived at is impossible. The data in Table 5.2, for example, would be stated as 48.8 percent substitutions, with no necessary recognition of the fact that almost all of these are the letter *A*. To make matters worse, most traditional studies categorized misspellings with respect to standard spelling, as the term 'substitution' suggests. So even one's basic point of view—that children are attempting to *represent sounds* rather than to *imitate spellings,* affects the generalizations that one is able to make.

Nevertheless, as exciting as it is to uncover what appears to be a valid generalization about a significant fact, you can also see that the observational level of adequacy can be profoundly unsatisfying. *If* this is a valid generalization, and *if* the children's spelling is indeed not random, then there must be some reason for it. Until we find that explanation, there must remain some doubt about these two *if*'s. The significance of our generalization, and even its validity, are suspect until we achieve some explanation for it.

2. Toward Descriptive Adequacy

Our task, then, is to find and test explanations for what we have observed. We have already considered two possibilities—that our data may be unrepresentative, so that our generalization is simply not valid, and that the spelling may be simply the result of choosing letters in a random fashion. Both of these possibilities would explain our observations and at the same time deny their significance. Since these accounts seem to be incorrect, let us seek others.

One possibility arises from the choice of the letter *A*. Could it be that as children search the alphabet for a spelling, they simply stop with the first candidate, the first letter of the alphabet? And could the choice of *A* reflect the fact that children are most familiar with this letter, having learned their A, B, C's—literally? It could indeed, and this explanation again seems to reduce our observation to triviality. In fact, if we accept this explanation in an extreme form, it suggests that young children might use the letter *A* to represent any sound, vowel *or* consonant, which does not correspond to a letter-name. This is by no means impossible.

But we have already seen some evidence that suggests that this explanation is by no means correct. Consider again the example of the letter:

HOW R YOU WAN YOU GAD I CHANS
SAND IS OL I LADR
RAD R YOU TACEG CAR IV
YORSALF

Recall that there are *two* consistent nonstandard spellings of vowels in the message. Before reading on, you may wish to identify the four instances of the second nonstandard vowel spelling and consider its bearing on this discussion.

The second spelling is seen in the following examples:

I   a (twice)
IS   us
IV   of

Here the letter *I* seems to correspond to three different letters in standard spelling, but in each case it represents what would be a reduced vowel, [ə] or the higher [ɨ], in running speech. Again, it is clear that the child had to invent a spelling for these vowels; they do not occur in any letter-names. The significance of this spelling is that he did not simply use *A* to represent every such vowel.

The question of whether or not other children use this same spelling is a bit complicated. The computer tables suggest that they do; *I* is the most frequent spelling of [ə] except for omissions, which have a special explanation. My reservation is that Sam (the writer of the letter) and other children seem to have created this spelling for different reasons. This inference comes from examining the spelling of each child closely, an activity which doesn't suit our purposes here. At any rate, the conclusion for our purposes is the same: none of the children simply used *A* to stand for every non–letter-name vowel, let alone consonant. Rather, the children created particular spellings for each vowel, and what is more, different children created similar spellings.

We could go on proposing and testing superficial explanations for this spelling, taking into account such factors as the shapes of the letters and the order in which children learn them; one can hardly exhaust the supply of *conceivable* explanations. But the fact is that none of the superficial ones that I have thought of, or which others have suggested to me, seems to have any support in the evidence. Nor do the spellings reflect peculiar pronunciations. It seems that we must look deeper, that is, for a more complex (and more interesting) mental operation by the children.

Having seen that children adopt different spellings for different vowels, perhaps we should look at another example. This one is a

Table 5.3. *Spellings of [i] with E*

SEP	ship	SEK	sink	HEMM	him
FES	fish	WEL	will	DRENK	drink
EGLIOW	igloo	LETL	little	DOEG	doing
FLEPR	Flipper	PEL	pill	SOWEMEG	swimming

picture of a fish-like creature amidst wiggly blue lines. The caption reads:

FES SOWEMEG EN WOODR

Here again we have several nonstandard spellings, but of immediate interest are the spellings of [i]:

FES   fish
SOWEMEG   swimming
EN   in

In four instances, the spelling of [i] is *E*. Once again this turns out to be quite common among our preschool spellings. Table 5.3 presents some examples.

Again, if we look at the frequency of this spelling as compared with others, we find that it is by far the most frequent nonstandard spelling. It is less frequent than *I*, the standard spelling, but it is far more frequent than any other nonstandard spelling, certainly too common to be considered a random choice. See Table 5.4.

We have now seen three examples of frequent nonstandard spellings: *A* for [e], *E* for [i], and *I* for [ə], as well as the use of the letters to represent the vowels that form their names. In searching for an explanation, let us consider the possibility that these spellings have a phonetic basis; let us look at the spellings in relation to the articulatory position of the vowels. First, Table 5.5 summarizes the spellings that we have examined so far.

3. A Proposed Explanation

Figure 5.5 is a diagram of the place of articulation of the most common vowels in American English, with the sounds that are spelled alike grouped together within dotted lines. As you examine this diagram, bear in mind that the spellings of the sounds [īy], [ēy], and [āy] are given by letter names. But what is striking is that in each instance, a

Table 5.4. *The Frequency of Spellings for the Sound* [i]

Age:	Under 6		Unknown		6 or Over		All	
Spelling	Freq.	Pct.	Freq.	Pct.	Freq.	Pct.	Freq.	Pct.
I	157	64.9	82	69.5	110	73.8	349	68.6
E	55	22.7	18	15.3	20	13.4	93	18.3
(omit)	12	5.0	13	11.0	4	2.7	29	5.7
A	5	2.1	1	0.8	2	1.3	8	1.6
O	2	0.8	0	0.0	1	0.7	3	0.6
Y	2	0.8	0	0.0	1	0.7	3	0.6
EI	2	0.8	0	0.0	7	4.7	9	1.8
IE	2	0.8	0	0.0	0	0.0	2	0.4
EE	2	0.8	1	0.8	0	0.0	3	0.6
U	1	0.4	1	0.8	1	0.7	3	0.6
CH	1	0.4	0	0.0	0	0.0	1	0.2
OO	1	0.4	0	0.0	0	0.0	1	0.2
II	0	0.0	1	0.8	2	1.3	3	0.6
IA	0	0.0	0	0.0	1	0.7	1	0.2
LI	0	0.0	1	0.8	0	0.0	1	0.2
Totals	242	100.0	118	100.0	149	100.0	509	100.0

vowel that is phonetically similar to one of these letter-name vowels is spelled the same way.

Note that all the names of vowel letters involve glides: A, E, I, O, and U are pronounced [ēy], [īy], [āy], [ōw], and [yūw] respectively. Children spell [i] as well as [īy] with E. These are the vowel sounds of *itch* [ič], and *each* [īyč]. [īy] includes the sound [ī], somewhat higher than [i], but nevertheless similar. One can confirm this by starting to say *each* but shortening the vowel sound so as to take off most of the glide up to [y]. The more you do this, the more the word will sound like *itch*. A comparable relationship holds between [e] and [ēy], both of which children spell with A. One can do an experiment with *etch* [eč] and the letter name H [ēyč]: change "H" into something like *etch* by just shortening the vowel sound. Finally, children spell [ə] as well as [āy] with I. This time the short vowel is higher than the vowel that

Table 5.5. *Summary of Spellings Examined so Far*

Vowel Sounds	Children's Spelling
[īy] (as in "feet")	E
[i] (as in "fish")	E
[ēy] (as in "snake")	A
[e] (as in "Red")	A
[āy] (as in "like")	I
[ə] (as in "of")	I

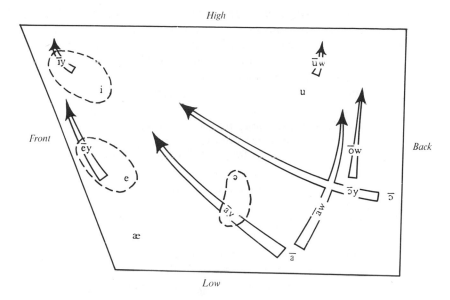

Figure 5.5. *Diagram of the Articulatory Gestures of Major English Vowels Showing the Sounds that Children Spell the Same Way*

begins the diphthong, but here again one can change [āys] into something like [əs] (*ice* into *us*) by removing the [y].

It looks as though children have devised a two-part principle for spelling English vowels:

> See if the sound of the vowel corresponds to the name of a letter. If so, use that letter to spell the vowel. (This strategy applies to the vowels of "feet," "snake," and "like.") Otherwise, find a letter-name that is *phonetically close* to the sound of the vowel and use that letter to spell the vowel. (This part applies to the vowels of "fish," "Red," and "of.")

Unless we regard the phonetic similarity of the vowels that are spelled alike as mere coincidence (or as the effect of some unknown third factor), we must suppose that children spell these vowels alike because they sense that the vowels *are* alike. Children seem to assume that if we must spell different sounds with the same letter, the sounds thus grouped together ought to be related phonetically.

The relationship between [īy] and [i] and between [ēy] and [e] as they are grouped in children's spelling are precisely the groupings that many phoneticians and phonologists have traditionally made by dividing vowels into high, mid, and low. Since the children seem to have arrived at these same groupings, without phonetic training, and since the phonologists have independent reasons for their classifications—such as the behavior of these vowels in various languages—we must say that these two independent analyses support each other. The phonological classification makes what the children do seem plausible, and the children provide independent evidence for the naturalness of the phonological classification. In fact, the notion of "independent evidence"—two kinds of evidence converging on the same conclusion—is extremely important in linguistic reasoning.

Nevertheless, attributing to children a mental "map" of English vowels like that in Figure 5.5 is bound to be controversial. In fact, any mentalistic explanation is controversial, because there are those who feel that the notion of the "mind" is at best a convenient fiction for what is really a network of associations, established through the repeated pairing of elements in our experience. It is hard to imagine what repeated pairings, in the children's experience, might have led to the grouping in Figure 5.5. Rather, this proposed explanation assumes that the children can do more than merely recognize the *contiguity* of two items in their experience; it proposes that they have done a bit of untutored phonetic analysis.

Let us clear away an obstacle that I may have introduced by using words such as "recognize" and "analyze." I do not mean that children are necessarily *aware* of their grouping of vowels, or of the phonetic basis for it. In fact, people are ordinarily not entirely conscious of the reasons for their spelling, and they often make judgments of relationships among sounds without being aware of it. For example, consider the cocktail-party phenomenon in which you have a conversation under noisy conditions. Often the noise obliterates part of the incoming message, and you must make some informed guesses about what was said. Many factors influence your guesses, such as what you know about the topic, the speaker, and English syntax, but another such factor is your judgment of phonetic similarity. If you hear something like "chair," but that word doesn't fit, you are likely to think of "share," rather than "pair," as your next choice, assuming that the context allows either one. This is a tacit judgment of phonetic similarity. Likewise, children appear to choose spellings on this unconscious level.

It may be plausible to suppose that the nonstandard spellings come about because children tacitly group vowels for spelling purposes on the basis of phonetic relationships. But obviously we need additional evidence to test this explanation. One great advantage of seeking explanations is that they "go beyond the data" and predict additional instances. Precisely because they do so, they provide us with tests of the proposed explanation. If the predictions turn out to be correct, then the explanation gains greatly in force.

In this case, we are led to some predictions by looking again at Figure 5.5. If this map is correct, then we might expect children to make use of other such relationships in creating spelling. What other pairs of vowels might we expect to find spelled alike?

Perhaps the first prediction we might make concerns [ūw] and [u], which are related phonetically as are [īy] and [i]. Tables 5.6 and 5.7 present the spellings of these vowels.

As predicted, the spellings of these vowels are very similar, especially the four most frequent spellings. These similarities are not quite so striking as those for the other pairs of vowels, though. First, these vowels are much less frequent than [e] or [i], so that there are fewer examples. Second, there is a greater variety of spellings for each, rather than one or two main spellings. Evidently, the children did not uniformly settle on *U* to represent [ūw]; this in itself is interesting. Most important, two of the most frequent spellings, *U* and *OO*, may also be standard spellings for these sounds, in some common words like *rude* or *balloon* with [ūw], and *push* or *look* with [u]. Therefore, we cannot be sure that the children didn't learn these spellings from adults, even though they use the spellings in words in which they are nonstandard. That leaves us with *O*, which does seem to be an invented spelling, and which is third and second in frequency. On the basis of its

Table 5.6. *The Frequency of Spellings for the Sound* [ūw]

Age:	Under 6		Unknown		6 or Over		All	
Spelling	Freq.	Pct.	Freq.	Pct.	Freq.	Pct.	Freq.	Pct.
U	28	35.4	4	14.3	4	12.5	36	25.9
OO	20	25.3	8	28.6	14	43.8	42	30.2
O	10	12.7	7	25.0	6	18.8	23	16.5
(omit)	5	6.3	0	0.0	0	0.0	5	3.6
OW	5	6.3	2	7.1	3	9.4	10	7.2
W	2	2.5	0	0.0	0	0.0	2	1.4
OE	2	2.5	0	0.0	0	0.0	2	1.4
OU	2	2.5	0	0.0	1	3.1	3	2.2
E	1	1.3	0	0.0	0	0.0	1	0.7
EOW	1	1.3	1	3.6	0	0.0	2	1.4
UO	1	1.3	0	0.0	1	3.1	2	1.4
AW	1	1.3	0	0.0	0	0.0	1	0.7
LLW	1	1.3	0	0.0	0	0.0	1	0.7
D	0	0.0	0	0.0	1	3.1	1	0.7
IOW	0	0.0	3	10.7	0	0.0	3	2.2
AO	0	0.0	1	3.6	0	0.0	1	0.7
OOW	0	0.0	0	0.0	1	3.1	1	0.7
OOO	0	0.0	0	0.0	1	3.1	1	0.7
UOO	0	0.0	2	7.1	0	0.0	2	1.4
Totals	79	100.0	28	100.0	32	100.0	139	100.0

123

Table 5.7. *The Frequency of Spellings for the Sound* [*u*]

Age:	Under 6		Unknown		6 or Over		All	
Spelling	*Freq.*	*Pct.*	*Freq.*	*Pct.*	*Freq.*	*Pct.*	*Freq.*	*Pct.*
U	9	39.1	3	23.1	9	22.5	21	27.6
O	4	17.4	3	23.1	12	30.0	19	25.0
(omit)	3	13.0	1	7.7	0	0.0	4	5.3
OO	3	13.0	3	23.1	15	37.5	21	27.6
E	1	4.3	0	0.0	0	0.0	1	1.3
K	1	4.3	0	0.0	0	0.0	1	1.3
OY	1	4.3	0	0.0	0	0.0	1	1.3
OOA	1	4.3	0	0.0	0	0.0	1	1.3
UO	0	0.0	0	0.0	1	2.5	1	1.3
OG	0	0.0	2	15.4	0	0.0	2	2.6
OU	0	0.0	1	7.7	1	2.5	2	2.6
AW	0	0.0	0	0.0	1	2.5	1	1.3
OUL	0	0.0	0	0.0	1	2.5	1	1.3
Totals	23	100.0	13	100.0	40	100.0	76	100.0

name, *O* would be a reasonable invented spelling, for these vowels and the letter-name are all similar in articulation. In fact, children use *O* for all back rounded vowels. All in all, the spelling of [ūw] and [u] tends to support our hypothesis, though less forcefully than the spelling of other pairs.

Similarly, our hypothesis predicts that children might relate [āy] and [ā], that is, might use the letter *I* as a representation for the stressed vowel of *father*. In fact, there are quite a few examples of just such spellings in our data (see Table 5.8), but it turns out that most of these examples come from one child. The vowel is considerably less frequent than [e] or [i] to begin with, and most children evidently acquired the standard spellings, *o* and *a*. In frequency, the spelling *I* for [ā] is fourth, after the two standard spellings and omissions. Once again, the invented spelling occurs more frequently than any other nonstandard spelling, though not by the huge margin that we find in the other cases. This case is complicated by dialect differences, as well.

Now we have examined the most likely cases in which children might relate a vowel that they wish to spell to one of the letter-name vowels. The evidence of a tacit grouping of vowels is strong for [e] and [i], and we find a general grouping of back vowels in relation to [ōw]. Other instances, involving [u] and [ā], do not contradict our hypothesis—in fact, on the surface, they seem to provide support, but the support is weakened by other considerations.

At this point we are likely to seek other kinds of evidence to test

Table 5.8. *Spellings of [ā] with I*

GIT	got	IR	are
CLIC, CLIK	clock	HIRT	heart
BICS, BIKS	box	RICET	rocket
DIKTR	doctor	UPIN	upon
	SCICHTAP	Scotch tape	
	CIDEJCHES	cottage cheese	
	PIPS	pops	
	MIRSE	Marcie	
	BITUVMELC	bottle of milk	

our hypothesis. One type of evidence is simply children's spelling errors; if the young children who composed their own spellings at home or in nursery school are not atypical, and if children in general regard [ēy] as similar to [e] so that this judgment influences their spelling, then we might find the spelling *A* for [e] even among the errors of first-graders who are learning standard spelling.

In the course of pilot testing for another experiment, we had occasion to ask a class of first-graders to spell a variety of words, so we included the words *left, pest,* and *rest.* An adult read each word aloud to the children and used each in a sentence, so that the children knew what word was intended. The instruction was simply to print each word "as you think it should be spelled." Table 5.9 presents the spellings of the vowel.

This test was given to an upper-middle-class suburban first grade in February of the school year, so these children had some mastery of standard spelling, but still we see that about one-quarter to one-third of the spellings of [e] are *A*, and that this error accounts for almost all of the misspellings of the vowel.

This small test belongs in the category of pilot tests, perhaps, because there is a possibility that the results are too few to be representative, or that they were influenced by some factor, such as the experimenter's pronunciation (although we tried to make it clearly [e]). Nevertheless, they are suggestive.

Table 5.9. *Spellings of [e]; First Grade*

Word:	left	pest	rest
Spelling			
E	17	21	18
A	9	7	7
other	1	1	0
%A	33.3	24.1	28.0

4. Experimental Evidence

To find additional evidence, we might seek to get away from spelling altogether. Since one function of independent evidence is to narrow the range of alternative explanations, the more varied its character, the better. Furthermore, we must recognize that the information that we will get from children's spelling is limited to the special problems encountered in attempting to spell with the knowledge that children have. That is, we are learning something about children's judgments of [e] precisely because the alphabet leaves them with the problem of how to spell that vowel. The spelling problem evidently encourages them, although it does not require them, to relate this vowel to one that they know how to spell. It does not give us information about many other relationships, such as those between sounds both of which are of unknown spelling. Furthermore, our proposed explanation really makes two claims, only one of which has to do with spelling; it claims that children recognize the relation between [e] and [ēy], *and* that this recognition accounts for their use of *A* in spelling. It would be good to test the first and more basic of these claims in a fashion that is independent of spelling.

In order to do so, we would like to ask children a question like, "Do you hear a similarity between [e] and [ēy]?" But of course, one cannot simply round up children and ask them this question. My experience is that children will give a straight-faced answer to almost *any* question; they leave it up to you to be sure that the question and the answer are *valid*—that is, meaningful measures of what you want to know. Furthermore, there is a special problem with questions about absolute similarity: any two things can be regarded as similar in some sense or other; it all depends on what dimensions of possible similarity are to count, and how much similarity is required. So we would be asking the children a logically difficult question, and we could not count on them to elaborate or to indicate any puzzlement in their answer.

It is more to the point, and less perplexing, to ask them a question of *relative* similarity: is [e] more like [ēy] or more like some other vowel, such as [ōw]. If the vowels of English are simply discrete entities, distinct from each other and not mentally grouped in any particular way, then children should choose randomly in response to this question. Likewise, if for some other reason the question makes no sense or if the two pairs of vowels happen to be equal in perceived similarity, the children should choose randomly. Only if the children do indeed regard [e] and [ēy] as more closely related than the other pair of vowels should they choose this pair more frequently than chance dictates. If children choose randomly, we will conclude that a grouping of

[e] with [ēy] on phonetic grounds could not be the basis of the spelling; if they choose [e]-[ēy] predominately, we will conclude that they recognize this relationship, so that it *might* be the basis of the spelling.

Another issue is that these vowels are not perfectly symmetrical; [ēy] occurs at the end of words, as in *say*, while [e] does not. Consequently, if we produce these vowels in isolation, [e] will sound peculiar in a way that [ēy] will not. It is possible that this difference might influence children's judgments in some way. It seems that we had better put both vowels in context—the same context, naturally—and ask the children to compare pairs of words such as *led–laid* / *led–load*, in which only the vowels vary. This solution is not ideal, and a case could be made that it is better to compare the vowels in isolation, but that method is also risky.

Now we must design an experiment that presents children with this choice. It turns out that the details of the experiment are very important; small changes in the way the experiment is set up and the way the question is presented affect the children's understanding and thus the reliability of their answers. We find ourselves in a trade-off situation: for the sake of validity, we want to stay close to our original question, and for the sake of reliability, we want to embed this question in a context that engages children's attention. After a good deal of manipulating and pretesting, we have designed an experiment that seems to maximize these two virtues.

In the test, the experimenter sits facing one kindergarten child in a quiet room. The experimenter introduces a hand puppet whose name is Ed, and indicates that Ed would like to play a word game. The child then puts Ed on his hand and the experimenter explains the game. Ed, it seems, likes to find "words that sound like Ed"—for example, Ed likes *Ted, Jed, fled, sled,* etc. At this point the child has a chance to suggest words that Ed might like. Then the experimenter presents pairs of words and asks which one Ed would like; "would Ed like *bed* or *bead*?" "Would Ed like *food* or *fed*?" (An assistant transcribes the child's choices, along with any relevant comments and nonstandard pronunciations.) The experimenter corrects any incorrect choices and announces "Right!" for the correct choices before continuing. When the child has identified the rhyming word in five out of six of these examples, we assume that he or she is able to identify rhymes with *Ed,* and we go on to the experiment itself.

In beginning the experiment itself, the experimenter says, "Now I'll tell you some words that don't sound *exactly* like *Ed,* and you listen and see if you can tell me which one Ed would like—which word sounds more like *Ed.* Would Ed like *aid* or *owed*? Would Ed like *showed* or *shade*?" There are six test items of this type. The child's individual choices and those of all children are used to measure whether children judge [e] and [ēy] to be more closely related than [e] and [ōw], which share other phonetic properties.

Some controls were included in this basic schema. In the pretest, which establishes the rhyming class, we varied both order and the alternative vowel [īy] or [ūw], so that the child could not succeed merely with a position preference, and so that the alternative vowel would not bias the experiment. In the experiment, more "control" items of this type ("Would Ed like *bread* or *brood*? Would Ed like *speed* or *sped*?") were alternated with the six test items in order to remind the child that he was to find a word that "sounds like Ed," and to provide a check on whether children were indeed listening for this target throughout the experiment. We could then use scores on these control items as a measure of the validity of each child's judgment of the test items.

After the pilot testing and refinement which led to this experimental design, we tested kindergarten children in Nahant, Massachusetts, during April of the school year. About 82 percent of the children who participated achieved the criterion in identifying rhymes (five out of six correct), although about 25 percent required more than six trials to do so. Almost all children participated with evident enjoyment; in general, the experimental design was clearly successful.

Only when a child achieved the criterion in identifying the true rhymes did we go on to the experiment itself and the six control items that alternated with test items. We can have greatest confidence in the judgments of those children who correctly identified the true rhymes with *Ed* on these control items as well, that is those who clearly continued to seek words that "sounded like *Ed*" during the experiment. For this reason I will present the results from those children who made at least five out of six correct identifications of rhyme both in establishing the class and during the experimental list itself. In fact, the results of the experiments do not differ greatly if we adopt a less stringent criterion for correctness on these latter control items.

The essential result is that the twenty kindergarten children chose the phonetically related pair [e]-[ēy] to a degree that is statistically significant at the .05 level, that is, a degree that would not have occurred by chance more often than five times in one hundred trials. The appropriate statistical test here is one that compares the results with what might happen by chance, without making any assumptions about what *all* children would do on this test, since that is unknown. In tests of human judgments, especially with children, this level of statistical significance is usually accepted as sufficient evidence of nonrandomness. The clear implication is that these English vowels are not merely discrete contrasting speech sounds for kindergarten children, but rather that children tacitly recognize phonetic relationships among them. These relationships are such that they may explain the common pattern in children's spelling of [e].

We replicated this experiment with adults, with very minor modifications, such as not inviting them to put the puppet on their hands. If adults chose randomly, then in order to attribute the phonetic grouping to children, one would have to suppose that people lose the ability to recognize these relationships. In fact, the adults also chose the [e]–[ēy] relationship even more strongly than children, although five adults (out of twenty-two) consistently chose the [e]–[ōw] pair. This outcome suggests that most adults retain the ability which we are attributing to children, although adults have learned that these phonetic relationships are not reflected in spelling.

There is more to this story. It turns out that children's spelling of [e] is probably influenced also by their grouping it with [æ], the vowel of *cat,* which they know is also spelled *a.*[2] But the basic point of this description is the varied kind of evidence that one can bring to bear on a mentalistic explanation. With the experiment, we strengthened our hypothesis by finding that its presupposition seems to be true—that young children tacitly group English vowels on the basis of certain phonetic relationships. In the process, we developed an experimental technique that could be used, or adapted as necessary, to study other kinds of phonetic judgments by children, including those that are not seen in spelling. In this way, the attempt to achieve a descriptive level of adequacy—to account for our observations by identifying their general linguistic basis—has led to methodological progress as well.

In fact, we now have four lines of evidence which converge on our notion that children tacitly group vowels according to phonetic similarities and that this grouping is reflected in some common patterns in their spelling. First, there is the invented spelling of young children; second, the characteristic spelling errors of first-graders; third, the judgments of similarity made by children in our experiment; and fourth, the naturalness of the hypothetical grouping of vowels—the phonetic relatedness of the vowels that are spelled alike. There is also the fact that predicted similarities in the spelling of other pairs of vowels do occur. Although this evidence is confounded by other considerations, at least we did not find evidence *against* our hypothesis, in the form of entirely dissimilar spellings. Together, these four strands of evidence increase the plausibility of our proposed explanation considerably. They show that our hypothesis could be true and that some

---

2. For a more complete account see Charles Read, "Children's Categorization of Speech Sounds in English," Research Report no. 17 (Urbana, Illinois: National Council of Teachers of English, 1975). See the Suggestions for Further Reading at chapter's end for more information.

other possible hypotheses (for instance, that the preschoolers are unique in their spelling) are not correct. It is not difficult to think of other explanations for the spelling, but it is quite difficult to find other explanations that pull together all four lines of evidence.

Nevertheless, this is by no means a proven proposition or a closed area of inquiry—far from it. There is a sense in which we can never absolutely *prove* a hypothesis; there is always the possibility of an alternative explanation, no matter how rich and varied our evidence is. In this case, that is more than a remote possibility. Furthermore, research in this area is just beginning; you can no doubt think of many questions about whether or not and how children categorize speech sounds, how these categories are reflected in spelling, and what this relationship may tell us about the teaching of reading and writing. The purpose of this chapter is not to present a completed analysis, but rather to illustrate the processes by which we deepen and strengthen a linguistic explanation, and in particular, to illustrate the ways in which a mentalistic explanation can be tested. I hope it is obvious that the explanation is by no means completely adequate or thoroughly tested; it is not a point of general agreement in the field, either. However, I hope it is also clear how one might proceed to refine and test it further.

5. Toward Explanatory Adequacy

One natural refinement actually leads us toward a third level of generalization, a still higher level of adequacy. It has to do with the question of whether or not children's phonetic categories relate to the phonetic categories in other kinds of linguistic behavior by children and adults. Puns, slips of the tongue, historical changes in languages, and the phonological processes in languages all involve relationships among speech sounds. When a lecturer makes the standard but malodorous pun about the Great English Vowel Movement, or when a diner asks for a "cuff of coffee,"[3] it is significant that the pun and the slip involve pairs of sounds [v]–[b] and [f]–[p] that are similar in articulation and voicing. Puns are better (worse?) and slips of the tongue more likely with pairs of closely related speech sounds. Likewise, the aforementioned Great English Vowel Shift affected similar sounds; it raised the pronunciation of tense, or long, vowels, so that [ēy] in the Middle English pronunciation of *sweete*, "sweet" has become Modern English [īy]. Typically, we also find that current phonological pro-

---

3. Victoria A. Fromkin, "The Non-Anomalous Nature of Anomalous Utterances," *Language, 47,* 1971.

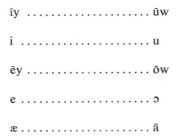

Figure 5.6. *A Possible Alternative Set of Vowel Relationships*

cesses involve closely related sounds, such as the alternation of [s] and [š] in words like *race–racial*. So children's spelling and other judgments are just two of several kinds of evidence about classes of speech sounds, and the question naturally arises, whether all these kinds of evidence will in the end point to a single basic (if complex) set of relationships among speech sounds, as judged by speakers of languages. Current research is just beginning to gather together the full range of evidence.

We can put the question another way. Assume for a moment that for children the prominent relationships are indeed those represented in Figure 5.5. We can seek a deeper explanation: why are people inclined to find these similarities salient, rather than some others? Speech sounds are, after all, related along many dimensions; why couldn't Figure 5.5 look like Figure 5.6 instead?—or any number of other possible groupings?

Part of the answer is simply that we do not yet know just how children group English vowels—whether there are several kinds of relationships and if so, which ones are most salient. Recall that the spelling problem was a special one: it required children (if they wished to devise spellings) to relate the 'short' vowels, which they did not know how to spell, to those 'long' vowels that correspond to letter-names. As I mentioned in connection with [e] – [æ], our experiments indicate that children can recognize relationships other than those needed for spelling.

Still, the question remains: why some phonetic categories and not others? There is an indefinitely large variety of distinguishable noises that we can make with our vocal apparatus, and it appears that we divide up this phonetic territory in specific ways, without any special training. Ultimately, the explanation for this fact will be a theory of the human capacity for language and how it interacts with the phonetic material. This theory will, presumably, have to do with all humans and all languages. Obviously, we can hardly even approach this level of generalization yet. It has been called the 'explanatory' level—perhaps not the best choice of terminology, since lower levels of generalization can be explanatory, too, in the ordinary sense of this term. Today, the effort to reach this explanatory level has led to questions about the relative importance of articulatory and acoustic qualities in the categorization of speech sounds, and to interesting proposals such as the *quantal* theory of speech production and perception. At any rate, recognizing this level of generalization helps us to describe the ultimate goals of linguistic inquiry.

6. Teaching and Learning

In the meantime, and at a more practical level, the study of what children know about the sounds of their language when they enter school has some immediate importance for teaching. First, we can now distinguish a type of frequent apparent error that deserves special consideration. Teachers have known for years that it is common for children to confuse mirror-image letter-shapes in reading and spelling: to write *b* for *d*, or *u* for *n*, for example. We also know now that this confusion has a basis in neurological maturation; it is not ordinarily a sign of visual disorder, nor is it a purely random error. Now, in spellings that arise from the way in which children relate speech sounds to each other, we can distinguish another type of common pattern that is not merely a random error—a stab in the dark—but which shows, on the contrary, that the child is performing a particular kind of analysis. The child who spells *let* with an *i* is probably just guessing; the child who spells it with an *a* may be just guessing, but may, more likely, be attempting to extend the letters available to represent the vowel sounds in a systematic, phonetically-justified way. Notice that this child is on the right track, generally; we do use a single spelling to represent more than one sound.

What the child does not know, and must be taught, is that we do not group sounds together for spelling purposes on a *phonetic* basis. Considering just vowels that we have discussed, the vowels that are spelled alike in English are, for instance, the vowels of *sane* and *sanity, recede* and *recession,* and *divide* and *division.* Figure 5.7 represents these relationships.

As you can see, the vowels that are spelled alike in standard spelling are not particularly closely related phonetically, in contrast with the relationships that children identify, as illustrated in Figure 5.5.

The standard arrangement exists largely because the pronunciation of English has changed historically, while the spelling has tended

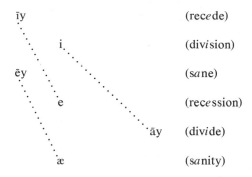

īy	(rec*e*de)
i	(divi sion)
ēy	(s*a*ne)
e	(rec*e*ssion)
āy	(div*i*de)
æ	(s*a*nity)

Figure 5.7. *Some Pairs of Vowels That Are Spelled Alike in Standard Spelling*

to remain the same. This arrangement persists, despite the efforts of spelling reformers over the centuries, largely because it serves a useful purpose; different forms of words that are related in meaning are spelled alike, as in pairs like *divide – division*. To the person who is reading silently for meaning, it is more to the point that these are two forms based on the same stem and with related meanings than that the pronunciation of the vowel differs.

Whatever the strengths and weaknesses of the standard spelling system, we have now characterized a large and central part of what children must learn in order to read and write English. The necessary learning is illustrated in the contrast between Figures 5.5 and 5.7. Once children have reached a stage of attempting to group speech sounds together in order to represent more than one sound with one spelling, then they have to learn that the basis for such grouping in standard spelling is not phonetic, but is more abstract. We should not be surprised to find that children are too close to the phonetic ground in their first attempts at spelling. The phonetic forms are, after all, their first and most basic information relevant to spelling. What is interesting is finding out that children have intuitions about phonetic relationships, and that these intuitions influence their spelling, so that the process of learning to spell, for many children, appears to be one of *replacing* one set of relationships with another, rather than a process of filling a void.

This insight may help to shape a teacher's comments in the classroom. It would seem that a teacher should distinguish between plausible and implausible spellings, both of which are nonstandard. In responding to a child's LAT for *let,* a teacher might even indicate that he or she understands that this is a reasonable attempt, that "it sounds as if it might be spelled with an *a.*"

I have chosen a few examples of vowel spellings for detailed consideration, to illustrate some of the processes by which we develop

133

linguistic descriptions and explanations. There are several other, equally interesting, characteristics of children's spelling and questions about how they categorize speech sounds. The questions that follow will suggest some of these to you.

Problems

1. See what you can learn from the following story written by a five-year-old. It appeared in a little folded booklet, with a picture on the front, a title page, and the story:

    HOO LICS HANE! HOO LICS HANE WAS OV PONA TIM
    THER WAS OV BER HOO LOVED HANE THE EAD

    The picture shows a little brown creature standing next to a tree.

    The spellings here are strongly influenced by standard spelling—the use of *OO* to represent [ūw], for instance. You will find, however, examples of omitted nasals, and of *I* and *E* used to represent their names.

    Sometimes children's spelling tells us what they know—or do not know—about how sentences divide into words and which word a particular pronunciation represents in a particular context. Note that OV is used twice to represent [ə]. Can you think why this might be reasonable? Does the pronunciation [ə] ever occur as the realization of a word that might be spelled OV? The spelling OV PONA reminds us that there are necessary steps in learning the language which we often take for granted (and which have been studied very little). Learning to read may help children to acquire information about their language which would be difficult to infer from the spoken form alone.

2. Consider the use of *D* in SDROGIST. From your knowledge of English phonetics, can you think of a reason why this spelling is probably not merely a mistake? If you or your instructor have a tape recorder and some splicing equipment, try recording normal pronunciations of *spy, sty,* and *sky* (or *spill, still,* and *skill*). Now move the tape slowly past the playback head of the recorder and splice out the [s] at the beginning of each word. Most people would expect that the remainder of each word would sound like *pie, tie,* and *"kye"* (or *pill, till,* and *kill*). What do they actually sound like? Why?

3. Consider the cases in which nasals have been omitted from the children's spelling:

SATU	(Santa)	(from problem one:)	
LOGIST	(longest)	WAS	(once)
SDROGIST	(strongest)	EAD	(end)

    This is in fact a very frequent phenomenon. See also Table 5.10 below.

    What do all these nasals have in common, with respect to the phonetic context in which they occur? Notice, from Figures 5.2, 5.3 and 5.4, and the data in problem 1, that these same children *do* represent nasals when they occur in other contexts, such as before a vowel. Is there any reason why nasals in these two kinds of contexts might be treated differently? Is there

Table 5.10 *Examples of Omissions of Preconsonantal Nasals*

BOPY	bumpy	MOSTR	monster	HACC	Hanks
NUBRS	numbers	PLAT	plant	THEKCE	thinks
ATTEPT	attempt	AD	and	AGRE	angry
GRAPO	Grampa	WOTET	want it	SEK	sink
STAPS	stamps	CAT	can't	NOOIGLID	New England

any phonetic basis for omitting nasals in just the contexts in which children tend to omit them?[4]

4. Try to collect some of your own examples of children's spelling and analyze them. You may or may not be able to find preschoolers who are making up their own spelling, and actual experimentation on children's judgments is a complicated and tricky business, but one approach that is usually fairly easy is to persuade a first-grade teacher to share some examples of students' spelling. You may even be able to propose some words to be used on a spelling exercise.

Bear in mind that the more experience a child has in reading and writing, the more his or her spelling will be influenced by the standard variety. As usual, a little knowledge can be misleading; children with a limited acquaintance with standard spelling often use standard spellings in nonstandard positions, such as the use of *CK* to spell [k] at the beginning of CKOBERA. Consequently, an explanation in terms of letter-names and phonetic relationships is often inappropriate for spellings by such children.

Nevertheless, some of the spelling patterns we have examined tend to persist in first or even second grade. Specifically, you may expect to find the use of *A* to spell [e] and the omission of preconsonantal nasals.

5. Think about the ways in which the study of children's spelling may be of use to teachers. What other kinds of frequent spelling errors are there? How might a teacher respond differently to a nonstandard spelling based on phonetic relationships than to a spelling that comes from inversion of letter-shapes (*b* for *d,* or *u* for *n,* for example)? How might a teacher distinguish between spellings based on phonetic relationships and misspellings based on incorrect discrimination of speech sounds? For instance, if a child has written SAND for *send,* how likely is it that he or she actually misperceived the word as *sand?* How could a teacher tell the difference? Why must a teacher be cautious about telling a child not to spell two different sounds with the same letter? Are some misspellings more sophisticated than others? Under what circumstances might a teacher encourage children to write a word "the way you think it should be spelled"? Is it possible that there is a trade-off between fluency of writing and standardness of spelling, at least at some ages? At what stage of development should children be urged to spell in the standard fashion? How could a teacher respond to a spelling such as SNACK for *snake,* in such a way as

---

4. Note: this question has more than one possible answer, and it involves some moderately technical phonetics. See Read op. cit., Section 2.4 and Chapter 4, for an extensive discussion and some experimental evidence.

to indicate to the child that the spelling is reasonable, even though "it is not the way they spell it in books"?

6. Here are two signs that my son made for my office:

    DOT MAK NOYS   THIS SI WER MI DADAAA WRX
    MY DADAAY WRX HIR   B CWIYIT

    • What characteristics of children's invented spelling can you identify?
    • In what respects is this spelling more like standard spelling?
    • Consider the spellings MY and MI. (These signs were made at the same time.) What common assumption about spelling do these violate?
    • Consider the two occurrences of WRX. How do these differ from the standard spelling of the third-person verb ending? What effect does that have on the communication of meaning through silent reading? Why do you think five-year-olds tend not to share the adult assumption that spelling should make it easy to identify the parts that make up a word, such as the stem and the ending in this case?
    • What does the writer assume that the reader knows? What sociolinguistic constraint is violated in "MY DADAAY"?

Suggestions for Further Reading

1. A detailed description of how writing began for one child: Chomsky, Carol. "Write First, Read Later." In *Childhood Education,* March, 1971, 296–99.
2. A summary, with examples and suggestions for encouraging spelling in an open classroom:

    Chomsky, Carol. "Invented Spelling in the Open Classroom." In *Word* 27, 1–3 (April–Dec., 1971). Child Language, 1975.

    What this reference means is that the article appears in a special issue of *Word* devoted to children's language. The issue was published in 1975, but it is officially the April–Dec., 1971, numbers of the journal.
3. More examples and illustrations of what can happen in a first-grade classroom where writing is encouraged. Chomsky, Carol. "How Sister Got Into the Grog." In *Early Years,* November, 1975.
4. A monograph on the spellings and on a series of experiments which investigated the phonetic basis of the spellings:

    Read, Charles. *Children's Categorization of Speech Sounds in English.* NCTE Research Report no. 17. Urbana, Ill.: 1975.

    This monograph includes tables of children's spellings for various phone-types of English (Appendices). It can be ordered from: National Council of Teachers of English, 1111 Kenyon Road, Urbana, Illinois 61801 (stock no. 06307).
5. Examples of stages of spelling development, with suggestions for primary teachers: Gentry, J. Richard, and Henderson, Edmund H. "Three Steps to Teaching Beginning Readers to Spell." In *The Reading Teacher,* March, 1978, 632–37.

Dialects

Chapter 6

Selections from Bengt Loman's "Conversations in a Negro American Dialect"

Timothy Shopen

Introduction

This chapter centers on the study of five conversations involving children ages 10 and 11, residents of Washington, D.C. These conversations are presented in Part 1 of the taped material for the chapter, which occurs at the beginning of the cassette accompanying this book. Five additional conversations are recorded on Part 2 of the taped material, conversations between three of the same children and adults. Each of these two parts runs approximately 11 minutes, and can be worked on independently.

1. Five Conversations

1.1 Initial Observations

CONVERSATION 1. Gregory J. (10) and Michael J. (10), cousins. *Suggested procedure:* listen first without reading; stop at the end of conversation 1 and go back to the beginning. Did you have difficulty understanding Gregory's and Michael's speech? If so, do you think they would have trouble understanding yours? Next, read the transcription below as you listen.

To those who had trouble understanding the first time through, is it easier to understand now? Why? Are the main differences between your speech and the speech here a matter of vocabulary and word order, or do they have to do with pronunciation? See if you can find

139

The Cassette, from the Beginning of Side I

Part I: Five Conversations (11:02)

Conversation 1:	Gregory J. (10) and Michael J. (10), cousins	(1:31)
Conversation 2:	Jacqueline D. (11) and Michael J.	(0:46)
Conversation 3:	Anita P. (10) and Jacqueline D.	(2:31)
Conversation 4:	Jacqueline D., Anita P., and Sandy B. (one of the interviewers)	(1:07)
Conversation 5:	Anita P., Margy G. (one of the interviewers), Michael J., and Jacqueline D.	(4:30)

Part II: Five Additional Conversations (11:09)

Conversation 6:	Gregory J. and his aunt Patricia J.	(3:13)
Conversation 7:	Gregory J. and Patricia J.	(1:39)
Conversation 8:	Gregory J. and Margy G.	(2:14)
Conversation 9:	Jacqueline D. and Margy G.	(1:56)
Conversation 10:	Anita P. and Margy G.	(1:42)

any vocabulary that is foreign to your speech; if there is any, ask yourself if you have trouble understanding it. Next, see if you can find any instances where the way words are combined to form sentences appears different. Now compare these factors to pronunciation. Do you have an impression of what the social and economic background of these children is? If so, jot it down, and jot down what features of their speech have led to this impression. Listen to this conversation until you can understand it without reading. As you do so, describe to yourself the kind of conversation it is. What is going on between the two boys? A transcription of the conversation on the tape:

GJ: You come here with you shirt going all a-way down here, and your shirt sticking out . . .

MJ: Who?

GJ: You!

MJ: I don't wear no shirts like that. Do you see this one? . . . way, way, way . . .

GJ: I thought you say you don't wear no shirts that go all a-way down to here.

MJ: I didn't say that.

GJ: You did so say that.

MJ: This one's supposed to go there.

GJ: Don't do that. Shut up!

MJ: I bet you I got more money than you. I got cash money in my pocket now.

GJ: You ain't got no cash money . . .

MJ: You want to bet? (LAUGHS)

GJ: You ain't got nothing but fifty cent, and you got to buy a notebook with that. (LAUGHS)

MJ: I got a notebook and paper now.

GJ: You ain't got no notebook and paper, so be quiet, big mouth!

MJ: . . . one, two, three, four, five, six, seven, eight, nine, ten, eleven . . .

GJ: . . . four . . . You got six cent . . . You got six cent.

MJ: Ain't this cash money?

GJ: No, that's not cash money, that's not even over a dollar.

MJ: I bet you it is. This cash money when you got fifty cent. That's cash money.

GJ: That ain't no cash money, that's half a dollar.

MJ: It is, boy.

GJ: You don't know what you talking about.

MJ: What's cash money?

GJ: It ain't that. That's why you so dumb in school because you always calling fifty cent cash (LAUGHS) money.

MJ: So why you have to borrow—borrow my pencil because I let you use it now?

GJ: I know and it wasn't your pencil; it was the teacher's pencil.

MJ: So.

GJ: I know and you have just let somebody else use it.

MJ: So you got teacher pencil in your pocket!

CONVERSATION 2. Jacqueline D. (11) and Michael J. Again, listen both with and without the transcription as an aid. Keep an ear and an eye open for what appear to you as distinctive grammatical features. Classify the style of each conversation, what the goal of the communication seems to be for each of the speakers. Particularly in the next three conversations, 2, 3, and 4, take note of what is revealed about the life and attitudes of these children.

JD: You pointing at my foot looks like.

MJ: I'm pointing at you. You want to do something about it? You want to use this?

JD: Did I ask you to use that old smelly thing?

MJ: Well let's see your one.

JD: Well I don't carry such.

MJ: I know you don't carry such because you can't afford such . . . ha ha!

JD: I have more than what you got.

MJ: I bet you you don't. Do you got a twenty dollar coat? No, you got a twenty dollar pair of shoes. Yeah, right there . . . huh . . . Got a twenty dollar coat?

JD: I'm telling you the truth about it. I don't have one.

CONVERSATION 3. Anita P. (10) and Jacqueline D. There are two versions of the same story here. Note the variation.

AP: That's the story I'm telling.

JD: And mines ain't about no ghost.

AP: And all three of them men, and so, so one . . . the white man went there first . . . and the, and the ghost scared him out. And so he ranned out . . . And so, . . . mmm . . . And the Chinese man went in there and so he tried to eat them beans and the ghost scared him out . . . So the colored man went in there and he say . . . And he scared, and he was scaring the colored man . . . colored man say " . . I'm a kill . . . I'm a . . " no, the ghost say "I'm a kill you . . . " And the ghost say . . . and the . . . and the colored man say "I'm a kill you if you mess with these beans . . . " Something like that.

JD: See . . . it was a . . . it was a . . . a white man, a Chinese man and a colored man. So . . . so one morning they had . . . they had a whole houseful of food, you know. So one day it was Thanksgiving and they had a big old turkey and they put a whole lot of stuff on . . . no, on the . . . on the table you know . . . so . . . all . . . and then they cooked all that stuff and then all they had, and then that that evening when they finish eating they looked in the ice box and they say "All we have left is some baloney and beans," and so . . . ah . . . so they went upstairs, you know, and they say "The one that has the best dream, the one, the first person that has the best dream can . . . can . . . can . . . ah . . . eat the . . . the . . . the . . . beans and the hot dog," I mean "the beans and the baloney," you know, so . . . so they woke up that morning, so the white man said "What you have . . .," that white man say "How, what, what did you have . . ., what, what kind of dream did you have?" He was talking to the Chinese man. So he say, so the Chinese man say "I dream I was, I was sitting down at a silver table, eating out of silver plate," and he say "I . . . I dream that I had all of this good food on my table," and so the colored man, so the, so the white, so the other white man said . . . say . . . ahm . . . what, what did, what did you, what did you . . .," and then the colored man say "What did you dream about?", told, asked the white man what did he dream about. So he, he say, so he say "I, I dreamed I was, I was . . . ah . . . riding in a golden car and I had a chauffer," . . . What's the name of those things?

CONVERSATION 4.   Jacqueline D., Anita P., and Sandy B. (one of the interviewers). The text:

JD: And sometimes, we make them laugh, we, they, we make somebody laugh when we be doing that, you know, whoever it be crying we make them laugh so hard that they, they, that, that they be steadily, they be steadily crying and laughing back. And then we used to say, and then we used to say, when they do that we used to say "Crying when you laughing!" (LAUGHS) We used to say all like that. We'll say "Crying when you laughing!"

AP: Who is "we" now?

JD: People in our our house and everybody start laughing.

AP: Crying when you shaking. Sandy go and see is the tape over.

SB: Oh, it isn't. We got a long way to go.

JD: Sandy, you know what?

SB: What?

JD: I, I know . . . ah . . . ah . . . people cry and . . . I know people, I know that people would, ah, when they come back from a funeral home, that they, that they, that they have a party or something and drink and stuff for to, just to make them happy.

SB: Yeah . . . Who told you that?

JD: My, my teacher.

CONVERSATION 5.   Anita P., Margy G. (one of the interviewers), Michael J., and Jacqueline D. After the first several remarks, this selection consists entirely of two stories, one about "Who killed Abraham Lincoln?" told by Anita P. and the second "Little Red Riding Hood," told by Jacqueline D. This time the transcription will not be provided. If you needed the transcription as a listening aid in the first conversation, you will probably find it much easier to understand now without reading. Could this be because you have become more used to the speech of these children? There is another factor to consider. Until conversation 4, there was no indication the children were including anyone else in the sphere of communication. In conversations 4 and 5, on the other hand, we can tell that one of the interviewers is present. Could that make a difference? If so, why?

As you listen to "Who Killed Abraham Lincoln?" and "Little Red Riding Hood," jot down your observations about the structure of the plot in each case and the style with which the stories are told. Conversation 5 ends the taped material for Part 1 of this chapter.

1.2 Analysis and Discussion

(1) In conversation 5, transcribe, with standard spelling, a passage of about fifty words, starting with either (a) the point after Anita P. starts her story by saying "and so this boy said . . . so this boy . . . so the teacher asked the children 'Who killed Abraham Lincoln?' . . ." or (b) after Jacqueline D. begins hers by saying "Once upon a time (LAUGHTER) it was, it was Little Red Riding Hood and her, and her

mother. . . ." In the passage you transcribe, underline or circle the parts of each word where the pronunciation is markedly different from your own.

(2) Give five words in the passage you have transcribed that illustrate a difference in pronunciation between you and the person talking. Give the best phonetic transcription you can in each case for your pronunciation and the pronunciation on the tape.

(3) In comparing your pronunciation to that of the children on the tape, you may be considering only one of the styles in which you talk. Many of the pronunciations used by these children which have been stigmatized as "substandard" occur as completely acceptable variants in the informal speech of "standard" speakers. Social class distinctions in speech often depend on the contexts in which a person uses a nonstandard form. All speakers vary between the socially acceptable pronunciation of the *ing* suffix and its "dropped *g*" variant. Notice how you say a sentence like "What are you working on?" and see if you don't sometimes say *workin* instead of *working*. A similar situation exists for the *th* at the beginning of words like *the, this, that, these,* and *those*. On the tape, Anita P. varies between *this* and *dis* for "this." Many more speakers than realize it (or would care to admit it) use a *d* pronunciation in informal speech. Try something like "What are you going to do with the canary cage?" and see what happens to the pronunciation of "the." Spend some time listening to people talk in a natural and informal style and see if you can hear variation in the pronunciation of the *-ing* suffix or of the *th* sound in words like *the* and *this*. Report your observations about the variation you have heard and discuss who was talking and in what situation.

(4) One of the major innovative processes at work in the speech of these children is consonant cluster simplification, the elimination of one or more of a group of consonants that come together in the stream of speech. If you sometimes leave out the *d* sound in "good-bye, bad-boy," etc., you are simplifying the consonant cluster *db*, a cluster created by putting a word ending in *d* in front of a word beginning with *b*. Consonant clusters also occur within words. Note the *t* in the words "Christmas," "chestnut," "fasten," "hasten," "listen," "soften," "castle," and "whistle." The *t* sound was pronounced by the English-speaking world in these words at one point, giving sequences of three consonant sounds in a row, *stm, stn, ftn,* and *stl*. Now the *t* is silent and retained only in the spelling. The *t* in "often" is teetering: a relative minority of American English speakers pronounce it. The consonant

clusters that get simplified in the speech of these children occur most often at the ends of words, never at the beginning. The words "bring," "truth," "three," "dream," "cry," "grandmother," "school," "smelly," "stuff," "quiet," and "twenty" all have clusters of consonant sounds at the beginning, which are fully pronounced on this tape.

Check the variation in your speech and in that of others around you in the pronunciation of the final consonant clusters in "ask" and "ghost" (both of these words occur on the tape) in contexts such as the following:

ask They ought to ask him.
       He asks too many questions.
       Bill asked me yesterday.

ghost He said there was a ghost in his dream.
         He said there were some ghosts in his dream.
         It was a ghostly dream.

By putting the endings *-s, -ed, -ly,* etc. on these words, the consonant clusters *-sk,* and *-st* are made longer. "Asks" gives us *sks,* "asked" gives us the sounds *skt,* "ghosts" gives us *sts* and "ghostly" gives us *stl.* The question is whether or not people always say all of these consonants, and if they don't, what ones they leave out. Report your observations.

(5) To enlarge the scope of your observation, consider verbs like "lisp," "roast," and "frisk," nouns like "wasp," "waist," and "desk": these words end with the consonant sequences *-sp, -st,* and *-sk.* Find endings that can be put on these words that will lengthen the sequences of consonants. They can all take an *-s* ending. The verbs can take an *-ed* ending (which will have the effect of adding a *t* sound except when the verb root already ends in a *t* sound). In addition, you can put words immediately after that begin with consonants, as in expressions like "wasp nest," "waist line," and "desk drawer." These expressions produce the sequences *spn, stl,* and *skdr.* But do you or the people around you always pronounce all these sounds in natural speech? Write down the additional data you consider and your observations. If you have found that there can be simplification of the consonant clusters you have examined here, describe what principle is involved. What sounds can be left out? In what context?

(6) In the same vein, consider what happens to the voiced and voiceless *th* sounds when they occur at the end of word roots. How do you say the verb "clothe"? The same unit of meaning occurs in the

noun "clothes." Is there variation in respect to the *th* sound? Check other speakers to see if they say "clothes" the same as "close" as in "Close the door!" Similarly, compare "breathe" with "breathes." Is one of them pronounced like "breeze"? What is your plural for "moth"? Does it sound the same as "moss"? Related to this is the pronunciation of fractions. Do people ever pronounce "eighths" in "3/8" so that it rhymes with "hates"? Consider the pronunciation of fractions like 2/5, 5/6, 6/7. Write down the additional examples you consider and your observations. Describe the principle determining when people are likely not to pronounce the *th* sounds.

(7) Conversation 1 is a competition between the cousins Gregory and Michael, a kind of verbal jousting match. It has a distinct structure with each boy in turn trying a ploy to put the other one down. Outline the structure of the conversation in terms of Gregory and Michael's ploys and counterploys.

(8) Give examples of five negative sentences in conversation 1 and write how you would express the same meanings in your own speech.

(9) Write down the equivalents in your speech for the parts of the following lines in italics:
  (a) (Con. 2, line 5) MJ: "Well let's see *your one*"
  (b) (Con. 2, lines 6–7) JD: "Well I don't carry *such . . .*" MJ: "*. . . such . . . such . . .*"
  (c) (Con. 2, line 10) MJ: "*Do you got* a twenty dollar coat?"
  (d) (Con. 3, line 2) JD: "And *mines* ain't about no ghost."
  (e) (Con. 3, lines 9–10) AP: "*I'm a kill* you"
  (f) (Con. 3, line 13) JD: "*it was a . . . a white man . . .*"
  (g) (Con. 4, line 2) JD: "*whoever it be crying*"
  (h) (Con. 4, line 4) JD: "*they be steadily crying*"
  (i) (Con. 4, line 10) AP: "go and see *is the tape over*"

(10) Fill in the blanks:
Examples: It's their house.   It's ___THEIRS___
             It's your house.   It's _____
             It's our house.   It's _____
             It's her house.   It's _____
             It's his house.   It's _____
             It's my house.   It's _____

In what way could the form *mines* in question (9d) above be called a regularization? Give the question that corresponds to each of the following statements.

Examples: You're laughing.   <u>ARE YOU LAUGHING?</u>

                You've been crying.   _____

                You could be mistaken.   _____

                You can swim.   _____

                You'll come.   _____

                You like Ernie.   _____

                You need a pencil.   _____

What principle do you follow to turn a statement into a question? What statement corresponds to (9c) *Do you got a twenty dollar coat?* How would MJ make that statement? Find evidence in conversation 1 to support your hypothesis. Then is MJ following the same rule that you do for forming questions?

(11) Comment on the story "Little Red Riding Hood" as told by Jacqueline D. in conversation 5. Consider it as verbal art. First, is there a 'correct' form of the story? Does Jacqueline tell the story the way you have read it in books? Should an English teacher encourage this kind of imaginative retelling, or should he correct her and get her to tell the story in its traditional form? Second, what does Jacqueline's rendition of the story reveal about her life, our lives, and the contemporary scene in the cities?

(12) Write briefly what you would consider to be a likely biography of one of the young people in this tape. Include a characterization of social and economic background. Then comment on what it is in the way these children speak that enables you to know as much as you do about them, or to put the matter differently, what it is in the way these children speak that might be important to them as part of their sense of social identity?

2. Five Additional Conversations

Listen to the rest of the tape for this chapter where five conversations take place between adults and children. Featured in conversations 6, 7, and 8 is Gregory J., the same boy you heard in conversation 1. In conversations 6 and 7 he is speaking with his aunt, Patricia J. In conversation 8 he is talking with Margy G., the interviewer you heard in conversation 5. In conversation 9 Margy G. talks with Jacqueline D., the girl you heard in conversations 2, 3, 4, and 5. In the final conversation, conversation 10, Margy G. talks with Anita P., the girl you heard in conversations 3, 4, and 5.

    Comment on the form and function of the speech in these conversations. There are a number of interesting questions to consider. For example, do the children talk differently when talking to adults than when talking to other children? Do they have different goals in those two contexts? What do the goals of the adults appear to be here? Who directs the course of the dialogues? If you conclude that the adults are trying to teach the children something, what kind of speech do they use for this purpose? Do they tell them what to do directly in every case? One detail worthy of note is the way in which the adults use very polite language to criticize the children. Note the use of questions in this regard.*

Suggestions for Further Reading (and Listening)

This chapter is based on selections from the fine tape recordings made by Bengt Loman for his study *Conversations in a Negro American Dialect,* Washington, D. C.: Center for Applied Linguistics, 1967 (book and tape). Interested persons may wish to listen to all of this tape: it is fully transcribed in the book.

Dillard, J. L. *Black English: Its History and Usage in the United States.* New York: Random House, 1972. Especially Chapter VI entitled "Who Speaks Black English." Dillard's work should, however, be read with some caution since he seems to exaggerate some of the differences between Vernacular Black English and other varieties.

Burling, Robins. *English in Black and White.* New York: Holt, Rinehart and Winston, 1973. This book gives a readable account of some of the main characteristics of the variety of English exemplified in this chapter, along with some relevant educational considerations.

Labov, William. *Language in the Inner City.* Philadelphia: The University of Pennsylvania Press, 1972. It gives a detailed account of Black English; some of it requires considerable linguistic background, but important portions of it are accessible to any interested reader, such as the brilliant chapter "The Logic of Nonstandard English." It is an invaluable resource book on which much of the discussion in current literature is derived.

Kochman, Thomas E., ed. *Rappin' and Stylin' Out.* Urbana: University of Illinois Press, 1972. This book is concerned with the functional uses of language in the Black community and is therefore complementary with descriptions of linguistic features.

Fasold, Ralph W. and Wolfram, Walt. "Some Linguistic Features of Negro Dialect," in *Teaching Standard English in the Inner City* (Urban Language Series 6) edited by Ralph W. Fasold and Roger Shuy, Washington,

---

*The author wishes to thank the Center for Applied Linguistics for making material from Bengt Loman's study available, and Bengt Loman for having made such excellent-quality recordings. In addition, the author expresses gratitude to Charles Bird, Wayles Browne, Walt Wolfram, and especially Richard Wright for very helpful suggestions.

D. C.: Center for Applied Linguistics, 1970, pp. 41–86. It is a fairly concise treatment of the linguistic features of Vernacular Black English that should be readable for the nonlinguist, although it covers many of the linguistic rules characteristic of the variety.

Smith, Arthur. *Language Rhetoric and Communication in Black America*. New York: Harper and Row, 1972. This book is a fairly comprehensive anthology of the scope of language in the Black community, focusing on functional aspects of communication and rhetoric.

Chapter 7

The Speech of the New York City Upper Class

Geoffrey Nunberg

Geoffrey Nunberg has taught linguistics at the City University of New York and is currently a fellow at the Institute of Human Learning at the University of California at Berkeley. His research interests include semantics, sociolinguistics, and poetics and stylistics. He is very middle class.

Introduction: The Upper Class in America

The term "social class" has been used in several different ways. For most American sociologists, to say that someone is "working class" is simply to place him at a certain point on the socioeconomic scale; to characterize him in terms of those factors—income, education, and occupation—that determine status in American society. Used in this way, "working class" is a convenience term that chops off a certain slice of a continuum in the way that "cold," "cool," "tepid," "warm," and "hot" divide up the scale of temperature.

But a class may be more than this; the term is also used to refer to groups whose members share common social attitudes and feel closely connected to one another. Most Europeans feel a strong sense of identification with their class group, and so social classes in Europe have tended to act in concert politically and socially. But in America, "class loyalty" is not a strong force; many Americans feel stronger ties to ethnic and racial groups and are not accustomed to thinking of themselves as members of such-and-such a class. If pressed, they will generally identify themselves as "middle class," whether they work as bus drivers or bank presidents. The English writer George Orwell wrote that, in school, he was very much aware of his status as a member of the "lower upper-middle class," but few Americans would be capable of making such a fine determination. Of course, factors like income and occupation determine where people live and who they associate with, and these in turn are important in determining social behavior, including language habits. But all of these factors are subject

---

The Cassette, 22:11 from the Beginning of Side I

Part I: Local Features in the Dialect   (6:42)

Section 1.1 How to Say "Coffee" and "Dog" (Passage A)   (1:14)
Bryan L. (middle-class Californian, student, 24)
Judy E. (lower-middle class, secretary, 27)
Robert H. (working class, route manager, 23)
Barbara D. (upper class, book editor, 32)
Robert N. (upper class, college teacher, 31)

Section 1.2 How to Say "Aunt" and "Fast" (Passage B)   (2:44)
Judy E., Robert H., Barbara D., Robert N., and
Peyton M. (upper class, student, 24)

Section 1.3 Studied Indifference (Passages A and B)   (2:21)
Passage A: Judy E., Barbara D., and
David L. (middle class, advertiser, 37)
Passage B: Judy E., Robert N., and David L.

The Cassette, from the Beginning of Side II

Part II: The Features in Time and Space   (16:51)

Section 2.1 Changes in Upper Class Speech (Passage C and
conversation)   (6:42)
Reading: Robert H., Robert N., Leo G. (working class,
student, 25); *Conversation:* Leo G., Robert N.;
Reading: Jane C. (upper class, housewife, 44);
Conversation: Lawrence M. (upper class, diplomat, born 1903),
Carter C. (upper class, publisher, born 1897), Henry S.
(upper class, politician, born 1880)

Section 2.2 The New York City Upper Class and the Upper Class
Elsewhere (Passage D and conversation)   (3:42)
Reading: Robert N., Barbara D., Peyton M., Judy E.,
Bryan L., Leo G., Weston T. (Boston upper class, art
dealer, 32), Nancy G. (Boston upper class, political
activist, 27); *Conversation:* Robert N.; *Reading and
Conversation:* Betty W. (Boston middle class aspiring
to upper class, college teacher, 33)

Section 2.3 It Takes One to Know One (conversation)   (6:04)
Barbara D., Peyton M., Jane C., Weston T., Peyton M.

---

to casual change. When the children of a bus driver go on to college and professions, their social status changes, and with it, their social behavior.

The American upper class, however, is in many ways an exceptional case. Membership is not determined solely by education and income; the most important determination is lineage; i.e., family background. Jones and Smith may have gone to the same college, live next door to one another, and work at similar jobs for the same company; but Jones may nonetheless be considered upper class, while Smith is not. In this respect, the American upper class has been compared to a "caste," a social group whose membership is determined entirely by lineage, such as is found in India. Perhaps "upper class" is a misleading term, since one can enjoy considerable power and prestige without being a member of it. Some writers have preferred to talk about "society," or "metropolitan 400"—a term we'll discuss below.

In the nineteenth century, and before, the quotes around "upper class" would not have been necessary. The class was then an elite group consisting of the descendents of old families who had made their fortunes in finance and industry. Throughout this period, there were attempts to consolidate the upper class into a fixed aristocracy, of the sort found in European countries. Lists of "good" families were compiled, and leaders here and there tried to set themselves up as arbiters of who should and should not be included in "society." (The expression "the 400," often used to refer to the urban upper class, comes from the remark of Ward McAllister, the nineteenth-century New Yorker who made up the first "social register," that there were really only 400 people in New York society. "If you go outside that number, you strike people who are either not at ease in a ballroom or else make other people not at ease.")

But these efforts did not succeed in closing off the upper classes; the children and grandchildren of the newly rich and powerful soon gained access to society drawing rooms. In 1870, Mrs. Astor (the descendent of an old New York family and the reigning duchess of New York society) tried to snub Mrs. Vanderbilt (of a more recently acquired railroad fortune); by 1883, she was forced to recognize the upstart. Abraham Lincoln was far too rough and uncultured for the nineteenth-century upper class; but his son, Robert Todd Lincoln, played a central role in the upper-class community. By contrast, for all the political and financial success that the Kennedy family has achieved, they have never been accepted by the Boston aristocracy. In the twentieth century, the upper class has become much more of a closed group. (We'll talk later about some of the reasons for these social changes, in connection with the discussion of the restoration of *r* in upper-class speech.) The effect has been to increase the social isolation of the upper class, which has lost a large part of its social and cultural "authority," as membership in it becomes less and less a prerequisite to obtaining power and success.

Probably because power has never been centralized in any one American city, we do not have a national upper class, as does England, where the nobility and gentry of all regions have functioned as a cohesive, close-knit group since the seventeenth century. The children of a London banker, of a Manchester industrialist, and of a Cambridge warden are packed off at an early age to one of a few "public" schools and later to the same universities; here they meet and form friendships that transcend their regional origins. (One important result of this process is that they emerge from school speaking very much the same dialect, wherever they may have been born. This dialect is called "Received Pronunciation" or RP, and although it shows some variation, according to the age and precise social level of its speakers, it is remarkably uniform throughout Britain.)

In America, by contrast, aristocracies tend to be local products. Philadelphia, New York, Boston, San Francisco, Baltimore, Chicago, Pittsburgh—each of these cities has its own hierarchy of "good" families. While there is a lot of contact between the groups, they do tend to socialize with people from the same region and to send their children to local schools. In New York, for example, both boys and girls are likely to attend a private grade school within the city; after this, the boys, but generally not the girls, will attend a New England prep school. As a result, the speech of the upper class in New York, like the speech of other upper-class speakers, always shows marked regional characteristics.

The members of the upper class in any large city will have a number of things in common. Most will be listed in the local *Social Register*. There are at present thirteen regional editions, which purport to give the names of "those families who by descent or social standing or from other qualifications are naturally included in the best society." The *Social Register* gives names, addresses, club and university affiliations, and, most important, schools. Among the upper class, what matters most is attendance at the "right" secondary school, not at a good college. (Admission policies at the best eastern universities have by now become so stringent that even graduates of the "best" eastern prep schools may have to attend universities in other parts of the country.)

After schooling, members of the upper class usually go on to careers in business or the professions. Despite the fact that their absolute power may have diminished in this country, they remain an important force; directly or indirectly, they control many huge fortunes and they sit on the boards of the banks, museums, universities, and city clubs that dominate much of the political, cultural, and economic life of the community. Social connections are maintained through membership in town and country clubs, at summer resorts, and through sports (riding, yachting, skiing, and tennis). It is still unusual to marry outside the class, probably because young people are unlikely to meet members of other classes.

The upper class is a curious institution, flourishing in the midst of a pluralistic, avowedly democratic society. Most people who have come into extended contact with it wind up having strong feelings about it, though these feelings are often suppressed. And the members

153

of the class are themselves aware of this; their consciousness of the position they occupy, and of their anomalous role, plays an important part in determining their social behavior.

Language is social behavior *par excellence,* and the speech of the upper class mirrors in many ways its position in American society. In particular, we can see in the speech of upper-class New Yorkers markers of all the communities in which they function. There are features that are shared by many other New Yorkers, features shared only with the upper classes of other regions, and features that reflect the influence of a "general American" middle-class pattern, because it is with all of these groups that members of the New York upper class interact.

There will be two main parts to the discussion. First we will examine several of the local features of New York City upper-class speech and see it as very much a part of the language of the city as a whole. In the second part we will expand to a wider context of time and space; here we will see roots in the general population of New York, but on the other hand we will also see a special sense of identity with upper-class speakers across the eastern seaboard.

How to Use This Chapter

In this chapter, we'll look at some of these features and try to relate them to the social position of the upper class. The chapter is designed to be used along with the taped material on the cassette accompanying this book. The work for the chapter can be done in two parts, each corresponding to the two main parts of the chapter. For each of the two main parts there will be three sections containing selections from speakers who are identified by first name and initial—as "Judy E.," "Robert N.," and so forth. The social background of the speakers will be given in the text, but you may find it useful to consult the table at the end of the chapter, which lists the age, native city, and social background of each of the speakers on the tape. With that table is also a list of the order in which the speakers appear in the various sections of the tape.

It will probably be easiest to use the tape in the following way. First read the section of the text that discusses a given linguistic feature; this will tell you what part of the tape to play and what to listen for. Then play the relevant section of the tape over several times until you can hear clearly the different pronunciations. Some of the differences are rather subtle; you will find it easier to hear them if you try to imitate the pronunciations as you play them, comparing yourself to the tape. Once you have "got" the pronunciations, reread the portion of the chapter that discusses them.

1. Local Features in the Dialect of the New York City Upper Class

Though upper-class children are often sent away to school and college, they remain very much a part of the New York City speech community, and this is evident in their speech. For example, it is characteristic of New York speech to say "I was waiting *on* line" and to ask for "change *of* a dollar"; upper-class New Yorkers share this feature. But the linguistic affinities go much deeper than this—into the basic patterns of pronunciation. A good example is the way in which they pronounce the vowel sound of words like *call, dog,* and *awful.* This vowel is subject to considerable variation in most parts of America. In some regions, such as the Northwest, the vowel of *call* and *caught* is sounded the same as the vowel of *collar* and *cot* ([ā]), with the mouth wide open and the lips unrounded, as in *father.* We can call this variant *AH.* In other regions, the vowel in *call* and *caught* is produced with the lips slightly rounded ([ɔ]); we'll call this *AW.* In some parts of the Northeast, particularly in New York City, these words are pronounced with a vowel that sounds almost like the vowel of *coal, coat* ([ōw]); the lips are quite rounded, and the mouth is somewhat less open; this is the *OH* variant.

1.1   How to Say *"Coffee"* and *"Dog"*

In this portion of the tape, speakers can be heard reading a passage that contains a number of words in which these variants can be heard:

Passage A.   We *always* had *chocolate* milk and *coffee* cake around *four* o'clock. My *dog* used to give us an *awful* lot of trouble; he jumped *all* over us when he *saw* the *coffee* cake. We *called* him "Hungry Sam."

Before playing the tape, read this passage aloud, and then listen to how you say the *stressed* vowel in each of the italicized words. Do you say *call* as "cAHl," for example, with the same vowel as the first syllable of *collar?* Many speakers use one vowel in *call,* and another in *awful,* or pronounce *chocolate* and *coffee* with different vowels. Try saying just the first syllable of each of these words, and see if you pronounce them with the same vowel.

The first speaker is Bryan L., 24, a middle-class Californian (his

155

father is a naval officer). He generally uses the AW vowel in the underlined words. Play his passage over several times and try to imitate his pronunciation of words like *call* and *coffee*. Check to see whether your lips are more rounded when you imitate his pronunciation than when you pronounce the word in your own way. If they are much more rounded, then your own pronunciation is probably OH; if they are much less rounded, then you probably say AH.

The second speaker is Judy E., 27, a lower-middle class New Yorker (she works as a secretary; her father is a supervisor for the phone company). She pronounces the italicized words with the OH variant: listen to the way she says *saw, coffee,* and *call,* and try to imitate her. This pronunciation is characteristic of most New York City speakers, though to varying degrees; it is most marked in the speech of the working class. Listen to the third speaker, Robert H., 23, a native Manhattanite of working-class background—his father is a factory foreman. His pronunciation of the OH vowel should be quite distinct, especially in the words *coffee* and *dog.* If you have trouble hearing it at first, play the tape over, and try to imitate the pronunciations you hear as closely as possible. Notice how rounded your lips are when you make the OH vowel that Robert H. uses.

The fourth speaker is Barbara D., 32, an upper-class New Yorker (her father is the minister of a fashionable church). The final speaker is Robert N., 31, also upper-class (his father is the president of a large advertising agency that was started by his grandfather). Both of these speakers attended "good" eastern prep schools. Play both of these speakers together. Notice that both of them use the OH variant, like Judy E. and Robert H., except in one of the italicized words— you should be able to identify this exception. There is a slight difference between the way in which the upper-class speakers say *call* and *coffee* and the way in which Judy E. or Robert H. says them: you may or may not be able to hear it. But the four New Yorkers are much closer in pronunciation to each other than any of them is to Bryan L., the Californian.

1.2 How to Say *"Fast"* and *"Aunt"*

The next passage to be heard contains a number of words with "short *a*":

Passage B. We used to play "kick the *can.*" One *man* is "it," and you run *past* him as *fast* as you *can,* and you kick a tin *can* so he *can't tag* you. *Sammy* used to *grab* the *can* and *dash* down the street; we'd chase him with a baseball *bat* and yell, *"Bad* boy, *bad, bad!"* But he was too *fast.* Only my *aunt* could *catch* him. She could even make him *ask* for a *glass* of milk. That was *rather* clever of her, don't you think?

(In this part of the tape, as well as in some of the parts that follow, different speakers may read slightly different passages, or may misread parts of the passages, leaving out phrases. Not all of the speakers read a version of this passage that ends "That was rather clever of her, don't you think?" To give us another occurrence of the short *a* vowel, we have left in the end of the preceding passage with the word "Sam.") The pronunciation of short *a* varies even more from dialect to dialect than does the pronunciation of the AW/OH words in passage A. Some speakers pronounce it as Æ, the vowel [æ] as in *bad,* with the mouth wide open. Others pronounce it as EH, with the mouth slightly closed and the lips spread; more like the vowel of *bed* ([e]), but drawn out long. Which variant is used depends, not only on the regional and social background of the speaker, but on which sounds follow the vowel. Some speakers use EH only when the vowel is followed by a nasal sound, as in *can, can't, Sammy,* and *man;* in other words, they use Æ. Other speakers use EH, not only before nasals, but also in words where short *a* is followed by a voiceless fricative sound (that is, *f, th, s,* and *sh*), as in *past, fast, dash, ask,* and *glass.* Some people also use EH in words where short *a* is followed by a voiced stop sound (*b, d, g*), as *tag, grab,* and *bad.* And some speakers use EH in all words, no matter what the following sound is.

To get straight on this, try reading the passage aloud before playing the tape. Check your own pronunciations of the words against Table 7.1. For each class of sounds, see whether you say EH (with the lips spread) for Æ (with the mouth wide open. Note: some speakers who use EH before nasals may nonetheless use Æ in the auxiliary verb *can,* as in " . . . as fast as you *can.*")

The first speaker to read Passage B is Judy E., the lower-middle-class New Yorker. Notice that she uses the EH vowel in all but one of the classes of words listed above (except for the auxiliary *can*). This is characteristic of most New Yorkers. (The use of EH in class IV like *catch* and *bat* is a feature of many midwest dialects.) The second

Table 7.1. *Four Classes of Words for the "Short a" Sound*

	I	II	III	IV
Words	*a + nasal* (can, man, Sammy, aunt)	*a + s, sh* (past, fast dash, ask, glass)	*a + b, d, g* (tag, grab, bad)	*other words* (bat, catch, rather)
Vowels	Æ			
	EH			

speaker is Robert H., working-class. The third speaker is Barbara D., upper class. She used EH in the words in classes I and III above, but uses Æ in words in classes II and IV. In two words, she uses AH instead of short *a;* these should not be hard to identify. The fourth speaker is Robert N. Although he is of roughly the same background as Peyton M., his pronunciation comes closer to that of Judy E. and Robert H.—compare him and Peyton on the words *past* and *fast* and note that he uses AH in one of the words in which Barbara D. and Robert H. use EH—we'll talk about this particular word later on. The final speaker is Peyton M., 24, another upper-class New Yorker. Note his pronunciation of the word on which Barbara D. and Robert N. differed—which pattern does he follow? Note also his pronunciation of the word *rather,* which was not contained in the passage read by Barbara D. and Robert N.

Once you have listened to this section of the tape several times, try to fill in Table 7.2. For each word, indicate whether each speaker has EH, Æ, or AH. (For some words, it will be hard to tell; in those instances put a question mark.)

Despite the differences between them, it is clear with "short a" words that all the speakers again show a similar pattern; they share

Table 7.2. *Summary Chart for the Reading of Passage B. For each word indicate whether each speaker has EH, Æ, or AH.*

| | | Speaker | | | | |
| | | Judy E. | Robert H. | Barbara D. | Robert N. | Peyton M. |
Word Class	Words					
I. (-n, -m)	can (noun) man Sammy aunt					
II. (-s, -sh)	past fast dash ask glass					
III. (-b, -d, -g)	tag grab bad					
IV. (other)	bat catch rather					

certain features that are characteristic of the region, but there remain indications of the social distances between them.

1.3   Studied Indifference

Inasmuch as the New Yorkers we have listened to are so much alike in their pronunciation of words in passages A and B, one would expect that other New Yorkers would all show the same linguistic pattern. But surprisingly, this is not the case. The first three speakers here are all reading passage A ("We used to have chocolate milk . . . "). The first is Judy E. (lower-middle class). The second is Barbara D. (upper class). Both show the same pattern of OH pronunciations—note that Barbara D., like Peyton M. and Robert N., says AH in *chocolate*. But the third speaker, David L., 36, has a pronunciation that is much closer to the AW shown by the Californian, Bryan L. David L. is a middle-class New Yorker whose father ran a small business. His pronunciation is not uncommon among other middle-class speakers and presents us with a real puzzle. How is it that people at the lower and upper ends of the social scale come to do one thing, and those in the middle another?

Next we have Judy E. (lower-middle class), Robert N. (upper-class), and David L., reading passage B ("We used to play . . . "). Here again, while the first two speakers generally have EH, David L. has Æ in most words, excepting *tin can, can't, bad,* and *aunt.* This is even more curious, since the words in which he says Æ do not correspond to any of the classes I–IV outlined in Tables 7.1 and 7.2; he says *mÆn*, but *tin cEHn,* for instance. Here again, however, David L. is typical of the middle-class pattern.

The reasons for the inconsistency of the middle class lie in the history of the New York City dialect. Originally, we can assume that the AW and the Æ pronunciations were standard for most words in most American dialects. Some time ago, AW began to change to OH, and Æ to EH—the change may have started as long ago as a hundred years. There is good motivation in the phonetics of the language for this sort of change (which is called "vowel raising," since the tongue is slightly raised for the EH and OH variants). Similar changes often occur in other languages and have occurred before in the history of English. In fact, all languages are in a constant state of change, so that over a relatively short period of time, a language can become unrecognizable; scarcely a word of English is pronounced today as it was in Chaucer's time, 600 years ago, and a number of word meanings and syntactic constructions have changed as well. And Chaucer's English was very different from what was spoken three centuries earlier at the time of the Norman Conquest.

But a linguistic change doesn't happen all at once, with every speaker of the language suddenly adopting a new variant. Consider the way in which a new word, for instance *hippie,* enters the language: it is first used by a few speakers in a small community and gradually spreads to other regions and social groups. Changes in pronunciation are similar; they begin among a small group of speakers, and spread out. The speakers who are geographically and socially closest to the original innovating group will acquire the innovation first, and they in turn will pass it on to other speakers.

But sometimes a change may fail to spread to other groups, or start to spread and then stop and reverse itself. This is particularly often the case when the group that initiates the change has low status within the community. Suppose, for example, that the lower classes begin to use a new word X. Speakers from other groups may come to associate the use of X with the lower class, so that to use the word is to risk being thought of as "uncultured" or "vulgar." This is what has happened, in fact, with forms like *ain't* and *he don't* and is why these forms have never been accepted as standard American usage.

The changes of AW to OH and use of Æ to EH probably began in New York among working-class speakers. When we look at the patterns of older speakers, who learned the language a long time ago, we find that EH and OH are used by middle-class speakers very infrequently, but by working-class speakers very frequently; we can assume that, sixty years earlier, the use of EH and OH was largely confined to the working class. Among middle-aged middle-class speakers, EH and OH are used somewhat more frequently; from this we infer that these vowels did not begin to spread to the middle classes until some sixty years ago. But among still younger middle-class speakers, the vowels OH and EH are *less* common. This is because these pronunciations have become *stigmatized;* that is, have been associated with "the way a laborer speaks." When a middle-class child says *bEHd* or *mEHn,* he will be corrected by parents and teachers, and told that the "correct" pronunciation is *bÆd* or *mÆn.* New Yorkers are accustomed to make social judgments about each other according to whether or how often the EH and OH pronunciations are used. If a speaker does not "speak correctly"—that is, if he does not avoid EH and OH—he may lose out on getting a job, or find that his business associates look down on him. So speakers like David L. make a conscious effort to avoid the EH and OH pronunciations that they probably used naturally as children; they "correct" their speech to the more acceptable AW and Æ pattern. This correction is particularly noticeable in careful speech, as when a passage is being read aloud; hence the pattern we saw in this section of the tape. When David L. is talking casually about the Knicks, he uses EH and OH much more frequently since he is much less self-conscious then.

But what about the upper-class speakers; why have they adopted the EH and OH patterns? If these pronunciations are stigmatized, surely they should use them least. The fact is, however, that the upper class takes a very different attitude towards correction. The middle class is characteristically "success oriented"; a premium is put on education and hard work, which are the ways to social and economic betterment. Parents hope that their children will surpass their own achievements and ultimately make it to the top of the ladder. But members of the upper class usually feel that they *have* made it; their children, the descendents of senators, bank presidents, and industrialists, cannot look forward to surpassing the achievements of previous generations. Consequently, there is little pressure to "improve oneself" in order to get ahead; someone who pays overly careful attention to his speech, manners, and dress will often be thought of as showing some insecurity about his social position. As one upper-class writer said, "Whenever I meet someone who takes pains to say *who* and *whom* correctly, I know I am in for a boring half-hour with a self-made man." Rather, the upper class stresses a kind of "studied indifference," with an aim towards giving the impression of being so secure in one's social position that one can afford to be careless about personal habits. At one point, the narrator of John Barth's novel *The Floating Opera* says of an upper-class friend, "There were three little flecks of mayonnaise on his upper lip. As he spoke, an occasional crumb blew over to me. I admired the casual bad manners that one often encounters in finely bred animals like Harrison." This indifference carries over to linguistic habits; for most upper-class New Yorkers, making a conscious effort to correct EH to Æ, or OH to AW, would be equivalent to admitting that one was seriously worried about being taken as working class.

It shouldn't be surprising then, that the upper class often behaves linguistically more like the lower class than like the middle class, or that they have by and large resisted any temptation to correct their speech. The same pattern can be found in other countries; in England, for example, the pronunciation *huntin'* for *hunting,* and *frustratin'* for *frustrating* has long characterized both the lower classes and the nobility, as has the use of *ain't*. In France, there is a certain pronunciation of *alors,* "then," that one hears only among the workers and the aristocrats. The New York pattern is consistent with these. The change from Æ to EH, and from AW to OH, may have spread to the upper class from the working class; more likely, it developed independently at about the same time as it did in the working class; what is important is that the upper class has not tried to correct its speech in order to avoid a working-class pattern.

2. The Features in Time and Space

2.1. Changes in Upper-Class Speech

This is not to say, however, that the upper class has not modified its speech as a result of social pressures, but rather that these pressures have been somewhat different from those that operate on the middle classes. An important part of the upper-class style has often been to *avoid* giving the impression that one is a snob. This is particularly true in America, where we like to preserve at least the semblance of "equality of opportunity." Marietta Peabody Tree, the descendent of an old Boston family, recalls that her grandmother slapped her only once—when she referred to an acquaintance as "very middle class." After the slap came these words: "There are no classes in America—upper, lower, or middle. You are never to use that term again." What Mrs. Tree's grandmother meant, of course, was not that there were really no classes—her grandmother knew better than that. It simply wasn't polite to mention the fact. (You don't slap a child, after all, to teach her that there is no Santa Claus.)

Now, just as a word or pronunciation may come to be associated with a lower status group, and be called a "vulgarism," so it may come to be associated with an upper-status group. In this case, it may be used particularly by people who want to be identified with that group, so that others will stigmatize it as an affectation. The pronunciation *tomAHto,* for example, is usually held to be affected; so is the pronunciation of *aunt* with AH. (Some people make fun of an affected accent by using the AH vowel for words like *potAHto,* or *fAHncy,* where in fact no one says them that way.) When this happens, the upper class will often drop the offending pronunciation, lest it be thought snobbish. Note that only two of the three upper-class speakers that you heard reading passage B said *AHnt,* although the other one—Barbara D.—admitted that that was the pronunciation that her parents used. Similarly, many upper-class speakers now say *rather* with a short *a* instead of AH. This has in part to do with the prestige that is accorded English RP in this country. If a pronunciation sounds "too English," it may be thought that the speaker is putting on airs, even though the pronunciation may have arisen quite independently in his own speech.

A case in point involves the pronunciation of *r* in New York City speech, in words where the *r* precedes a consonant (*card, heart*) or is the last sound in the word (*before, car*). In New York City speech this "post-vocalic" *r* is often dropped. For example, listen to the first speaker in this part of the tape, Robert H., the working-class New Yorker we heard earlier. The passage he is reading contains a number of words with post-vocalic *r:*

> *Passage C.* I remember where he was run over, not far from our corner. He darted out about four yards before a car, and he got hit hard. We didn't have the heart to play ball or cards all morning. We didn't know we cared so much for him until he was hurt.

Note that Robert H. drops the *r* from a number of words, such as *our, far, darted, yards,* and *heart.* The second speaker in part IV is Robert N., upper-class; he too drops a few of the *r*'s, such as in *our* and *heart,* but he pronounces most of them. The next speaker is Leo G., working-class. Both of these speakers pronounce almost all of the *r*'s in the passage. But from what was said above, you may be justifiably suspicious that people may do things in reading style that they do not do in casual speech. After Leo G.'s reading passage, there is a stretch of his conversation—note that, while he pronounces *r*'s when reading, he routinely drops them in casual style, when he is less self-conscious. Listen to his pronunciation of the words *repair, artifacts,* and *cultures.* Following this are several snippets of conversation from Robert N.; note the dropped *r*'s in *structure, sure, they're, clearly, weird, Walter, familiar, more,* and *armies.* In general, however, the working-class speakers produce *r* much less frequently than the upper-class speakers on the tape. We might assume from this that loss of *r* is a working-class innovation, which has only begun to spread to the upper class. But when we listen to older upper-class speakers, we find that they drop *r* almost invariably. One is the next speaker on the tape, Jane C., 44, reading passage C. Note that *she* drops *r*'s even in the reading passage; listen to her pronunciation of *far, corner, darted, four, hard, heart, cared,* and other words. This tendency to drop *r*'s is even more pronounced in still older upper-class speakers, such as the next speaker on the tape, Lawrence M., who was born in 1903. He drops just about all his *r*'s; listen to him say *four, before, for, part, four, powers, years.* Note, by the way, that Lawrence M. in particular uses EH and OH in many words; this is an indication that the changes from Æ to EH and from AW to OH must have begun some time ago. He is followed by Carter C., born in 1897, who drops *r*'s in his pronunciations of *over-keen, part, or, fairly, Harvard, varsity,* and *sports.* We can conclude that when Carter C. and Lawrence M. acquired their speech patterns, around 1905 or 1910, *r*-dropping was a standard feature of upper-class speech.

The last speaker in this section is Henry S., who was born in 1880 in New York City. (He moved to New Jersey and entered politics in his thirties; thus the reference to Mercer County, New Jersey, as "home"). Henry S.'s pattern is twenty years older than that of Carter C. and Lawrence M. Interestingly, he produces *more r*'s than they'do. Note his pronunciation of *our, term, Mercer,* and *before.* But Henry S. still drops the *r* in many words, such as *Jersey, Forbes,* and *heard.* (This tape was made some time ago, and the quality is not good—you may have to strain to hear the pronunciations.) We can assume that the loss of *r* began some time before Henry S. learned to speak, but that it was still spreading in the 1880s; this would explain why he drops *r* in some, but not all, words. Twenty years later, it had reached its greatest extent, as witness the speech of Lawrence M. and Carter C.

From the turn of the century to the present time, *r*-dropping has been in gradual retreat among the New York upper class. Carter C. and Lawrence M., born around the turn of the century, drop almost all their *r*'s. Jane C., born in 1933, drops a large number of *r*'s. Robert N., born in 1945, drops *r* only occasionally. And younger upper-class speakers drop *r* almost never.

It's easiest to trace the change in pronunciation of post-vocalic *r* in upper-class speech if we set up a table like Table 7.3.

Looking at Table 7.3 it's clear what has gone on. *R*-dropping must have begun sometime around the middle of the nineteenth century and spread throughout the upper class. Sometime after the First World War, however, this spread was first checked and then reversed, until, today, *r*-dropping has pretty much disappeared.

As it happens, we see roughly the same pattern among working-class speakers, except that here the *r* is not so far along on its way to restoration—remember that Leo G. still drops many *r*'s in casual speech. For the working class, however, we have an explanation for the restoration of *r*; like OH and EH, *r*-dropping became associated with "vulgar" speech, so that younger speakers make a conscious effort to pronounce their *r*'s. (Observe Leo G.'s use of *r* for all the words in the reading passage.) But we noted above that upper-class speakers do not share the tendency to "correct" their speech; thus

Table 7.3. *Degrees of* R-*dropping for Upper-Class Speakers*

| | Speakers born around: | | | |
	1880	1900	1930	1945
	Henry S.	Carter C. Lawrence M.	Jane C.	Robert N.
Frequency of r-*dropping:*	frequent	very frequent	frequent	occasional

they use the EH and OH variants with great frequency. Then why should they make an effort to pronounce their *r*'s? *R*-dropping, like the raising to EH and OH, is a "natural" sound-change: the tendency in this sort of linguistic change is usually to simplify pronunciation, and a sequence of vowel + *r* + consonant is not as simple as a sequence of vowel and consonant alone—it's easier to leave things out than to stick them in. So if the upper class has been busily *restoring r,* it must be as a result of social pressures operating from outside the linguistic system, and not because this is the natural thing to do.

It appears that *r*-dropping is evaluated by New Yorkers in a curious way. When working-class speakers drop their *r*'s, the pronunciation is perceived as vulgar and stigmatized. So younger working- and middle-class speakers make an effort to pronounce their *r*'s, on the assumption that this is what an educated speaker does. When upper-class speakers drop their *r*'s, however, the effect is the opposite; the pronunciation is thought to be an affectation. This is partly a consequence of the fact that upper-class Bostonians and British RP speakers also drop their *r*'s, so that an American who happens also to be *r*-less might be taken to be affecting a British or Boston brahmin accent.

Now there is an apparent contradiction here: we have said that a New Yorker who drops his *r*'s could be perceived as either uneducated or affected. But how can people make opposing judgments about the same linguistic feature? The answer is that they do not make these judgments in a vacuum; they evaluate the pronunciation in the light of other things that are known about the speaker. When one meets an Irish-American factory foreman or Jewish tailor who drops his *r*'s, one takes the *r*-dropping as a mark of working-class background. When the speaker is a bank president, or a college dean, one takes the same pronunciation as an upper-class marker. There are many other linguistic and nonlinguistic cues to class background; the fact that Archie Bunker and William F. Buckley, Jr. both pronounce the word *car* without an [r] is not going to lead many people to assume that they are from the same social class. So the upper-class speaker who drops his *r*'s is not likely to be worried about being taken for a working-class speaker—there is too much distance between the groups. But he may be concerned that a middle-class speaker, perhaps from another part of the country, will take him for an affected snob.

This concern over the reaction of the middle class has grown considerably in the twentieth century. In the nineteenth century, the upper class dominance in politics, finance, and culture was taken for granted; if a gentleman wanted to rise to the top, he had to gain entrance to the upper-class circles. In the twentieth century, as we noted earlier, power has been spread across a much broader base; the upper class has become only a small part of an interlocked "power elite," as the sociologist C. Wright Mills called it. These changes have been linked by sociologists to various factors. E. Digby Baltzell has suggested that the upper class was not sufficiently flexible to absorb the large numbers of ethnic Americans—Jews, Italians, Slovaks, and others—who have risen to positions of power in the twentieth century. (Even today, the upper class is largely Protestant, though there has always been a small separate group of upper-class Catholic families, largely the descendents of French and English Catholic settlers, or of Irishmen who arrived before the 1840s.) Other social scientists have laid the change to the growth of universities, of the government, of the labor movement, and to the creation of new industries, all of which provided opportunities for advancement that were too widespread to be controlled by a single small group. Whatever the causes, members of the upper class now find themselves working and going to school alongside of people from very diverse backgrounds, who are less overwhelmed by the credentials of their upper-class associates than they might once have been. Members of the upper class feel a greater pressure to get on with their middle-class colleagues and are more likely to drop habits that might be regarded as snobbish affectations.

With these changes has come a change in the political attitudes of the upper class. In the nineteenth century, the upper class controlled the Republican party and were naturally conservative in matters affecting their own interests. In the last fifty years, however, the political right has been largely taken over by other groups. (Nowadays a military career is no longer "acceptable" for upper-class youths.) Franklin Roosevelt was regarded as a "traitor to his class" by his Groton and Harvard schoolmates, but he was by no means an anomaly, and today there are many liberal Democrats and radicals among the members of the upper class—though most, especially of the older generation, remain Republican. Averell Harriman, William Sloane Coffin, Alger Hiss, Archibald Cox, and Benjamin Spock are all of upper-class backgrounds. Private schools have been making an effort—sometimes under pressure—to accept large numbers of students from different backgrounds, and there are Blacks in the exclusive clubs of Harvard, Yale, and Princeton. Many of these changes are cosmetic only, made in an effort to "look more democratic" in a pluralistic culture. But a deliberate change in language habits, like a change in dress, is exactly this sort of adaptation—it represents an attempt to correct the impression that one is making.

Finally, there has been a shift of power within the upper class itself, as the midwestern and western elite has attained a social importance equivalent to that of the upper classes of the east coast cities. The non-eastern upper classes are of more recent origin, and the loss of *r* never occurred natively in their dialects, though some older speakers, who went East to school, acquired the *r*-dropping habits of their Boston and New York schoolmates. Today, the midwestern families are far more assertive and secure than they were when a nervous F. Scott Fitzgerald arrived at Princeton, and it may be in part out of deference to them that eastern speakers have made an effort to restore their *r*'s.

The restoration of *r* among younger upper-class speakers can be seen as a response to all of these social forces. It is not a "correction" to an established prestige form, like the restoration of *r* among working- and middle-class speakers. Rather, it represents an attempt to downplay the differences between upper- and middle-class speakers and to assimilate to a more democratic style. By pronouncing *r*'s, one comes to sound more "American" and less self-consciously different.

2.2 The New York City Upper Class and the Upper Class Elsewhere

The New York City upper class belongs, not only to the New York City speech community, but also to a sort of national upper class as well. A working-class New Yorker will have relatively little contact with working-class Bostonians or Philadelphians; he will likely go to school, find a job, and raise his children in the same neighborhood. If he goes to college, it will be to one of the divisions of the City University, where he will socialize only with other New Yorkers. By contrast, an upper-class New Yorker is likely to have a great deal of contact with upper-class Philadelphians and New Englanders. He will first meet them at prep school and then at college. Later, when he goes to work in a law firm, a government bureau, or at a university, he will likely have colleagues who are members of the upper classes of other regions; if he buys a summer house, whether upstate, in Maine, or on Long Island, his neighbors may well be from another city. Out of this sustained contact grows a certain set of linguistic features that are common to the upper classes of a number of regions; these, in turn, enable an upper-class New Yorker to identify an upper-class Bostonian or Philadelphian when they meet. These features are not likely to be those that are most commonly associated with upper-class speech, such as *r*-dropping; if a feature is too widely recognized, it is likely to be stigmatized as an affectation, as we have seen; moreover, it is easier for an outsider to imitate it, so that it loses its value as a sure token of shared social background.

This section of the tape involves two such features; the pronunciation of the vowel in words like *play,* and in words like *neck.* The short *e* vowel of *neck* ([e]) is usually made with the tongue higher, and the lips a bit more spread, than the vowel of *knack* ([æ]); it is also a bit shorter than the vowel of *knack* in most American dialects. Among upper-class speakers of most eastern regions, however, this vowel is longer, with the mouth wider open, so that *neck* sounds a good deal like *knack;* working-class New Yorkers and Bostonians do not have this feature. We'll call the upper-class pronunciation E, as opposed to the more common [e].

The second feature is related to the first. The vowel of *play* ([ēy]) is really a diphthong, much like a sequence of two vowels sounded together. The first half is [ē], the tensed version of the vowel of *neck,* and the second is like the EE vowel of *see* ([īy]). If you say [e] and then EE fast in succession, you will hear something close to the diphthong of *play.* In upper-class pronunciations of *play,* however, the longer, wider E is used as the first element, so that the word comes out sounding closer to *ply* ([plāy] instead of [plēy]). You'll hear several speakers reading passage D:

> *Passage D.* When I was nine or ten, I had a lot of friends who used to come over to my house to *play.* I remember a kid named Henry who had very big feet, and a boy named Billy who had no *neck,* or at least none to look at.

(Some of the speakers read a passage in which *Fay* was substituted for *Billy.*) The first speaker is Robert N., upper-class New Yorker. Listen to the way he says *play* and *neck;* try to imitate his pronunciation to see how it differs from your own. The second and third speakers, Barbara D. and Peyton M., are also upper-class New Yorkers; their pronunciations are very like those of Robert N.

By contrast, the next speaker, Judy E., does not have the E pronunciations—recall that she is a lower-middle-class New Yorker. Nor does the next speaker, Bryan L., the Californian. But now listen to the speakers who follow these. Leo G., the next speaker, does not have these pronunciations—he is, you will remember, a working-class New Yorker. Weston T., 32, is an upper-class Bostonian, as is the next speaker, Nancy G., 27. Note that both of them use the same E vowel that is used by the upper-class New Yorkers. These passages are followed by several snippets of conversation in which this vowel is used by Robert N.; listen to the way in which he says *way, state, nectar, say,* and *today.* The last person to read passage D is Betty W., 33, a middle-class Bostonian, educated at a good Catholic girls' school; from there, she went to an eastern college, where she was made very much aware of the social differences between herself and her upper-class schoolmates. She changed her dress, her manner, and her speech in such a way as to become accepted by them, and to a certain extent, she succeeded; most of her current friends are upper-class New Yorkers. But note her pronunciation of *play* and particularly *neck;* while she has picked up a number of upper-class linguistic patterns, she still has the middle-class vowel in these words. (Listen also to the way she says *ladies* and *legs* in the snippet of conversation following her passage.) Upper- and middle-class speakers are generally not aware of this particular feature, in the way that they are of *r*-dropping, so Betty W. has not acquired it. Nonetheless, it serves as a subtle unconscious cue for class identification and marks her as an outsider. When her tape was played for Weston T., an old-family Bostonian, he was puzzled, and finally said, "She certainly speaks well. Is she an actress or something?"

2.3   It Takes One to Know One

Upper-class speakers are very good at identifying one another, even on the basis of voice alone. (In a later passage on the tape, one of the informants discusses this.) Lewis Lapham, himself an upper-class New Yorker, writes that, "The old rich recognize one another by small and elusive signals: a tone of voice, a name in common, a summer once at Fisher's Island, the recollection of a bunker below the thirteenth green at a course at Southampton." In discussions of this sort, language keeps coming up as the most important indicator; Stephen Birmingham claimed that "Trying to duplicate the American society accent has provided the greatest stumbling block for the *parvenu*." It is virtually impossible to acquire another dialect with native facility after adolescence, and it is this difficulty that betrays the interloper, even after he has mastered the "look" and can throw the right names around.

It is because of the importance of the upper-class accent as a social indicator that phonological features play such an important role in it. These are learned young and are very difficult to acquire later. By contrast, lexical features (that is, the use of certain words and expressions) are relatively easily learned by the non-native speaker. (An American can learn to write correct, and even elegant French, starting at the age of twenty; but he will never sound like a native Parisian.) Lexical features are most important for groups like teenagers, where turnover in the membership makes them useful to use a code that changes rapidly; the constant introduction of new words ensures that the teenagers of the last decade will not be able to share the slang of the next.

But the upper class requires a code that will remain relatively fixed over several generations of speakers, so that speakers who went to the same schools can identify each other twenty years later. Phonological features change more slowly than the word-stock. Moreover, the code must be difficult for the enterprising intruder to crack. To be sure, there are occasional "vogue words" that enjoy a

169

temporary popularity among upper-class speakers; for example, *attractive,* used in a certain ironic way, as in "That's such an *attractive* salad." But these tend to be remnants of prep-school slang and play only a marginal role in social identification. (Some constructions seem to have a slightly longer life, such as the use of the adverb *awfully* to modify verbs—not adjectives, as in *It's awfully late.* In this final portion of the tape, for example, the first speaker says, "My parents ridiculed it awfully"; this use is not common nowadays in the speech of the middle class.)

In addition to its phonological segments, the most important characteristic of upper-class speech is its intonational pattern. It is in fact this, rather than phonological variables, that has struck most of the social scientists who have written about the "society accent." Because of its very obviousness, the intonational pattern *can* be mastered by non-upper-class speakers, and it is often abandoned by younger upper-class speakers who find it affected, but who generally retain the subtler phonological features of which they are not aware. But the intonational features are nonetheless widespread and serve a definite purpose.

Intonational patterns are difficult to describe in print; the last section of the tape contains several characteristic samples of two primary features. First, the voice itself has a slightly nasal, creaky quality. Second, stress is handled differently. In most American dialects, there is a distinct rise in the pitch of the voice when a word is stressed, but in upper-class English this rise in pitch tends to be a bit suppressed—the effect is of something like a drawl, with the flattened pitch giving the voice what has been perceived as a "bored" quality. Listen first to Barbara D.; note the way in which she says *loathed, knew,* and *back.* Like most younger speakers, she generally moves in and out of the upper-class pronunciation pattern; interestingly, here she introduces it while she is criticizing the affected accent of her high-school classmates. The next speaker is Peyton M. The upper-class stress pattern is quite evident here; listen to the way he says *tend, live, quarter, group, do,* etc. Significantly, he is here defending his fraternity against the charge that it is "cliquey." The next speaker is Jane C., 44, who has the upper-class "voice" more than the stress pattern; but listen to how she says, "all these things that people could *do,*" and "absolute *gold-mine.*"

Again we have Weston T., the Bostonian. In the first part of his section, he uses the nasal voice, but not the stress pattern, of the upper class. (This section is interesting for another point, however; note the way in which he corrects himself on the word *class,* from *clAHss* to *clÆss.* In Boston, the AH vowel in words like *class, past* has a status rather like *r*-dropping—it is a stigmatized feature when used by working-class speakers, but is regarded as an old-fashioned affectation when used by members of the upper class. Younger upper-class Bostonians make a conscious effort to avoid this pronunciation; this is especially true of Weston T., who now lives in New York, where the pronunciation is not heard even among upper-class speakers.) But Weston T. does use the upper-class stress pattern on occasion, as when he is talking about the public school system; note the way in which he stresses *say*.

The taped material for this chapter ends with another passage from Peyton M.; the voice, but not the stress pattern, is evident here. This passage is most interesting for its content; he is talking about a characteristic New York intonational pattern that is called "Locust Valley Lockjaw," which involves an extreme version of the upper-class stress pattern. (In Boston, a similar pattern is sometimes called the "Massachusetts Malocclusion.") This is particularly interesting because it indicates how aware upper-class speakers are of the stress pattern, while few, if any, take note of the vowel in *neck*. As we noted above, the easy accessibility of the stress pattern makes it possible for non-native speakers of the dialect to acquire it and makes it unsuitable as a primary indicator of social class. But at the same time, this accessibility makes it easy to turn the stress pattern on and off. It is no accident that most of the passages in the final section involve discussions of the upper class itself, or of class characteristics. While speakers may use this stress pattern in any circumstances, it is most pronounced when the topic of conversation is intimately connected to upper-class values. Speakers fall into the stress pattern most easily when they want to underscore their social identity, much as a working-class New Yorker will fall into a characteristic voice and intonational pattern when he is talking tough. Barbara D. is parodying the upper-class intonational pattern when she talks about the "Friday accent," but in the very next sentence she uses the flattened stress on *loathed,* as if to say, "I am myself of this group, and can criticize their affectations without it being thought that it's just sour grapes." Peyton M. is responding to the accusations of outsiders. And Weston T. is talking about why he would not send his child to public schools; the "fourth-grade syndrome" is the contention that one can send one's children to public schools until the fourth grade, without their having problems; he goes on to say that he is skeptical, and would be fearful of the violence that they might encounter. (To be quite fair, he is talking about the New York City schools.) In each instance, it is as if there is a middle- or lower-class speaker invisibly present in the room, whom the speaker is opposing by taking an upper-class point of view.

Every group shares characteristic values; the usefulness of a dialect feature like the intonational pattern is that it can be invoked when the speaker wants to reinforce deliberately his identification with the group in expressing these values. Speakers are sensitive to this, and when an intonational pattern is used in what they judge to be an inappropriate situation, they may be annoyed. For the upper class, in particular, the speaker may be perceived as unnecessarily stressing his class background and consequently as betraying some social insecurity. These people are the "snobs" whose speech is criticized by Barbara D. and Peyton M.

Suggestions for Further Reading

For a good discussion of social class in America, see W. Lloyd Warner, Marchia Meeker, and Kenneth Eells, *Social Class in America,* Harper, 1960; or, for a more modern discussion, from a different point of view, Gabriel Kolko, *Wealth and Power In America,* Praeger, 1962. Works dealing with the upper class in particular are E. Digby Baltzell, *The Protestant Establishment,* Random House, 1964; and G. William Domhoff, *The Higher Circles,* Random House, 1970. C. Wright Mills' *The Power Elite* (Oxford University Press, 1956) is an important, controversial book; a collection of essays discussing it can be found in *C. Wright Mills and the Power Elite,* edited by G. William Domhoff and Hoyt B. Ballard (Beacon, 1971).

There is no published study of upper-class speech in New York. An extensive discussion of social variation in New York speech can be found in *The Social Stratification of English in New York City* by William Labov (Center for Applied Linguistics, 1966). For briefer and less technical presentations of some of the same research, see *Sociolinguistic Patterns* by the same author (University of Pennsylvania Press, 1972).

Table 7.4. *Speakers in the Order of Their Appearance on the Tape*

Speaker	Age When Taped	Home City	SR*	Secondary School**	Occupation	Father's Occupation	Ethnic Background
Bryan L.	24	San Diego		Public	Student	Naval Officer	WASP
Judy E.	27	NYC		Public	Secretary	Phone Company Supervisor	German
Robert H.	23	NYC		Public	Route Manager	Shop Foreman	Czech
Barbara D.	32	NYC		Prep	Book Editor	Minister	WASP/German
Robert N.	31	NYC	x	Prep	College Teacher	Executive	WASP
Peyton M.	24	NYC	x	Prep	Student	Banker	WASP
David L.	37	NYC		Public	Advertising (Sales)	Small Businessman	Jewish
Leo G.	25	NYC		Public	Student	Service Station Manager	Jewish
Jane C.	44	NYC	x	Prep	Housewife	Lawyer	WASP
Lawrence M.	b. 1903	NYC	x	Prep	Diplomat	Businessman	WASP
Carter C.	b. 1897	NYC	x	Prep	Publisher	Lawyer	WASP
Henry S.	b. 1880	NYC	x	Prep	Politician	Lawyer	WASP
Weston T.	32	Boston	x	Prep	Art Dealer	Doctor	WASP
Nancy G.	27	Boston	x	Prep	Political Activist	Banker	WASP
Betty W.	33	Boston		Parochial	College Teacher	Doctor	WASP/Irish

*"SR"—speaker or immediate family listed in New York City or Boston *Social Register*.
**"Prep"—attended "good" private secondary school.

Dialect Encounters
Standard

On the Application of Sociolinguistic Information: Test Evaluation and Dialect Differences in Appalachia

Walt Wolfram and Donna Christian

Walt Wolfram and Donna Christian work at the Center for Applied Linguistics, where they specialize in the study of social and ethnic varieties of English. Wolfram also teaches at the University of the District of Columbia, and Christian, on leave from CAL, is teaching at the Adam Mickiewicz University in Poznań, Poland. A survey of their academic history reveals them to be dialect vagabonds, winding their way through Vernacular Black English, Southern White Rural English, Puerto Rican English, American Indian English, and Appalachian English. Along the way, they have also considered the educational implications of dialect diversity, looking at problems like the testing issues presented here.

Introduction

"What good is all this information on different dialects anyhow?" This is a question frequently asked in workshops where dialect differences are discussed. Apart from the interesting guesses that can be made about a person's social and geographical background, what does all this information have to do with the everyday world? From a professional standpoint, we can say that the investigation of language rules for different dialects can be an interesting introduction to one kind of scientific reasoning. From a social perspective, if we understand the rules governing dialect differences, we can appreciate the integrity of all language systems. However valid such reasons may be for studying theories of language use and variety, many people still ask a basic utilitarian question. Educators may still want to know what value such information might have in their educational setting. Or parents may

177

want to know how this information may be relevant to their children's welfare.

In this chapter, you will see how to use sociolinguistic information in a question of concern to both professionals and lay people: standardized testing. The importance that mainstream America places on testing is obvious. Standardized tests could be added to the small list of inevitables in our society, such as taxes and death. Before you entered elementary school, you were probably given a battery of tests to determine your readiness for school. Throughout your education, you have been taking standardized tests at intervals so that the schools could evaluate your educational achievement. If you planned to go to college, your preparation may have been evaluated by the Scholastic Aptitude Tests, and if to graduate school, by the Graduate Record Examination. As if these were not enough, your placement in some jobs may be determined by standardized tests, such as the Civil Service Examination, or the battery of aptitude tests given by the military to people entering the services.

Standardized tests serve, more or less well, a number of functions. They are designed to help society select the best-qualified people for various careers and to help individuals find careers best suited for them. They provide feedback on educational programs across the country, and they help decide whether or not people are ready for particular levels of education and work. With uses such as these, the quantified, objective results of standardized tests are difficult to resist. Although test scores may be difficult to resist, we are still faced with a serious question: whether or not the tests measure what they are supposed to measure, wherever they are administered.

One persistent question is whether standardized tests are appropriate for different cultural groups, including nonmainstream working-class groups, Chicano, Black, and rural white. Is the talent of these people for various careers properly and fairly measured? We are led to the question of which cultural differences have to do with true aptitudes for careers and which ones are irrelevant, as well as the question of whether or not reliable tests that will impose the same standard everywhere can be constructed. There is an analogue to formal testing in many other situations where people are evaluated with standards of behavior from outside their community. This can happen in the most informal meetings; it often happens when employers interview job applicants and when teachers judge pupils. Through tests we can hope to learn something about this wider phenomenon, and language is an appropriate aspect of culture by which to approach the problem. Most tests involve language, and some tests aim to evaluate language aptitude itself; moreover, differences in language structure from one area to another lend themselves to examination better than most other aspects of culture.

Standardized tests have shown disproportionately lower scores for nonmainstream groups in our society. We should ask why this is so. High socioeconomic groups achieve the highest test scores, an achievement that could be due to some kind of inherent superiority. Conversely, various nonmainstream groups could be genetically inferior in the intellectual skills being measured. This is an issue at least as old as Aristotle—broadly speaking, the question of whether poor people are poor because it is in their nature to be so. It has been brought to the fore again with data from standardized tests. An alternative explanation is that proportionately higher scores for mainstream groups result from an environment that provides them with certain cultural advantages, and, in some cases, perhaps even physical ones such as proper nutrition or health care. A third possibility is that the pattern of scores may reflect a bias built into the testing instruments themselves, and not at all important differences in the capabilities of the test takers. In fact, evidence from a sociolinguistic analysis of tests supports this third explanation and suggests that certain groups may be using language diversity to their advantage at the expense of others.

In this chapter we will be concerned with analyzing standardized tests for possible bias against particular cultural groups, with particular respect to test takers who are speakers of Appalachian English (AE). We will be concerned with both the use and the structure of AE, for test taking involves not only words but the conventions governing the use of words in social interaction. We will first examine the way a standardized notion of "correctness" is likely to affect speakers of AE when they take tests. Next we will present some sociolinguistic principles for evaluating tests. Finally, you will have an opportunity to evaluate a test according to these principles.

1. Testing and the Notion of "Correctness"

1.1 Testing as a Social Occasion

Testing creates a social occasion. It involves social interaction between the test administrator and the test taker. To this occasion, the test taker brings a set of expectations based on his past experience with other social encounters, expectations that will influence how he performs on the test. In one current intelligence test for children, in a section entitled "General Comprehension," the test taker is asked "What would you do if you were sent to buy a loaf of bread and the grocer said he did not have any more?" The most highly valued answer, worth two points, is the alternative solution, such as going to another store to look for bread or purchasing biscuits and rolls instead. The answer which involves checking with the original source for instruction for further directions (e.g., going back home) is worth one point, and an answer which involves accepting failure is worth zero points. How might a child's previous experience influence his reply on such a test item? To what extent does the question test "general comprehension"? What aspects of cultural attitudes or socialization might the answer reflect?

One aspect is what the test taker would actually do in such a situation, but what most concerns us here is the way the test taker chooses to respond to the test item. The child who does the most intelligent thing in real life situations may not give the most valued answers on a test. Real life situations are complicated: for example, the people who sent the child to buy bread may not like biscuits or rolls; they may be particular about which store they do their shopping in. It takes a special attitude to give answers freely about hypothetical situations. Furthermore, it matters who is asking the questions and the relationship to the person being asked: you the reader might reflect upon your own experience and consider how your response to questions can be affected by your relationship to the person presenting the questions to you.

Constructing tests requires elaborate plans to manipulate people's behavior. While procedures for taking standardized tests are presumably the same everywhere, test takers may respond quite differently to those procedures, and in ways having little to do with the skills being tested. How much is involved in the procedures for test taking is revealed in the following "hints" for successful test taking from a brochure on aptitude tests published by the United States Department of Labor (1968).

1. Get ready for the test by taking other tests on your own.
2. Don't let the thought of taking a test throw you.
3. Arrive early, rested, and prepared to take the test.
4. Ask questions until you understand what you are supposed to do.
5. Some parts of the test may be easier than others. Don't let the hard parts keep you from doing well on the easier parts.
6. Keep time limits in mind when you take a test.
7. Don't be afraid to answer when you aren't sure you are right, but don't guess wildly.

8. Work as fast as you can but try not to make mistakes. Some tests have short time limits.

If it is admitted that these hints may change how a person scores on a test, what does it imply about test administrators being able to interpret test results in an orderly way? What kind of skills can you see suggested by these hints that might have to do more with test taking *per se* rather than with real-life situations?

The linguistic performance of test takers can be determined by social factors that go beyond language itself. In a test designed to elicit conversation from children to determine how verbal they are, a child and a tester are seated at a table across from each other. The tester places a toy fire engine in front of the child and asks the child to tell him everything he knows about it. The child first says nothing, then later makes comments consisting of one word or short phrases, punctuated by long periods of silence. In a contrasting situation, the investigator sits on the floor with the same child and one of his friends. The children busily munch on potato chips as they engage in a rapid fire conversation about various toys and games, while the adult takes the role of an observer rather than initiator of the conversation. Why might the child appear "nonverbal" in one context and quite fluent in another? Assuming the child is given two independent rankings in respect to other children his age, a ranking for the verbalness he displayed in each of the two situations, which ranking would be the most valuable? How would you decide? Can you conceive of a purpose for which the first (presumably lower) ranking would be more useful than the second? And the complement to this: can you conceive of a purpose for which the second ranking would be more useful than the first?

It is common among the cultures of the world for people to feel uncomfortable about being asked lots of questions, especially when the person asking the questions is an outsider to the community. And in a testing situation, there is perhaps no aspect of culture likely to raise the issue of cultural boundaries in as conscious a way as language itself. People who speak nonmainstream dialects are made aware at an early age that the *way* in which they express themselves, including the very form of the words and sentences they use, conflicts with the norms of the wider society. They are used to being corrected by teachers; they notice that when people in their community are speaking carefully at the most formal occasions they tend to shift their language in the direction of the mainstream norms; they sometimes see or hear the typical speech of their community stereotyped and mocked. They can perceive a test on language abilities as an instrument designed to measure them according to someone else's standards, not their own.

This can put them at a disadvantage compared with mainstream speakers, where they have to follow a different strategy from the one the mainstream speaker follows. On each test item the mainstream speaker can follow his first intuitions about what is correct, because he knows the standard for the test is the one that he already knows. By contrast, the nonmainstream speaker must check his first intuition about what is correct, to determine whether he should express himself the way someone else would speak. To succeed on the test, he should specifically not have confidence about his first and most natural choice. Here again, then, the matter of how well one performs in real life may be one thing, and how well on tests may be quite another. The most articulate person, the one best able to express complex thoughts clearly, may not be the one who receives the highest test score.

1.2 Correctness in Appalachian English

Listen to the tape that goes with this chapter, the final portion of the cassette accompanying the book. Two speakers of AE each tell a story, and the transcription of what they say is in Appendix B at the end of the chapter. Listen first without reading and see if you have trouble understanding any of what is said. If you do, listen again, and read the transcription as you listen: note the passages you had trouble understanding and see if you can pinpoint what the problem is in each case. Ask yourself what you would have to learn to talk like one of these people. How much of it would involve vocabulary or the way words are put together syntactically, and how much of it would be simply a matter of pronunciation?

Now go through the transcription of the two stories and note what forms or constructions reveal dialect differences that would be relevant to a *written* test. The most common standardized tests concern written English, so that few of the subtle differences in the way dialects sound are going to affect test performance. (Note that pronunciation differences do enter into another less formal but equally important kind of evaluation in the education process, and that is in the frequent instances when teachers evaluate reading comprehension by having pupils read aloud; it is not uncommon for a child to be corrected as he reads aloud, not because he didn't understand what he read, but because he read aloud with a pronunciation that was not standard.)

In ''An Appalachian Ghost Story,'' the first story on the part of the tape that goes with this chapter, the speaker says:

I hear him a-talking, a-setting over there . . .   (line 5)

The prefix *a-* combined with verbs ending in *-ing* is a notable feature of AE.[1] As with most of the distinctive forms of AE, forms like *a-talking* are *variable* with mainstream forms: referring to the same situation, the speaker can also say *I hear him talking.* The *a-* prefixed forms are used above all in narratives and seem to have special stylistic effect: there is something more vivid about saying *I hear him a-talking* rather than just *I hear him talking.* Here are some additional examples recorded from other texts. Take note of the patterns in which the *a-* prefix can appear:

(1) I knew he was a-telling the truth, but still I was a-coming home.

. . . and he says "Who's a-stomping on my bridge?"

Well, she's a-getting the black lung now, ain't she?

It was a dreadful sight, fire was a-flaming everything.

He was really a-running.

He's been a-jumping from one job to another for years.

This man'd catch them behind the neck and they'd just be a-rattling.

. . . and John boy, he come a-running out there and got shot.

All of a sudden a bear come a-running and it come a-running towards him and he shot it between the eyes.

They wasn't in there no more and I went down there a-hunting for them.

. . . and then I took off a-riding on a minibike.

He just kept a-begging, and a-crying and a-wanting to go out.

Then send the rope back down, just keep a-pulling it up til we got it built.

You just look at him and he starts a-busting out laughing at you.

(2) . . . and I heard something a-snorting coming up the hill and I said "Aw heck!"

1. The data and analysis of the *a-* prefix on which this discussion is based is presented in Wolfram and Christian, *Sociolinguistic Variables in Appalachian English,* NIE Final Report, Grant Number NIE–G–74–0026 (Center for Applied Linguistics, 1975).

. . . and I turned around and I seen that old snake a-laying there all coiled up, his mouth was open like this, getting ready to bite me.

I know you might have heard of peppermint a-growing along the streams of the water.

Well, it brings back memory to me, when I was a child a-growing up, just about the same way that they played.

Well, let's say you had a little headache or something, or maybe a bone a-hurting, your leg a-hurting, mother would get you up some kind of sassafras tea.

I had twelve children and I got two dead and ten a-living.

No, that's something I hadn't ever got into, with dogs a-fighting.

(3) . . . you was pretty weak by the tenth day, a-laying in there in bed.

. . . one night my sister, she woke up a-screaming—crying, hollering and so we jumped up.

He nearly died a-laughing so hard.

. . . say Chuck would come by and want to spend a hour a-talking, I always figure I'm not too busy to stop.

. . . of course a lot of times you can't, and grow up a-hunting with them instead of hunting for them.

(4) Then the big Daddy Bear says, "Who's a-been eating my porridge?"

I went a-deer hunting twice last year.

He was going up there a-squirrel hunting.

The final group of examples (4) are not as common as the first three, but they lend themselves to the same generalization as the others, which is that the *a*- prefix is used with verbal expressions ending in *-ing*. The verbal expressions in (4) each contain two words: *been eating, deer hunting, squirrel hunting*. The verbal expression that takes the *a*- prefix is usually just the *-ing* word itself.

Go through the text of the two stories and see what additional examples of the *a*- prefix you can find. Take care to note cases where words ending in *-ing* do not work in construction with the *a*- prefix.

One reason why AE has -*ing* forms without the prefix is because the prefixed forms are variants used only part of the time for stylistic effect.

There is another reason. The *a*- prefix is used with -*ing* forms only in certain constructions. There are a number of instances where -*ing* forms can be used where the grammar of AE would not allow the *a*- prefix: if you were trying to speak AE and you put the *a*- prefix in any of the wrong places, it would sound very bad indeed to the ears of AE speakers.

One cannot, for example, use the *a*- prefix on most -*ing* forms that are not being used as verbs. English makes productive use of verbs ending in -*ing* both as adjectives and as nouns. One can say not only *The boy was running,* but:

The running boy

The running was fun.

with *running* being used as an attributive adjective and as a noun. No AE speaker ever says either of the following phrases (* means 'ungrammatical'):

*The a-running boy

*The a-running was fun.

What is involved here is a sense of which *part of speech* a word belongs to, which is to say in this case whether a word is a verb, a noun, or an adjective. This division of words into distinct parts of speech is systematic in every dialect of English, but an outsider who wanted to learn AE might need some conscious means of testing an -*ing* word to see if it is one of those parts of speech where one should avoid placing the *a*- prefix. Nouns generally allow the insertion of a determiner such as *the.* Thus, you can predict which of the following pair will not allow the *a*- prefix:

He enjoyed swimming.

He went swimming.

Just one of them allows the insertion of *the:*

He enjoyed the swimming.

*He went the swimming.

This shows that the *swimming* after *enjoyed* is a noun, while the one after *went* probably is not, and on the basis of this test at least, we could guess that the *swimming* of *went swimming* is some kind of verb and allows the *a-* prefix. And we would be right. An AE speaker's judgment on the insertion of the *a-* prefix would be as follows:

*He enjoyed a-swimming.

He went a-swimming.

The distinction between verbs and adjectives is in some ways more subtle. Consider:

The man was charming.

No one ever says *The man was a-charming*. Word for word *The man was charming* might appear to involve the same construction as *The boy was running,* but in fact the syntax is quite different. *Charming* is being used as an adjective, not as a verb the way *running* is. Adjectives generally allow intensifiers such as *very* or *quite,* and verbs never allow these expressions. Just so, we can modify *charming* with *quite* or *very,* but in no way can we do this with *running:*

The man was quite charming.   The man was very charming.

*The man was quite running.   *The man was very running.

To be a good speaker of AE, one would have to learn to use the *a-* prefix *variably:* if one used the *a-* prefix every time the grammar of AE allowed it, that would be unnatural; no one talks that way. In addition, one would have to be sure never to use the prefix incorrectly. To use it with any noun would be wrong. To use it with most adjectives would be wrong as well.[2] One more syntactic constraint will be noted here: the *a-* prefix may not be used on a form that is the object of an immediately preceding preposition. This means one can say all of the following:

He died working so hard.   She thought of Billy coming to visit us.

He died a-working so hard.   She thought of Billy a-coming to visit us.

but not the ones that follow marked with an asterisk:

---

2. Ibid., p. 107. See the few adjectives and adverbs that have been noted with the *a-* prefix. These forms are rarely used and make up the small list of exceptions to the generalization that *a-* is used only on verbs.

He died from working so hard.   She thought of coming to visit us.

*He died from a-working so hard. *She thought of a-coming to visit us.

Two constraints concern pronunciation. The prefix is not per-mitted on verbs that begin with an unstressed syllable. Thus there are two possibilities for *bréaking,* but only one for *destróying:*

He's breaking the boxes.   He's destroying the boxes.

He's a-breaking the boxes.   *He's a-destroying the boxes.

The other pronunciation constraint is that the prefix is not per-mitted on words beginning with a vowel sound.

She's chewing corn.   She's eating corn.

She's a-chewing corn.   *She's a-eating corn.

You are invited to try your hand at a test on the material that has just been explained. It concerns an aspect of grammar that has been mastered by anyone who is a fluent speaker of AE, but not one for which you would get credit on a standardized test, because it is not a feature of the norm dialect. Indicate which of the following examples would be correct with an *a-* prefix added to the *-ing* form, and which ones incorrect (ungrammatical). The examples are presented in pairs. In most cases, one member of a pair is correct and the other is not, but there are instances where both are either correct or incorrect. In each case where you identify an example as not allowing the prefix, see if you can state why this is so.

(1) a. He likes sailing.

     b. He went sailing.

(2) a. Alice kept looking.

     b. Alice started looking.

(3) a. I've never messed with dogs fighting.

     b. I've never messed with fighting dogs.

(4) a. Sally was eating real fast.

     b. Sally was drinking real fast.

(5) a. The man was confessing his crime.

b. The man was hollering at the dogs.

(6) a. The woman was coming down the stairs.

b. The movie was shocking.

(7) a. She got sick working so hard.

b. We thought hunting would be good for her.

(8) a. We go walking in the woods.

b. We went walking in the woods.

(9) a. Sadie was waiting for an answer.

b. Sadie kept waiting for an answer.

(10) a. He makes money by building houses.

b. He makes money building houses.

(11) a. Sam was following the trail.

b. Sam was entering the cave.

(12) a. The horse ran off galloping.

b. The show was fascinating.

(13) a. Gary kept denying the accusation.

b. They kept asking the same questions.

(14) a. He got sick from running so much.

b. He got sick of going over there all the time.

From this you have perhaps gotten a bit of an idea of the rule-governed regularity that characterizes AE, as indeed rules are involved in any dialect, standard or not.[3] Besides productive processes such as

---

3. Here are the sentences in which it would be incorrect to add the *a-* prefix: (1a) "sailing" is a noun, (3b) "fighting" is an adjective and is immediately preceded by a preposition, (4a) "eating" begins with a vowel, (5a) "confessing" begins with an unstressed syllable, (6b) "shocking" is an adjective, (7b) "hunting" is a noun, (10a) "building" is preceded by a preposition, (11b) "entering" begins with a vowel, (12b) "fascinating" is an adjective, (13a) "denying" has an unstressed first syllable, (13b) "asking" begins with a vowel, (14a) and (14b) both "running" and "going" are immediately preceded by prepositions. On all other *-ing* words in the test it is grammatical to add the *a-* prefix.

a- prefixing, there are also many details in the form of words that one would have to learn to be a good speaker or writer of AE, forms you may have noticed in the stories on the tape and that you would have to learn on an individual basis if you wanted to master AE, for example (from the first story):

> . . . so Ingo, he'd went over to this man's house . . . (line 2)

> . . . I got down there and I hearn something shut the church-house door. . . (line 7)

In Appendix A, you will find an illustrative sketch of some of the grammatical rules of AE that differentiate it from mainstream varieties of English. You should read this sketch and gain an overall familiarity with the structure of the dialect. In each instance consider how the variance between AE and mainstream English might become involved in a test of grammatical correctness.

1.3 Test Taking as a Task for AE Speakers

One of the features of AE commented on in Appendix A concerns noun plurals. Consider the following forms:

Appalachian English	*Standard English*
two *pound* of nails	two *pounds* of nails
a two-*pound* box of nails	a two-*pound* box of nails
three *gallon* of gas	three *gallons* of gas
the three-*gallon* container	the three-*gallon* container
It's twelve *inch* long	It's twelve *inches* long
It's a twelve-*inch*-long ruler	It's a twelve-*inch*-long ruler
two *mile* to the store	two *miles* to the store
a two-*mile* hike	a two-*mile* hike
He's six *month* old	He's six *months* old
He's a six-*month*-old baby	He's a six-*month*-old baby
in five *hour*	in five *hours*
a five-*hour* hike	a five-*hour* hike
four *boys* over there	four *boys* over there
a four-*boy* team	a four-*boy* team
three *boxes* of it	three *boxes* of it
a three-*box* limit	a three-*box* limit
six *dogs* out there	six *dogs* out there
the six-*dog* attack	the six-*dog* attack
five *desks* for working	five *desks* for working
a five-*desk* office	a five-*desk* office

189

eleven *bag* of it   eleven *bags* of it
the eleven-*bag* container   the eleven-*bag* container

Without for the moment checking back to Appendix A, carry out the following analysis: identify from the above list the AE and standard English items that are alike in taking a plural *-s* (or *-es*). Identify the items where AE and standard English are alike in *not* talking a plural *-s*. What types of patterns do these occur in? In what patterns do differences occur between the two dialects? Can you state a general rule that accounts for the differences? If stated correctly, the rule should predict new forms not already in the list, for example, that in AE one would say *two foot off the ground, eleven bushel of apples,* and *He is fourteen year old.*

With the rules of the two dialects in mind, consider a language test which focuses on plural forms. Suppose this test admits as correct only plural forms that match the standard English rules. In a test item such as the following:

$$\text{This car needs eight } \begin{Bmatrix} \text{pints} \\ \text{pint} \end{Bmatrix} \text{ of oil.}$$

You can see immediately that there is a clash between what is correct in the grammar of AE and what is correct in the grammar of standard English. The AE speaker has to refer to two standards of correctness, one for communicating in his community and the other for taking the test: the standard English speaker need refer to only a single standard. But even in an item where the two dialects agree, the AE speaker can have an extra dimension to his task that never touches the standard English speaker.

$$\text{I have a two } \begin{Bmatrix} \text{pound} \\ \text{pounds} \end{Bmatrix} \text{ box of nails.}$$

It is not grammatical here in either dialect to add the plural suffix. The standard English speaker can exclude the response *pounds* without a moment's hesitation: it doesn't sound right. But the AE speaker always has to check his first most natural choice: it doesn't sound right to him either to add the plural suffix, but can he be sure? His own native sense of correctness is not enough. *Sometimes* it clashes with the mainstream norms, and that being the case, he must always be on guard. He'll probably be correct on this one, but making the choice is a complex task.

2. Principles for Test Evaluation

2.1 An Illustrative Case and Some Erroneous Assumptions Exposed

Here is a test that examines the child's ability to identify the "correct" language forms according to standard English usage. This test is similar to some actual and widely used tests. Using the grammatical principles of AE that you have just become acquainted with, try to determine which choices the AE speaker might make if he were to use the rules of AE grammar. How many of these are "incorrect" according to standard usage? The number of items you mark "incorrect" in this way is the measure of dialect interference.

> *Directions:* Each sentence below has two words placed one above the other. You are to circle the one you think correct in each sentence.

(1) He $\begin{Bmatrix} \text{are} \\ \text{is} \end{Bmatrix}$ my cousin.

(2) Can you $\begin{Bmatrix} \text{go} \\ \text{went} \end{Bmatrix}$ out now?

(3) Beth $\begin{Bmatrix} \text{come} \\ \text{came} \end{Bmatrix}$ home and cried.

(4) We $\begin{Bmatrix} \text{were} \\ \text{was} \end{Bmatrix}$ told to sit down.

(5) My sister $\begin{Bmatrix} \text{am} \\ \text{is} \end{Bmatrix}$ six years old.

(6) He $\begin{Bmatrix} \text{run} \\ \text{ran} \end{Bmatrix}$ all the way to school.

(7) I didn't hear $\begin{Bmatrix} \text{no} \\ \text{any} \end{Bmatrix}$ noise.

(8) There $\begin{Bmatrix} \text{were} \\ \text{was} \end{Bmatrix}$ no ducks on the lake.

(9) He $\begin{Bmatrix} \text{can} \\ \text{may} \end{Bmatrix}$ read very well.

(10) She will give me $\begin{Bmatrix} \text{them} \\ \text{these} \end{Bmatrix}$ dolls.

(11) She $\begin{Bmatrix} \text{doesn't} \\ \text{don't} \end{Bmatrix}$ read well.

(12) I just $\begin{Bmatrix} \text{began} \\ \text{begun} \end{Bmatrix}$ my lessons.

(13) I have just $\begin{Bmatrix} \text{wrote} \\ \text{written} \end{Bmatrix}$ a poem.

It would be wrong to assume that these questions measure the same ability and knowledge for all speakers. This is at least potentially not so: speakers of standard English can answer all items by simply applying the rules of their dialect quite intuitively. But if speakers of nonmainstream dialects were to do the same, they might answer various questions incorrectly. The mainstream English speaker has nothing to learn to answer the questions: the "correct" answers are defined by the rules of his dialect. This biases the test in his favor.

A second and complementary error is the assumption that all test takers will agree on the definition of "correct." But correct for whom and in what context? In this test, the designer is using "correct" in two possible senses. On the one hand, "correct" refers to forms that the rules of both standard and nonmainstream varieties would predict. Thus, the alternative for *go* in (2), *went,* would not be acceptable in either standard English or any other variety of American English. An item like this is one all test takers will tend to get correct.

On the other hand, another sense of "correct" refers to the acceptable status of an item in standard English in opposition to other forms acceptable in some other dialect. In (3), for example, the choice is between the standard English form *came* and the nonstandard form *come*. Both of these alternates are, of course, governed by specific linguistic rules, but one belongs to a socially more acceptable variety of English, and the other to a socially stigmatized one. So this second sense of "correct" refers to social (or school) acceptance. For speakers of nonmainstream English, it might mean "school English" or "school correct": a separate set of language options.

The second notion of correctness is the stumbling block for the speaker of nonmainstream English. The first two items of the test follow the first notion of correctness. If he decides the test is asking for forms of correctness according to the rules of his language, he will quite regularly miss the items later on for which he has dialect interference. To get them right, he would have to change in the middle of the test and switch to the imperative of "correct" according to "school English." The standard English speaker has no such stumbling block: he can process all items successfully with only one definition of "correct."

The confusion that can arise in such a test in the use of the notion "correct" reflects on a further and widely held erroneous assumption: it is that forms that do not agree with the rules of standard

English do not follow *any* rules. From our exploration of some of the features of AE grammar, we have seen that this is not so. Let's look more closely at how an AE speaker might fare with this test.

2.2 An Analysis of Specific Items

The first item in the sample test deals with agreement between a third-person singular subject and the verb *be*. In the standard agreement pattern, the correct form would be *is*. But what about *are?* We have to check the grammar of AE to determine whether in that position *are* is a possible form. Looking at the section on *Agreement* in Appendix A (Section 2) we see that most of the difference from the standard pattern involves contexts where there are plural subjects—which is not the case here. The one instance of nonstandard agreement with singular subjects is with the auxiliary *don't,* so there is no conflict here. In a similar way, (2) does not present any conflict either, with its *go* vs. *went*.

In (3) the choice is between two forms of the verb *come,* and it is clear that a past tense is required, as indicated by the past form of the verb *cry* after *and* and also by the two choices themselves. Since in the agreement pattern shared by AE and standard English, an *-s* ending is required for a subject like *Beth* in the present tense, and since no choice is offered with an *-s* ending, the intended answer cannot be in the present tense: in the present tense of either AE or standard English, the form would have to be *comes*. Therefore, it must be the nonpresent, i.e., the past, that is called for.

So far the standard English speaker and the AE speaker will have been able to reason in the same way. But now there is a special problem for just the AE speaker. As you can see in the section on past-tense irregular verbs in Appendix A (Section 3), irregular verbs like *come* can have past-tense forms in AE that differ from the standard representation. One of the variants of *came* is *come,* so the choice of *come* on this item would conform to the rules of AE. AE *come* is like *cut, hit,* etc.: they can have either a past or a present meaning, e.g., "We cut flowers yesterday, we cut flowers every day." But the AE usage is variable in that a speaker might use either *come* or *came* as a past-tense form (the way some people fluctuate between *dived* and *dove*): an AE speaker could consider both choices acceptable.

The next item (4), involves agreement again, but this time the subject is plural. This is one of the situations where the Appalachian English agreement system can differ from the standard one: *was* would be consistent with the rules of this variety. (5) also deals with agreement, but it does not represent a case where AE conflicts with standard

English. *My sister am six years old* would not be a response that could be explained as one of a test taker's having followed the rules of AE.

(6) deals with the past tense of an irregular verb and is very much like (3). (You might have noticed by now that, for this test at least, there are a few features that appear repeatedly. It is interesting to consider what purpose is served by focusing in on these particular features.) The choice here is between the standard form of the irregular past tense, *ran,* and the basic word form *run.* There are no clues in the rest of the sentence that indicate a past context, so the choice of *ran* rests solely on eliminating *run* as a possible response. In both AE and standard English, *run* would be rejected as a present tense form, since there it would need the *-s* suffix to agree with *he.* Speakers of both dialects would conclude that a past-tense form is needed, but AE would allow *run,* whereas the standard only *ran.* The choice of *run* then would not signal a lack of knowledge about the third-person singular *-s* suffix for the present tense for a speaker of AE, but would rather be simply an alternate form for the past tense.

The next item, (7), focuses on a different grammatical feature, negation, particularly on the form of an indefinite following a negative verb. Standard forms of negation would require *any* because another negative particle is already present on the verb. We can now look at the inventory for AE to see what possibilities are open to a speaker of that dialect. Section 10 in Appendix A treats negation, and in 10(a) we see that a negative can occur both on the verb and on indefinites that follow it. That means that the choice of *no* rather than *any* would result in an acceptable sentence for AE speakers. The pattern with two negative words comes close to a word-for-word translation in standard Spanish "*No* escuche *ningun* ruido." Many languages pattern this way.

Consider one more item on the above test, since we can make some observations that are somewhat different from the kinds we have made so far. (9) asks the test taker to choose between *can* and *may,* with *can* being the response that would be scored as correct. Checking the appendix, we find no feature of AE that would seem to apply here, so we would not expect dialect interference to be a problem. If you look at the item a little more closely, though, you should notice that either of the alternatives would provide an acceptable sentence of English. The distinction being referred to is probably the traditional, prescriptive one between *can* in the sense of *ability,* as opposed to *may* in the sense of *permission.* Most of us can probably remember incidents when we asked "Can I go outside now?" and received an answer such as "I'm sure you can, but you *may* not." However, the fact that *may* can be used to refer to possibility is completely overlooked in (9), as in "It *may* rain today." In this sense, the choice of *may* results in an acceptable English sentence.

An item such as (9) could well be confusing for all speakers of English. It is an instance where "school English" precludes a commonly used expression in standard English. A good test taker might realize that the *can/may* distinction in terms of ability and permission is the focus and so choose the alternative that would be scored correct. But someone who simply tried to figure out which one made a good English sentence could be confused, and end up having to guess which alternative will be marked correct.

These examples should give you an idea how to evaluate items from a sociolinguistic perspective. The objective is to find out whether a speaker of a particular dialect could give a reasonable answer in terms of his dialect but be marked as incorrect according to the dialect of the test maker. Do the same kind of analysis with the remaining items on the above test, consulting the appendix to determine which ones could be problematic for an AE speaker. So that you can check what you find, Table 8.1 gives a list of the items in the test, with those that could involve dialect differences marked with the number of the appropriate section to refer to in the appendix. In each case, the alternative that would be scored as correct according to the norms of the test is underlined. (For the complete item in each case, return to the test above.)

In nine of the thirteen items on the test the alternate form in the list of choices is a legitimate one in AE. One would have to concede that at least in terms of these nine items, there is a bias in favor of standard English speakers, but as we have attempted to demonstrate, even a numerical index of 9/13 may not tell the whole story: interference may have damage beyond the specific items where the rules of the two dialects conflict. As a result of the pervasive conflict of this kind

Table 8.1 *Choices on Test that Would be Scored as Correct*

Item	Choices	Appendix Section
1	are/*is*	
2	*go*/went	
3	come/*came*	3(b)
4	*were*/was	2(a)
5	am/*is*	
6	run/*ran*	3(b)
7	no/*any*	10(a)
8	*were*/was	2(a)
9	*can*/may	
10	them/*those*	13(b)
11	*doesn't*/don't	2(b)
12	*began*/begun	3(e)
13	wrote/*written*	3(d)

experienced by the test taker, in school in general as well as on tests, he might lose confidence entirely in his ability to predict "correct" and might even conclude that "correct" is whatever his language does NOT predict. Thus his performance could be vitiated on any test item.

2.3 Four Principles for Test Evaluation

From our evaluation of this test item, we might infer several principles for evaluating a test for dialect interference and bias against speakers of nonmainstream dialects of English.

PRINCIPLE ONE.   Consider the assumptions that underlie the test-taking task.
    We found at least two interlinking assumptions that can be made erroneously here: the assumption that all test takers will agree on the notion of "correct" and the assumption that for all test takers this is a test of the same kind of ability. We have seen that the nonmainstream speaker must operate with two definitions of "correct" and that only nonmainstream speakers have to learn "school English" in order to produce correct answers on a substantial number of test items.
    These are the primary assumptions concerning language that we should be aware of. There are other assumptions relevant to the evaluation of the fairness of the test-taking task. People can be in fluent command of their language but at the same time can be poor readers or unskilled in the sheer mechanics of test taking. A complete evaluation of tests will extend beyond language, but a sociolinguistic analysis should be a primary component.[4]

PRINCIPLE TWO.   Predict what specific items in the test will create a conflict between the rules of the standard dialect and the nonmainstream dialect.
    Do this with careful reference to the rules of the nonmainstream dialect: you will be looking for cases where the choice that is "incorrect" in terms of the standard dialect is a grammatical option for the test taker in his native speech.

PRINCIPLE THREE.   Compare what the test claims to be testing with what it actually tests.

---

4. For a comprehensive set of principles for test evaluation in terms of general standards and guidelines that extend beyond the scope of sociolinguistics, we would strongly recommend that all test users or evaluators become familiar with the principles set forth in *Standards for Educational and Psychological Tests,* published by the American Psychological Association, 1974.

Certainly our sample test could not measure accurately the AE speaker's language abilities as it might those of the mainstream speaker. It would measure the extent to which the AE speaker can substitute the forms of standard English for his own forms (a kind of translation skill). This has not so much to do with his language ability as with his having learned a set of social cues.

PRINCIPLE FOUR.   Determine how the results of the test must be interpreted for nonmainstream speakers.

It takes the AE speaker longer to acquire the rules of mainstream English because he does not come to school already equipped. Consequently, he will fall behind his grade level of achievement in these "language skills" until he has mastered the extra set of rules. For a nonmainstream speaker, then, a lag in score for his grade level would not necessarily measure less capability but could measure the time it would take him to acquire the additional knowledge—something requiring quite a bit of practice.

To be more specific, let's see how the test might be scored, how the test items might predict grade level achievement, and how AE speakers would fare in such a classification. This type of test may be given to students on several different levels and is most typically given to children who are in grades two to four. For the sake of discussion, let's assume that it is given at the conclusion of grade three. Let's further suppose that Table 8.2 places raw scores (number of items answered correctly) on a scale to correspond to grade levels of achievement in "language usage."

At grade three, an AE speaker is probably beginning to be aware that his dialect differs on several points from "school English" and may have picked up some of the new cues; thus, he might be somewhere closer to his grade level than his grammar might predict. Nevertheless, it is quite likely that he lags behind his peers who speak "school English" even as they begin school. The latter might, in fact, score above their grade level simply by using the intuitions of the language they brought to school with them. "Achievement" for the AE speaker should be scaled differently since he has more to learn, indeed

Table 8.2 *Hypothetical Table for Correlating Raw Score with Grade Level Norms*

Raw Score Interval	Grade Level Classification
0–4	1
5–7	2
8–10	3
11–13	4

he has something different and more subtle to learn than has the mainstream speaker.

The test designer needs to reassess the relationship between the tools of language the AE speaker comes to school with and the reasonable rate of acquisition of a new set of tools in the form of "school English." An important part of test scores involves the "norming" of raw scores. This means comparing the raw score of the individual test taker with the average raw score of some sample, presumably model, population. But comparing the score of an AE-speaking child with the average of children in grades one through four nationally will not give us an indication of the child's achievements or capacities in any conceivable way that could be said to be useful to society. Some of the children involved in a national average will be native speakers of standard English and some will be native speakers of a variety of other dialects. The only fair way to "norm" a particular test for AE children where dialect interference is a factor would appear to be by comparing them to other AE children.

3. Applying the Principles

As a basis for our exercises in applying the principles discussed above, we shall look at one section of a test of psycholinguistic abilities which has fairly wide distribution, namely, the Illinois Test of Psycholinguistic Abilities (henceforth ITPA).[5] The section which we shall focus on is entitled "Grammatic Closure." As this test is examined in terms of the principles and procedures we set forth earlier, you will see how you can arrive at a meaningful preliminary sociolinguistic analysis.

First of all, we want to look at the assumptions that underlie the testing task. In order to do this, we need to look at the instructions for the administration of the test and see what capabilities must be assumed on the part of the test taker. Below are the instructions for the administration of the test.

> *Procedure:* Examiner points to the appropriate pictures as he reads the given statements, emphasizing the underscored words and stopping abruptly at the point where the child is to supply the missing words.

---

5. Kirk, McCarthy, and Kirk, *The Illinois Test of Psycholinguistic Abilities* (Urbana: University of Illinois Press, 1968). Copyright 1968 by the Board of Trustees of the University of Illinois. Reprinted with permission.

Demonstration:

Examiner points to the first bed and says,
> HERE IS A BED.

He then points to the two beds and says,
> HERE ARE TWO _____.

If subject fails to respond or responds incorrectly, as with "two" or "more" or "yes," Examiner says,
> TWO WHAT? TWO BEDS?

Then Examiner repeats the item, pointing and saying,
> YES, HERE IS A BED.
> HERE ARE TWO *BEDS*[6]

Examine the instructions, identifying the capabilities necessary for the test taker to participate in this task. In what ways is this task like or unlike the types of language usage that might exist apart from this testing situation? Does the task involve a specialized language usage relating to testing? If so, what? How is the notion of a "question" defined in this task? Are there any other situations in which these types of questions might be common to a child taking this test?

The next aspect of the test we want to examine is the systematic differences between the items considered correct responses on the test scoring procedures and those responses which differ systematically according to the rules of Appalachian English. That is, we want to predict where speakers of AE might get an item "incorrect" simply because they use the dialect of their indigenous community. In order to do this, we must consider each of the items, the responses considered correct according to the test manual, and the possible alternate forms which might occur in the responses of Appalachian English speakers. We should make reference here to the rules of AE summarized in Appendix A. Listed below are the thirty-three items included in the test, with the responses considered correct according to the test manual underlined. Circle any Appalachian English alternate that would be marked incorrect. It might also be helpful to list the section in the appendix where it is found. If there is no alternate Appalachian English form different from the responses considered correct, assume that Appalachian English speakers would use one of the items considered as a

---

6. Ibid., Examiners Manual, p. 70.

correct response in the test manual. When you are through, tabulate the number of items where there is an alternate Appalachian English form. How many items have alternate forms? What does this exercise demonstrate concerning the possible prediction of alternate forms for a given dialect? What sort of preliminary knowledge is necessary in order to predict dialect differences of this type?

ITPA Grammatic Closure Subtest   (Descriptions of the pictures are given in parentheses for some of the items.)

1.   Here is a dog. Here are two *dogs/doggies*.
2.   This cat is under the chair. Where is the cat? She is *on*—or any preposition—other than *under*—indicating location. (Pictures: (1) a cat under a chair; (2) a cat on the seat of a chair.)
3.   Each child has a ball. This is hers; and this is *his*. (Picture: A girl and a boy, each holding a ball.)
4.   This dog likes to bark. Here he is *barking*. (Pictures: (1) a dog; (2) the dog with his mouth open and lines coming out, to indicate barking.)
5.   Here is a dress. Here are two *dresses*.
6.   The boy is opening the gate. Here the gate has been *opened*.
7.   There is milk in this glass. It is a glass *of/with/for/o'/lots of* milk. (Picture: A glass with a line around it to show it about 2/3 full of a liquid.)
8.   This bicycle belongs to John. Whose bicycle is it? It is *John's*.
9.   This boy is writing something. This is what he *wrote/has written/did write*. (Picture: (1) a boy writing; (2) a piece of paper with writing on it.)
10.   This is the man's home, and this is where he works. Here he is going to work, and here he is going *home/back home/to his home*. (Pictures: (1) a man, with a lunch pail, walking toward a house; sky dark, crescent moon, street light on; (2) the man, with a lunch pail, walking toward a building, sun in the sky.)
11.   Here it is night, and here it is morning. He goes to work first thing in the morning, and he goes home first thing *at night*. (Pictures: same as item 10.)
12.   This man is painting. He is a *painter/fence painter*.
13.   The boy is going to eat all the cookies. Now all the cookies have been *eaten*. (Pictures: (1) a boy sitting at a table, a plate of cookies on the table in front of him, putting one cookie up to his mouth; (2) the boy at the table with an empty plate in front of him.)
14.   He wanted another cookie; but there weren't *any/any more*. (Pictures: same as item 13.)
15.   This horse is not big. This horse is big. This horse is even *bigger*.
16.   And this horse is the very *biggest*.
17.   Here is a man. Here are two *men/gentlemen*.
18.   This man is planting a tree. Here the tree has been *planted*.
19.   This is soap and these are *soap/bars of soap/more soap*. (Pictures:

(1) one rectangular object with SOAP written on it; (2) two such objects, each with SOAP written on them.)

20. This child has lots of blocks. This child has even *more*.
21. And this child has the *most*.
22. Here is a foot. Here are two *feet*.
23. Here is a sheep. Here are lots of *sheep*.
24. This cookie is not very good. This cookie is good. This cookie is even *better*. (Picture: A series of four gingerbread men—the first with no decoration and legs and arms not complete; the second complete in shape but no decoration; the third complete in shape with some decoration; the fourth with the most decoration.)
25. And this cookie is the very *best*. (Picture: same as item 24.)
26. This man is hanging the picture. Here the picture has been *hung*.
27. The thief is stealing the jewels. These are the jewels that he *stole*.
28. Here is a woman. Here are two *women*.
29. The boy had two bananas. He gave one away; and he kept one for *himself*. (Pictures: (1) boy (A) holding two bananas; (2) the boy (A) handing one of the bananas to another boy (B); (3) boy (A) holding a partially peeled banana.)
30. Here is a leaf. Here are two *leaves*.
31. Here is a child. Here are three *children*.
32. Here is a mouse. Here are two *mice*.
33. These children all fell down. He hurt himself; and she hurt herself. They all hurt *themselves*. (Picture: Three girls and two boys, all sitting or kneeling.)

We are now ready to look at what the test claims to be testing in relation to what it actually tests for Appalachian English speakers. In order to do this, we should first look at the stated goal of the test, which is given as follows:

This test assesses the child's ability to make use of the redundancies of oral language in acquiring automatic habits for handling syntax and grammatic inflections.[7]

Given the systematic differences for Appalachian English speakers that were predicted on the basis of the examination of the specific items, do you think that it is a valid test for assessing the acquisition of inflectional endings? (Inflectional endings include plurals, past-tense markings, the third-person singular present-tense marking, and the comparative -*er* and superlative -*est*.) What is the test actually testing in terms of these items? What types of assumptions must be made about the dialect of the test taker in order to obtain any type of meaningful results with respect to the acquisition of certain grammatical forms? How does the analysis of the specific items help

---

7. Ibid., Examiners Manual, p. 11.

you to ascertain what the test claims to be testing in relation to what it is actually testing for the Appalachian English speaker?

We now want to look at the ways in which the results from the test have to be interpreted in terms of the speaker of Appalachian English. This test, like many tests of language acquisition, provides a correlational table in which the raw score (i.e., the number correct out of the total number of items) is correlated with a "psycholinguistic age norm" (i.e., the "average" score for a given psycholinguistic age level). Table 8.3 gives the correlation of the raw scores (in terms of the number of items correct out of the total of thirty-three) with psycholinguistic age norms.

The correlation table will allow us to see the extent to which a speaker of Appalachian English might be penalized for using his indigenous dialect in this test.[8] Suppose we had a ten-year-old speaker of Appalachian English who systematically used his dialect wherever possible in his responses. In terms of the standard scoring procedure, what would his psycholinguistic age be?

Now suppose he used alternate Appalachian English forms in only one-half of those responses where he might have used them. What would his psycholinguistic age be now? How drastic is the penalty for

Table 8.3. *Correlation between Raw Test Scores and Psycholinguistic Age*

Raw Score	Psycholinguistic Age Norm Years/Months	Raw Score	Psycholinguistic Age Norm Years/Months
0		16	5/10
1	2/2	17	6/0
2	2/6	18	6/2
3	2/7	19	6/5
4	3/3	20	6/8
5	3/7	21	7/0
6	3/10	22	7/3
7	4/2	23	7/7
8	4/5	24	7/11
9	4/8	25	8/2
10	4/10	26	8/6
11	5/0	27	8/10
12	5/2	28	9/2
13	5/4	29	9/8
14	5/6	30	10/4
15	5/8		

---

8. Ibid., Examiners Manual, p. 102.

speaking the dialect of his community in terms of the psycholinguistic age norm classification? Given the standardized scoring procedures for the test, how accurate a picture is it possible to obtain from this test for the speaker of Appalachian English? How must we interpret the results? Are there any suggested changes in the scoring technique that might allow us to obtain a more accurate picture of language acquisition for this speaker?

Now suppose you were in the position of administering the ITPA to a group of nine-year-olds, many of whom seem to you clearly to be speakers of Appalachian English. One of these children has given the following set of answers to the thirty-three items of the grammatic closure subtest:

1.	dogs	9.	wrote	17.	men	25.	best
2.	sitting down	10.	back home	18.	planted	26.	hanged
3.	his	11.	of the night	19.	soaps	27.	steals
4.	barking	12.	painter	20.	more	28.	women
5.	dresses	13.	ate	21.	most	29.	him
6.	left open	14.	no more	22.	feet	30.	leafs
7.	of milk	15.	bigger	23.	sheeps	31.	children
8.	a bicycle	16.	biggest	24.	better	32.	mice
						33.	theirselves

How would you score these responses? If the answers were marked strictly according to the test manual, what would the raw score be? If dialect interference were taken into account (i.e., you gave the child credit for getting an appropriate dialect form), what would it be? Compare the two psycholinguistic ages that might be assigned based on these two scores. (Consult the table of norms given above.) Are there any items that seem problematic, that is, you are not sure whether or not to score them as correct, apart from dialect differences? If so, why are they hard to score? If you were given the task of interpreting these test results for this child, what recommendations would you make?

Suggestions for Further Reading

A number of articles are recommended for the reader interested in pursuing the question of sociolinguistic aspects of test bias. Wolfram's "Levels of Sociolinguistic Test Bias" (In Harrison and Trabasso, eds., *Black English: A Seminar*. Maryland: Lawrence Erlbaum Associates) gives more detail on the levels of potential bias identified in our previous discussion, although it essentially covers much of the same material included here. More general information on the principles of test construction can be found in the American Psychological Association's manual *Standards for Educational and Psychological Tests* (American Psychological Association, 1974), which is not limited to a sociolinguistic vantage point. More specific information on current models for evaluating test performance in the schools can be found in Cicourel, et al., *Language and School Performance* (Academic Press, 1974). The relation of language bias in reading tests is investigated in Meier's "Reading Failure and the Tests," and its relation to language development tests is treated in Roberts, "An Evaluation of Standardized Tests as Tools for the Measurement of Language Development" *(Language Research Report Number 1: Language Research Foundation,* 1970). Labov, in his article "Systematically Misleading Data from Test Questions" *(Urban Review* 9(3):146–69, Fall, 1976) discusses the problems of drawing conclusions about ability from children's performances in testing situations. He finds explanations for these problems in the nature of tests and more generally in the conflict between the cultures of certain groups and that of the schools.

Much more comprehensive information on the linguistic characteristics of Appalachian English is found in Wolfram and Christian's *Appalachian Speech* (Center for Applied Linguistics, 1976) for the reader interested in pursuing the distinctive aspects of this variety. Other educational considerations of language in the schools are also treated in that volume.

Some Grammatical Characteristics of Appalachian English

The following inventory contains some of the grammatical features that characterize Appalachian English. We have presented only grammatical features since they are the ones that may produce interference in the tests under consideration here. It would be possible, however, to prepare and consult a similar list on other kinds of features for evaluating tests that deal with those aspects of language. (For example, you would want to consider an inventory of phonological features to evaluate an articulation test.)

The inventory presented here is neither complete nor detailed, but it should be a useful guide as you look for potential interference in items on standardized tests. (A more complete account is given in Wolfram and Christian [1975]. See footnote 1 for complete reference.) While some of the features mentioned are specific to Appalachian English, a number of them are found in other nonmainstream varieties of English as well. Another point to remember as you look through the list is that the features occur variably. That is, speakers of Appalachian English would not necessarily use these particular variants 100 percent of the time, but would fluctuate between these and nonstigmatized alternate forms.

Verbs

1. *A*-verb-*ing*   This is found much more frequently in Appalachian English than in other varieties. An *a*- can be prefixed to a following verb that has an -*ing* participial form. These verb forms may function as progressives [as in (1)] or as certain types of adverbials [(2)–(4)].
   (1) I knew he was *a-telling* the truth.
   (2) I went down there *a-hunting* for 'em.
   (3) He just kept *a-begging* and *a-crying*.
   (4) One night my sister, she woke up *a-screaming*.
   These forms do not occur when the verb form functions as a noun or an adjective (as in *The movie was shocking*). An *a*- prefix also cannot occur with a form that begins with a relatively unstressed

syllable or with a vowel, so that we do not get *a-discovering* or *a-asking*.

2. Agreement   (a) Plural subjects can take verbs that are marked, with respect to the standard pattern, for singular agreement. This type of agreement is found more often with the verb *be* (giving *they was, the cars is*) than with other verbs *(some people makes, their friends has)*. Plural pronouns rarely have singular agreement except with the past-tense forms of *be,* so that *you is* or *we goes* would not be so likely to occur. Forms like *you was* or *we was* occur quite frequently.
    (b) The only time a singular subject does not have singular agreement is with the verb *do* used in auxiliary constructions with third-person singular subjects. *The car don't work* is then an alternate form for *The car doesn't work.*

3. Past Tense: Irregular V̇erbs   (a) Regularized Forms: Some verbs with irregular past forms can instead have the regular past-tense suffix, *-ed,* added—*knowed* for *knew/known, heared* for *heard, drinked* for *drank/drunk, gived* for *gave/given.*
    (b) Uninflected Forms: Some verbs can have the past-tense forms represented by their basic uninflected form: *come* for *came, eat* for *ate/eaten, run* for *ran, begin* for *began/begun.*
    (c) Different Irregular Forms: A small set of verbs have irregular past forms that are different from the standard ones: *brung* for *brought, set* for *sat, hearn* for *heard.*
    (d) Simple Past for Past Participle: For many of the irregular verbs where the two past forms in the standard pattern are different, the simple past may be extended to serve the past participle functions as well: *have went* for *have gone, have took* for *have taken, have rode* for *have ridden, have saw* for *have seen, have broke* for *have broken.*
    (e) Past Participle for Simple Past: For some verbs that have two different past forms in the standard pattern, the past participle form can be used for the simple past: *seen* for *saw, done* for *did, drunk* for *drank.*

4. Completive *done*   *Done* with a past form of a verb gives a completive aspect to the activity represented by the verb, as in *I done forgot, She's done sold it.*

5. *liketa, supposeta*   These items are accompanied by a past form of a verb: *It liketa scared me to death, I liketa never went to sleep, It was supposeta been there. Liketa* indicates that the activity in the sentence came close to happening, but didn't. *Supposeta* (or

sposeta, poseta) is closely related to its standard counterpart, *(be) supposed to have.*

Adverbs

6. Comparatives and Superlatives   The *-er* and *-est* suffixes may be extended to words of two or more syllables that end in a consonant where the standard pattern uses the adverbs *more* and *most* *(awfulest, beautifulest)*. In some cases, the comparative adverb and the suffix are both used, as in *more older, most stupidest*. There is also a regularization of some of the irregular comparatives, where the suffix is added to the base word or to the irregular form, as in *baddest, worser, mostest.*

7. Intensifying Adverbs   The intensifier *right* can be used in a wider set of contexts than it can in its standard distribution. These include before adjectives *(right large, right amusing)*, with an expanded group of adverbs *(right loud, right quick)*, and in construction with *smart (a right smart while)*. Another intensifier, *plumb*, occurs with adverbs, verbs, and some adjectives, and refers to completeness *(burn plumb down, scare you plumb to death, plumb foolish).*

8. *-ly* Absence   For some of the adverbs that require the *-ly* suffix according to the standard pattern, the suffix may be optional, giving *original* for *originally, terrible* for *terribly, sincere* for *sincerely.*

Negation

9. *ain't*   *Ain't* may be used for the negative counterparts of *have/has* and *am/are/is*. An alternate pronunciation is *hain't (I ain't been there, I ain't scared, Hain't that awful?).*

10. Multiple Negation   (a) Negative Concord: The negative may be attached both to the main verb and to all indefinites that follow it *(They don't have no work, I didn't have nothing to do)*. A negative in an indefinite before the main verb may also be attached to the verb and all indefinites that follow it, giving *Nobody didn't see him, Nobody wouldn't say nothing.*
    (b) With Negative Adverbs: Within a sentence, both a negative adverb, like *hardly* or *never,* and another negative element (a

second negative adverb, an auxiliary, or an indefinite with a negative attached) may be used, as in *They can't hardly see, We hardly
never go out*.

(c) Inversion: A negative auxiliary in the main verb *(didn't, can't,
ain't)* which follows an indefinite may be placed immediately preceding the indefinite. *Nobody didn't get hurt* can become *Didn't
nobody get hurt*.

(d) Across Clause Boundaries: Multiple negation may apply
across clauses so that a negative is attached to the auxiliary in the
second clause. This process is fairly rare but gives sentences like *I
wasn't sure that nothing wasn't gonna come up*.

Nouns

11. Plurals   (a) Plural Absence: For nouns that refer to weights or
measure, the plural suffix may be absent *(two pound, three foot,
twenty year ago, how many bushel)*. This occurs most often when
the noun is preceded by a numeral.

(b) Irregular Plurals: Plurals that are represented by an internal
change *(foot/feet, man/men)* or by no change *(sheep, aspirin)* may
be regularized to the *-s* suffix. This gives *deers, squashes, fire-
mans.* In some cases, the internal change may be made in addition
to the suffix, giving *mens, oxens*.

(c) Plurals that involve a change in the final sound of the base
word before the suffix is added *(wife/wives)* may be regularized.
The appropriate form of the plural suffix is added to the unchanged base word, giving *wifes, lifes*.

Pronouns

12. Reflexives   The form *-self* may be added to all personal pronouns. The possessive form used in reflexives for first and second
persons *(myself, yourself)* can be extended to the third person,
resulting in *hisself* and *theirself*.

13. Object Pronouns   (a) The objective forms *(me, her,* etc.) may
also function as subjects in coordinate constructions, giving sentences like *Me and him goes out there*.

(b) The objective form *them* may be used where the corresponding standard form would be the demonstrative *those,* giving *Them
guys were there,* or *Did you see them books? Here* and *there* can
also be added to demonstratives giving phrases like *this here one*.

14. **Possessives** When a possessive pronoun does not modify a following noun phrase, *-n* may be added to it, resulting in forms like *yourn, hisn,* and *ourn.* These may be found in sentences like *That's yourn.*

15. **Relative Pronoun Deletion** A relative pronoun *(that, who, which)* may be omitted whether it functions as a subject or an object of the subordinate clause. According to the standard pattern, deletion is possible only when it replaces the object, as in *That's the house _____ I built.* In this variety, the relative pronoun may also be omitted when it serves as a subject, giving *I got some kin people _____ lived up there, There was a snake _____ come down the road.*

16. **Prepositions** (a) The preposition *of* may be used with times of the day or seasons of the year, where other varieties of English would have a corresponding *in* or *at.* This results in phrases like *get up of the morning, if you plant of the winter.*
    (b) Other less general lexical differences: *at* with movement verbs *(I just go at my uncle's), agin* corresponding to standard *against (I got up agin it), beside of* for standard *beside (The river was right beside of the railroad),* the use of *upside (hit him upside the head, upside the jaw).*
    (c) Some prepositions may be omitted where they would be present in a corresponding standard construction, as in *I lived _____ Coal City.*

Two Illustrative Narratives from West Virginia

Passage 1. An Appalachian Ghost Story

I was always kinda afraid to stay by myself, just me, you know, it
was getting about time for me to get in, so Ingo, he'd went over to
this man's house where we carried our water from, and to get some
water, and, ooh the moon was so pretty and bright and I thinks
5   well, heck hit's dark, I hear him a-talking, a-setting over there in
the field where the spring is, I'll just walk down the road and meet
him, you know, ooh it was so pretty and light. I got down there
and I hearn something shut the churchhouse door but I didn't see
a thing, and the moon, oh the moon was as bright as daylight and I
10 didn't see nothing. And he come out on the walk, pitty-pat,
pitty-pat, pitty-pat, and I just looked with all my eyes and I
couldn't see a thing, come out that gate, iron gate, slammed it and
hit just cracked just like a iron gate, it well just slam it there. And
all at once, something was right in front of me. Looked like it had a
15 white sheet around it and no head. I liketa died. That was just a
little while before Florence was born. I turned around and I went
back to the house just as fast as I could go, and about that time,
Ingo come along and he says, "I set the water up," and he sayd
"I'm going down to the churchhouse," he said, "I hearn somebody
20 go in," he said, "They went through the gate," and he walked
across there and he opened the door and he went in the
churchhouse. And they had him a-looking after the church, you
know, if anybody went in, he went down there. He got—seen
something was the matter with me, I couldn't hardly talk. I told
25 him, I said, "Well, something or other, I hearn it, I seen it,
whenever I started over to meet you, and I didn't, I couldn't get no
further." So he went down there and he took his lantern, of course,
we didn't have flashlights then, took his lantern, had an old ladder,
just spokes, just to go up beside of the house, he looked all behind
30 the organ, all behind every bench, he went upstairs and looked in
the garret, not a thing in the world he could find. Not a thing. Well,
it went on there for a right smart little while and one day Miss
Allen was down there. Her girls come down there very often and
sweep the church and clean it. So one evening they come up to the
35 house, you know, and I's telling them. They said, "Honey, don't
feel bad about that," she said, "long as you live here, you'll see
something like that." Said "they was, in time of the war, they was

40

45

50

55

a woman, that somebody'd cut her head off and they'd buried in the lower end of the grave down there,'' and said ''There'd been so many people live in the house we live in, would see her,'' and said ''That's what it was, said it just had a white sheet wrapped around it.'' And we didn't live there very long cause I wouldn't stay. He worked away and aw heck—I's just scared to death but still Miss Allen told me, she said ''Don't be afraid because hain't a thing that'll hurt you.'' Said ''Just don't feel afraid.'' But you know how you'd feel. But now, but honey, that's the first thing that I've ever seen that I was even scared about, but now, I'll tell you, now that was, that was scary. Just, you just hear something like that and you look and you don't see a thing. Can't see it and then something right in the road, right in front of you stops you, and it just looked like it had a big sheet just a-wrapped around him and no head. Now that's the way it looked. And I told Miss Allen, she said, ''Well honey, everybody that lives in that house has seen the same thing'' but, she said, ''hain't nothing that'll hurt you.'' Said ''because I wouldn't be afraid,'' I said, ''Oh my goodness!'' ''Be afraid,'' I said, ''why, when he was a little after dark, I was scared pink.''

Passage 2.   An Appalachian Hunting Story

5

10

15

20

We went up there and Jack supposedly had a sack to put the coon in if we caught one. We's gonna try to bring it back alive, so we tromped through the woods 'til along about six o'clock in the morning. The dogs treed up a big hollow chestnut oak, and we proceed to cut the thing down. It's oh, about three or four inches all the way around. About four foot through the stump. We tied the dogs and cut the thing down. Well, we cut it down and turned one dog loose, and he went down in that thing, way down in the old hollow of the tree and it forked, and we couldn't get up in there so he backed out and he tied him. And we's a-gonna chop the coon out if it was in there. I's a kinda halfway thought maybe it just treed a possum or something. Well, I chopped in and low and behold, right on top of the dang coon. Eighteen pounder, Paul Snead says, kitten coon. I run in with the axe handle down in behind him to keep him from getting out or backing down in the tree. He reached, fooled around and got him by the hind legs and pulled that thing out, it looked big as a sheep to me. Turned him loose, he said ''kitten, Hell.'' We had an old carbide light and he turned that over and the lights was . . . that's all the light we had. And, we had to hunt it then and the dogs took right after the coon right down the holler and caught it, the dogs caught it and Paul beat us all down there. Went down there and he's a-holding three dogs in one hand and the coon in the other hand. And they's all a-trying

to bite the coon and the coon a-trying to bite Paul and the dogs, and
25   Jack pulled out a sack and it wasn't a dang thing but an old pillow
case that Maggie had used, his wife, it was about wore out. So we
fumbled around there and finally got that coon in that sack and he
aimed to close the top of it and the coon just tore the thing half in
two and down the holler he went again. With that sack on him, half
30   of it, and we caught that thing, and you know, E. S. Hurst finally
pulled off his coveralls and we put that thing down in one of the
legs of his overalls, and tied that coon up. He's tearing up
everything we could get, we couldn't hold him he's so stout. And I
brought that thing home and kept him about a month, fed him
35   apples and stuff to eat so I was gonna eat him. Well, I did I killed
him and tried to eat that thing. I'd just soon eat a tomcat or a
polecat, I wouldn't make much difference. And, that's about the
best coon hunt I believe I was on.

An Afterword

The Accidents of History

Joseph M. Williams

If the particular grammatical forms of our language somehow reflected our intrinsic abilities to think, to solve problems, to understand complex matters of science, philosophy, and the arts, then we could rely on grammar tests to distinguish those who are intellectually able from those who are not. Unfortunately, language does not provide us with those forms, and even more unfortunately, a good many educators and test makers think it does. More than a few have claimed, for example, that because some speakers utter sentences that seem not to have a fully expressed verb:

My friend in the house.

or have a form of *be* that is uninflected:

My friend always be at home.

then those speakers must lack a sense of time. Because logically, two negatives make a positive, some have claimed that double negatives indicate illogical thinking:

He don't have no time.

And some have even claimed that children who answer questions such as:

Where is the squirrel?

with phrases like:

In the tree.

are so cognitively deprived that they have no sense of even what a

213

sentence is, and so must be unable to communicate on anything more than the most rudimentary level.

The connection between language and intellectual development seems like an easy one to make. Many people in our society speak forms of English that are different from the English of those who have gone through our educational systems, who have reached positions where they write tests, make judgments, and write books. And because many of those who speak those different dialects have not gone through that system, they are also poor, illiterate, and unemployed. And because of all this, they are often judged to be intellectually deficient.

Now it is true that intellectual deficiency does cause individuals to use language in ways that we judge to be incompetent. But it is equally true that the criteria we use when we make those judgments are often utterly misinformed, and that as a consequence we incorrectly judge highly intelligent children and adults as unintelligent, or even retarded.

We have to distinguish at least three ways in which we judge language behavior. First, there is the skillful use of language to express ideas and feelings and insights in ways that effectively inform and even move readers and listeners. The rudiments of that skill are often acquired in high school and college, and not many of us ever really develop those skills to any high degree. We write and speak well enough to do our jobs and live our lives. But the effective use of language is a skill that requires us to analyze and understand audiences, to shape discourses, to craft sentences and select words with exactly the right nuance, and so on. And for that matter, it is a skill that entirely uneducated speakers can acquire without the benefit of formal schooling. We all know articulate, moving speakers who have never had a course in public speaking or rhetoric and yet who argue forcefully and persuasively.

A second kind of competency is at the other end of the spectrum. It is the ability to use language at all, an ability that every person has who is not mentally retarded or profoundly deprived by handicaps such as aphasia or schizophrenia. Every speaker of English knows that *the* goes before a noun; that verbs usually go after subjects; that nouns and not verbs can have relative clauses attached to them. The amount of knowledge that even the most uneducated normal person has about his language is astonishingly large, once we realize what it consists of. But for the most part, it is not a body of knowledge that we are interested in testing, because anyone able to read and understand a test has almost certainly acquired that knowledge already. If a person has not acquired that knowledge, then he or she probably could not understand the test in the first place.

The exception to this, of course, is children. We can measure their intellectual growth by how well they acquire their language. But in measuring that growth, it is absolutely crucial that we measure this second kind of linguistic ability and not a third kind that lies between these two extremes.

Between these two extremes, the ability to use language expressively and creatively and the ability to use language at all, lies the area that most test makers are interested in. It is also the area where they are typically misled and mistaken about what they think they are testing.

The typical misapprehension that governs the worst tests is that those who have successfully negotiated the educational process and have proven themselves to be useful members of a management or technical society must use linguistic forms that are "naturally" correct. There must be something about the intrinsic logic and nature of language that demands that subjects agree with verbs, that certain pronoun forms naturally follow certain verbs, that double negatives must be illogical because they are illogical in mathematics. Since the "best" people, the most highly educated people, observe these rules, then the rules must reflect the intrinsically "best" forms.

Once this idea of "natural" correctness implants itself in the minds of educators, it is very difficult to convince them that every linguistic feature that sets one dialect apart from another is the result not of transcendental inevitability but of historical accident. There is nothing about consistent subject-verb agreement that is more or less logical or natural than the lack of subject-verb agreement. After all, English does not require subject-verb agreement in the past tense (except for the verb *be*), so why do we need it in the present? We may say *they work* and *he works* in the present tense, but in the past tense, *worked* serves for both singular and plural: *he worked, they worked.* *Knowed* as a past tense of *know* is, if anything, more logical than *knew* because it maintains the stem of the verb more consistently. *Ain't* is a perfectly logical contraction of *am not,* the only *be + not* sequence in English that does not have a standard contracted form.

What all these forms attest to is not an intrinsic corruption of language or speakers so intellectually deprived that they must speak in a debased form of the language. These dialect features exist simply because language has changed in different parts of the English-speaking world at different times and in different ways. What we call mainstream English or standard English is simply one dialect that had its origins several hundred years ago in the dialect of English spoken around London. Because London was the most powerful, most culturally advanced, most stylish city in England, its dialect became the prestige dialect that anyone seeking personal prestige had to adopt.

Through the centuries, the dialect of London—along with all the other dialects in Great Britain—changed. When the British migrated to this country, they brought their dialects with them. Because cultural and political prestige was first invested in the areas around Boston and Charleston, the dialects of those areas became our earliest prestige dialects. Because those who later settled the midlands of America were more rural and isolated from the cultural mainstream, their speech became identified with a way of life that was not valued: a life of backwoods culture, of little formal education, of isolation from the economic and social development of the east coast and the area along the Great Lakes. Those areas had a standard of speech somewhat different from that of Boston and that of Charleston. And because Appalachia was so "backwards" and culturally isolated, its dialect became associated with illiteracy and ignorance.

As a result of all this, when those who had acquired the linguistic features of mainstream English decided to test the linguistic competencies of children and adults (indeed, *had* to acquire that dialect in order to acquire the education that qualified them to be teachers and testers), it was easy for them to assume that mainstream English was the only correct form and that all other forms of English were somehow degenerate departures from mainstream English.

They thought (and many still do) that their dialect stands in a kind of central relationship to all other dialects:

Mainstream English (Northern)

Eastern New England	Appalachian
Southern	North Midland
Upper Midwestern	South Midland

Actually, what some call "General American" is only one dialect among many:

Upper Midwestern   Eastern New England
        Northern
            North Midland
            South Midland
                    Appalachian
            Southern

Curiously enough, many of the features that characterize Appalachian English in particular were at one time acceptable to educated, literate speakers and writers of earlier British dialects. Some of the irregular verbs that at one time occurred quite frequently in AE were forms that reflected older standard forms: *holp* and *clum* as the past-tense forms of *help* and *climb*, for example. The completive *done* was not uncommon in the sixteenth and seventeenth centuries:

He's done gone now.

The *a-huntin'* form in:

He's gone a-huntin'.

goes back to an older prepositional phrase:

He's gone on-hunting.

Ain't was not too long ago a respectable contraction of *am/are/has/ have + not:*

We ain't ready yet.
He ain't been here for a while.
I ain't finished.

Multiple negation was not only common in older forms of the English language, but it is not uncommon in other languages. The absolute form of the possessive pronoun: *hisn, hern, ourn, yourn* as in:

It's not hern, it's mine.

were at one time common forms in the midland British dialects.

For purely accidental reasons, these features have not been adopted by mainstream English, but they have survived in many non-mainstream dialects. In other cases, nonmainstream dialects have evolved forms that have not yet been adopted in mainstream English but follow entirely consistent historical developments. The regularized verbs: *knowed, heared, drinked, gived,* and so on simply join *helped, climbed, carved, yielded, yelled,* and many others as regularized past tenses. The reflexive pronouns *hisself* and *theirself* regularize the pronoun into the possessive form to fit the others: *my-self, her-self, your-self, our-selves.*

In every case, Appalachian English—and every other dialect of English, for that matter—exhibits characteristics that were either quite acceptable at one time or follow perfectly normal forms of historical linguistic evolution. No dialect develops forms that are more intrinsically "correct" or "natural" than any other. They are simply different.

If London had been located two hundred miles north of where it is, if the original British migration had been from the West Counties, if the colonists had settled only around Philadelphia, if New York instead of Boston had become the cultural hub of the early colonies, if . . . , if . . . , if. . . . Only historical accident is responsible for the distinctions among dialects and only historical and geographical accidents are responsible for any one of those dialects emerging as the prestige dialect. What, then, do we measure when we ask children who speak a nonmainstream dialect to answer questions about mainstream English?